KENTUCKY STATE PARKS

A Complete Outdoor Recreation Guide for Campers, Boaters, Anglers, Hikers and Outdoor Lovers

Bill Bailey

Glovebox Guidebooks of America

To our readers: Travel outdoors entails some unavoidable risks. Know your limitations, be prepared, be alert, use good judgment, think safety and enjoy Kentucky's terrific outdoors. Be bold!

Special thanks to Phil Gray, Director of Marketing and Advertising for the Kentucky Department of Parks, and to all the staff at all the units. Kentucky has the finest parks---and staff---in the nation!

Cover design by Dan Jacalone
Cover photo courtesy of the Kentucky Department of Parks
Editor, Bill Cornish
Managing Editor, Penny Weber-Bailey

Published by **Glovebox Guidebooks of America**
1112 Washburn Place East
Saginaw, Michigan 48602-2977
(800) 289-4843 or (517) 792-8363

Library of Congress, CIP

Bailey, William L., 1952-

Kentucky State Parks Guidebook
(A Glovebox Guidebooks of America publication)
ISBN 1-881139-13-1

Printed in the United States of America

10 9 8 7 6 5 4 3 2 1

KENTUCKY
STATE PARKS

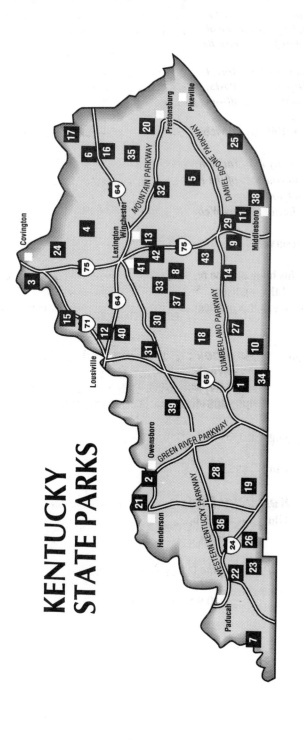

Contents

State Parks and Recreation Areas

Foreward

Kentucky is the vacation land you've been looking for...a land of friendly and hospitable people, a rich cultural heritage and great natural beauty. We Kentuckians take great pride in our state and want to share its riches with you through our nationally recognized state park system.

When you visit us, you will discover why our parks are known as the "the nation's finest." From dedicated employees working all over the state to the finest facilities designed to provide every comfort. We constantly strive to make our diverse park system the very best.

Our diversity is reflected in the quality of all 47 of our parks, from the tiny Isaac Shelby Cemetery to sprawling Kentucky Dam Village. In our parks, you can explore thundering waterfalls, magnificent sandstone arches, wild rivers and serpentine caves. You can ride the wild rivers over foaming rapids or stroll through quiet forests. You can snow ski or water ski, sail our lakes or drop your fishing line in a quiet cove. No matter what your sport, you can always find a place to play at a Kentucky State Park.

Kentucky operates more resort parks than any other state in the country. From the verdant fields of Jackson Purchase in Western Kentucky to the evergreen forests of the Eastern Kentucky mountains, Kentucky State Resort Parks provide the finest in lodging, dining and recreational facilities.

Kentucky's 15 state resort parks offer a variety of recreational activities including water sports, golf, tennis, hiking and organized recreational and naturalist programs for the entire family. Musical shows, dances and interpretive presentations provide hours of entertainment for visitors to our parks. After you play, sample delicious Kentucky cuisine in our beautiful dining rooms, then retire to well-kept lodge rooms and cottages surrounded by stunning natural vistas.

During the winter, discover a spectacular moonbow or join friends around a crackling fire after an exhilarating day of skiing. Or cool off during the dog days of summer in a lodge pool or sparkling lake.

A visit to our historic sites is a great way to learn about Kentucky's exciting past. Boone, Clay, Lincoln, and Rowan are but a few of the famous names etched in Kentucky history and preserved in our 10 historic sites.

Our 22 recreation parks offer the perfect setting for a weekend of camping or just a picnic on a beautiful Kentucky day. Our swimming pools and miniature golf courses are popular stops for families gathered for reunions. Nine of our recreation parks also feature historic sites such as My Old Kentucky Home and Old Fort Harrod. John James Audubon State Park, unique for the park system, features the renovated and expanded John James Audubon Museum and Nature Center, home to a comprehensive collection of Audubon art and memorabilia.

Whether you prefer Kentucky history, a day on the water or a hike in the mountains, I believe that just one visit to any of our parks will bring you back again and again. You can always be certain that you will be met with Kentucky's special brand of hospitality.

Mark A. Lovely, Commissioner
Commonwealth of Kentucky
Department of Parks
Capital Plaza Tower
500 Mero Street, 11th Floor
Frankfort, Kentucky 40601-1974

Introduction

The bass bite harder in Kentucky. The leaves of towering trees are greener, wildflowers are more fragrant and colorful, mountain skies bluer, and the state parks are terrific. In fact, the Kentucky state parks may indeed be the nation's finest, and this is your comprehensive guidebook with all the details on how to enjoy them.

You will discover extraordinary quality in the parks and exceptional natural features, where you can explore thundering waterfalls, sandstone arches, wild rivers and caves, wooded ravines, and towering ridges and bluffs. You can ride the foaming wild rivers, snow ski, water ski, stroll ancient forests, look for hundreds of different songbirds, fish in quiet coves, or just plain laze-out at one of the beautiful modern resorts' lodges. It's no wonder the repeat business at Kentucky state parks and resorts is the highest in the country!

You can find a place to play or just "park it" at a Kentucky state park. For general information about the state park, group sales, scheduling, or handicapped accessibility call (800) 255-PARK (TDD equipped).

Most state parks are open all year. For travel information and a listing of annual special events, call (800) 225-TRIP (TDD equipped).

Bicycling

The back roads of Kentucky and the often quiet roads that criss-cross the state's 47 state parks offer scenic beauty, wildlife, shady rides, and plenty of places to go and see. Each park has slightly different rules for bicycling, trail system use, bike rentals, and information about local roads and trails.

Campgrounds

Twenty-six parks have campsites with electrical and water hookups. Primitive camping is also available. Camping sites are rented on a first-come, first-served basis. Check the campground section for each part in the book for our "best site" recommendations.

Central service buildings contain restrooms, showers and laundry facilities and are typically near a small playground. Some camping areas include horse camping sections, swimming pools, mini-golf, activity centers and beaches.

Canoeing and Rafting

There are 14 major river systems in Kentucky offering plenty of canoeing, kayaking and rafting for every age and level of experience. You can paddle many gentle riverways and smooth lakes, or go nuts at the many whitewater rafting and kayaking locations around the state. Cumberland Falls State Resort Park has one of the finest group rafting adventures anywhere.

For more information about the state's nine most scenic rivers that cover 114 miles and are designated as the Kentucky wild river (and other riverways), call the Kentucky Division of Water, 14 Reilly Road, Frankfort, Ky., 40601, (502) 564-3410. You can also call Canoe Kentucky at (800) K-CANOE-1 for additional information. Each state park has information about its particular opportunities for boating and canoeing.

Fishing

Some local anglers claim the fish often jump right into your boat without coaxing. Actually, most species in the network of freshwater lakes, streams and rivers need only a little amount of coaxing to bite your lure or bait. Kentucky waters offer anglers a chance to delicately wave a flyrod and toss tiny dry flies at finicky brook trout, cut stinkbait for delicious tasting catfish, or test your skills on tough-fishing striped bass in the spawning depths of a reservoir.

update by calling (502) 527-5952. For Lake Cumberland, call (616) 679-5655. A 38-page Kentucky fish booklet is also available. For a subscription to "Kentucky Afield" magazine, write Kentucky Department of Fish and Wildlife Resources, #1 Game Farm Road, Frankfort, Ky., 40601, or call (502) 564-4336 during regular business hours. A list of lakes where people with physical impairments can fish with relative ease is also available upon request.

Games - golf and much more

From shuffleboard to horseshoe courts, tennis and golf—lots of superior golf, both mini- and challenging regulation—visitors to the parks can enjoy. How about sand volleyball, a game of softball, video games, basketball, pool, table tennis or foosball? Kentucky state parks can keep you hopping from game to game and court to court or hole to hole. Bring your tennis racket or golf clubs, or rent theirs. Many golf courses require advance scheduling of tee times on weekends.

Hiking

Kentucky's state park system provides 135 miles of marked hiking trails at 27 parks. Most of the 20 state nature preserves also have marked trails that are open to the public. There are also 60 public wildlife areas across the state available for hiking. In total, there are about 1,500 miles of marked, maintained hiking routes in the state. They are great places for casual walks, day hikes or wilderness backpacking adventures.

Aside from the terrific state park trails in individual parks, there are two major trails in the state—the Sheltowee Trace National Recreation Trail and the Jenny Wiley National Recreation Trail. Both offer excellent scenic routes through eastern Kentucky.

Sheltowee Trace is marked for 257 miles through the Daniel Boone National Forest from north of Morehead to Pickett State Park in Tennessee. The Jenny Wiley Trail runs 185 miles from Kentucky's northeastern tip at South Shore to the Jenny Wiley State Resort Park in Prestonsburg.

There are also two connector trails off Jenny Wiley—the 25-mile Tygart Trail to Greenbo Lake and the nine-mile Simon Kenton Trail to Carter

Caves. If this isn't enough great hiking, try some of the 1,112 miles of trails in Kentucky's national recreation areas!

Historic sites

Nine state parks in the commonwealth offer excellent and fascinating historic information about our past. Many of the resort parks also work diligently to protect, preserve and interpret Kentucky's history, including outdoor dramas, museums, reenactments, guided tours and costumed interpreters and craftspeople.

Horseback riding

Clip, clop. From atop a horse you can see many wonderful natural areas in Kentucky state parks. The following parks typically offer supervised hourly horseback riding during the summer season: Kentucky Dam Village Resort Park, Lake Barkley State Resort Park, Barren River Lake State Resort Park and Lake Cumberland State Resort Park.

Lodges

Kentucky state parks are destination parks. They are large, well-developed and complete with amenities for just about every user. Fourteen of the 15 resorts, plus Audubon and Blue Licks Battlefield, also have fine equipped cottages. Reservations are accepted for lodge rooms and cottages up to one year in advance.

Virtually all of the fine lodges have neighboring swimming pools, gift shops, conference and meeting rooms, excellent dining rooms, scenic views, game courts and game rooms, walking trails, shady rest spots, fishing, boating, and lots more.

There are nine cottage types ranging from efficiencies to three-bedroom executive models. Pets are not permitted in lodge rooms or cottages. The resort state parks have recreation directors and busy schedules of activities for youth and adults.

For more information about the "nation's finest" state parks, call 1(800) 225-PARK, (TDD-equipped)

1   *Barren River Lake State Resort Park*

Land: 2,187 acres Water: 10,000 acres

"Barren" it's not! Don't be fooled by the name frontier settlers gave the area not understanding that Indians periodically burned large tracts of land to improve grassland grazing condition for buffalo herds. In fact, the lush rolling area is dotted with forests, lakes and farms, and criss-crossed by small streams and big rivers. The area is anything but barren!

The highly developed resort park was dedicated in 1965 and is a short drive from Kentucky's famous cave area, which includes Mammoth Cave National Park, the longest cave system in the world.

Mammoth has 51,000 acres in the geological complex and is one of the

Seven Wonders of the World. More than 144 miles of caves (and 340 miles of corridors) are carved in the limestone and these fascinating formations are some of the most visited of all natural features in the world. More than 200 species of plants and animals have been documented inside the caves.

The first group of tourists to Mammoth Cave came 4,000 years ago. Beginning in the late 1700s, an increasing number of curious visitors from around the world came to the Kentucky phenomenon. The cave was designated as a national park in 1941. Cave tours are offered, ranging from .25-mile to five miles in length. Call (800) 967-2283 for additional information about this Kentucky treasure.

Barren, Allen and Monroe counties were once a part of Green and Warren counties and were established in 1797. This expansive territory had been set aside for military service grants for veterans of the Revoluntary War.

In early 1960 the U.S. Army Corps of Engineers started construction on the 146-foot-tall dam that impounds the Barren River Lake. The earth and random rock dam is 3,970 feet long and drains a 940-square-mile area. The impoundment created the 10,000-acre lake that was put into operation in 1964. The lake has 140 miles of shoreline.

Information and Activities

Barren River Lake State Resort Park
1149 State Park Road
Lucas, KY 42156-9709
(502) 646-2151 - lodge
(800) 325-0057 - reservations

Directions: 44 miles southeast of Bowling Green, take I-65 north to the Cumberland Parkway east to U.S. 31E south. The park is 95 miles from Louisville and 35 miles from Mammoth Cave.

Lodge: The Louie B. Nunn Lodge, named for a former Kentucky governor, opened for business in 1971. The lodge has 51 rooms, each with views of the lake from private balconies with outdoor seating. The lodge is famous for honeymoon specials, '50s weekends, and other theme getaways.

A stone fireplace with overhead vaulted ceiling and natural tile floor underfoot, comfortable seating, and bustle makes the lobby a favorite resting area for guests. A selection of video games, art works and reading material makes the area a popular "hangout" for guests of all ages. A large screen television is particularly popular for watching college football games on Saturday afternoons in the autumn. From the lobby windows, guests have a partial view of the lake in the distance.

Barren River's gift shop (open seven days) is one of the largest in the park system. From T-shirts and ornate glassware to mugs and quilts, guests can find many nice items to take home. The hand carved wooden spoons are one of the most interesting objects at the lobby-side shop.

From the wall of windows in the 146-seat dining room, guests can enjoy gracious service and fine Kentucky cuisine while watching the activity on the lake.

Swimming pool: Behind the lodge, the sparkling nine-foot-deep pool is outlined by globe-like street lamps that illuminate the large deck in the evening. Deck chairs, lounges, umbrella tables and one elevated lifeguard stand surround the rectangular pool. The pool is for the exclusive use of lodge and cottage guests. Campers and day-use visitors are welcome to cool off and enjoy the nearby sandy swimming beach.

A 30-foot-long kiddies' wading pool near the main pool offers parents a safe and comfortable place for toddlers to play. The tiny, shallow pool is enclosed by an four-foot-tall iron fence. Also for youngsters near the lodge is a small play area with clean sand, climbing apparatus and other interesting play equipment.

Meeting facilities: Barren River has five meeting spaces of varying sizes. For dining and meetings, there are two private rooms that can seat 20 and 32. The executive conference room seats 33, a larger meeting room can accommodate 75, and the main ballroom can seat up to 400.

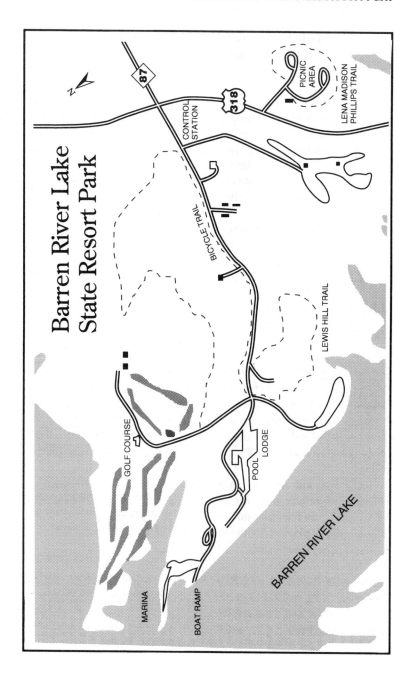

Cottages: Attractive globe-shaped lampposts and a meandering walk-way define the 22 cottages along a long ridge line on each side of the lodge. Modern and painted in pleasing pastel colors, the cottages nearest the lodge are built on a stilt-like foundation above the shoreline. Each of the cottages has two bedrooms and two baths, tableware, cooking utensils and linens. Cottages on the west side of the road have a view of the lake.

Cottages 513-522 are newer cottages near the beach. These two-tone cabins are perched on thick timber stilt-like foundations and offer guests an excellent view of the lake and cooling summer breezes. Several of the cottages have views down to the narrow swimming beach and tree-lined lake in the distance. The tasteful cabins also have free-standing grills, decks, side yards and additional parking.

Campground: Open from April 1 - October 31 (no advanced registra-tion), the hilly 99-site campground has utility hookups and two service buildings with laundry, showers and rest rooms. There are a mixture of camping sites that include large ones, private sites, pull-through and very small lots. The small campground contact station sells ice. A very nice day-use area with shelter house is adjacent to the campground entrance.

The park staff recommends sites 39-53, which are in a loop near the campground one-lane boat ramp and sites 69-79 are a wooded and shady section close to the rest rooms. Sites 80-92 are also popular, but farther from the service building. Other perennial favorites are sites 24-37 and 55- 69. The campground always fills up on holiday weekends. Many fishermen use this campground because of its proximity to good angling, boat trailer parking and a cozy boat ramp.

Site 24-37 and 55-79 are pull-through sites and can accommodate larger RV rigs. These camping sites are close to a playground that has a snail-like climbing apparatus with bulging green eyes and long antenna.

Fishing: Setting on a low ridge, looking down upon the expansive parking lots and marina, a cream-colored fish-cleaning station can be a busy place. The well-equipped facility has sinks, hoses, buckets, trash barrels, lights and running water.

The larger size limit for bass in Barren River Lake is testimony to the quality of the sport fishing. Light-colored spinnerbaits used in the upper reaches where dense weedbeds, stumps and other structures hold quality fish is a favorite method of serious anglers that flock to the impoundment.

Crappies are a sought-after species in the lake by casual weekend anglers. Stump beds, and humpbacks along submerged creek channels offer superb cover for hand-sized crappies during both the winter and summer seasons. Fish will often suspend in eight to 15 feet of water.

As the population of crayfish has increased, so has smallmouth bass numbers. Smallmouths tend to stay close to shale bluffs and gravel points in the lower Barren River Lake. Largemouth bass move more, often to the upper lake in the early spring and late fall and in the lower end of the winding lake during the summer and winter. Local experts say that during the summer, largemouth will suspend in submerged channels of the larger tributaries or the old river channels in deep water that can only be reached by deep-diving crankbaits, vertical jigging spoons or rubber worms.

Deep-water jigging includes a grape-colored, firetail rubber worm and a 1/8- to3/8-ounce jig. Jig the worm-rig off the bottom, across ledges. Fish will hit it on the drop. Other bass angling techniques include crayfish-colored crankbaits fished over deep points.

The lake also supports good populations of white bass, hybrid striped bass and big channel catfish that frequent shallow flats next to submerged channels.

Boating: You can run with the wind, ski all day, or putt about the lake on a pontoon boats. The large marina at the cove rents all types of watercraft, including fishing boats and motors, houseboats and wave runners. About 100 open slips and 40 covered slips, a launching ramp and small store serve visiting water enthusiasts. The small floating marina store sells T-shirts, PFDs (personal floatation devices), tools, packaged snacks, soft drinks, ice, marine supplies, fuel, live bait (minnows, crickets, nightcrawlers, meal worms, etc.) tackle, boat and water ski rentals.

Two fishing or small pleasure boats could launch at the same time from the ramp, but it is best that boaters go one at a time. The river channel is marked and virtually all of the shoreline is tree-lined and hilly. Pontoon boats are the most popular craft on the lake.

Hiking: Biking and hiking go hand-in-hand at Barren Lake. The many hard-surfaced trails and quiet park roads are excellent routes for a daily stroll, ride or jog. The seven miles of nature trails are open year-round and range from easy to difficult hiking.

The Lewis Hill Trail, a one-mile loop near the lodge and beach, is a popular trail for evening hikes and deer watching.

Riding stable: East of the lodge is the small horse barn where guests can enjoy guided horseback rides that depart several times a day, all summer. It is open seasonally.

Biking: The 2.5-mile hard-surfaced trail, and winding park roads at Barren River are perfect for an afternoon of bicycling. Bring your own bike.

Day-use areas: Outdoor game courts at Barren River include two shuffleboard courts behind the lodge, lighted tennis courts (a beach volleyball court is between the two courts), basketball goal and playground near the lodge. Overnight guests may check out sports equipment.

Golf: Eighteen holes of fun await players at the Barren River course. On a peninsula, the hilly course is densely wooded with evergreen and deciduous trees. The lake surrounds holes four and five; the ninth is a very tight par four. The fairways at Barren River are closely mowed and often tree-lined.

The timber-style pro shop is elegant and shaded by lofty pines. A long porch and outdoor seating near the practice green and first tee are heavily used by spectators and as a 19th hole lounging area for tired golfers. Indoors, a lounge with a television set and videocassette recorder is the focal point. The Barren River pro shop is well-stocked—one of the most complete in the system—with bags, clubs, clothes and golfing accessories.

Barren River has a well-stocked pro shop.

Swimming beach: Open seasonally, the small, light-colored sandy beach is a popular cooling off spot in the summer.

Planned recreation: The U.S. Army Corps of Engineers and the state park education and recreation staff collaborate on some programming, but most of the daily planned recreation activities are hosted in the park. Special events and traditional group recreation programs are offered. They include arts and crafts, game court tournaments, nature walks, hula hoop contest, Frisbee golf, dancing, musical activities, lake tours, morning hikes, bocce, poolside bingo, and more.

The game room in the lower level of the lodge features two ping pong tables and other games. The meeting rooms are next to the game room.

Special notes: The annual Trashmasters cleanup day yields tons of litter and is a very popular volunteer experience (700 volunteers annually pick up 15 tons of trash!) that helps the park stay clean.

The Glasgow Highland Games are a celebration of Scottish sport, featuring activities like piping, sheep dog demonstrations, battle ax throwing, clachneart (17-pound stone throw), 56-pound toss, caper toss, hammer toss, dance competition, tug of war, rugby, golf tournament and more. The popular event is generally held on four days in early June. Glasgow Airport is 17 miles from the park.

Golfers start registering for weekend tee times early in the week.

2   Ben Hawes State Park (golf course)

Land: 297 acres

They begin lining up outside the pro shop—sitting on the pro shop porch—and waiting in their cars on Wednesday mornings. They are the die-hard golfers, lining up for weekend tee times—days in advance. They are also a great bunch of guys—and gals.

More golfing stories are told on the big porch at Ben Hawes' Pro Shop than any other place in the universe. Knowing that, it's not surprising that Ben Hawes is the busiest golf course in the state of Kentucky. It's probably the friendliest, too.

The golfing stories continue inside the pro shop, too, where carts are rented, clubs examined and discussed, and greens fees paid. The pro shop reminded me of a Bennett Cerf quote that says, "The game of golf was launched at 11:10 a.m., the first lie about a scorecard at 11:22 a.m., and the first golf joke at noon."

I think some of these intrepid duffers are so accustomed to shaving their scorecard, they would card a hole-in-one as a zero. The park opened in 1975 and was named after a former Owensboro mayor.

Information and Activities

Ben Hawes State Park
400 Booth Field Road
Owensboro, KY 42301
(502) 684-9808 or 684-2011 pro shop

Directions: Off U.S. 60W, turn north onto Booth Field Road to the park. Three miles west of Owensboro. Audubon State Park is 25 miles away.

Golf course: Blending from the well-maintained neighborhoods, the 27 holes of golf look like an extension of the fine lawns and gardens of the quality homes in the area.

There's plenty of parking near the red-brick pro shop for guests and golfers who bring their own carts on tiny two-wheeled trailers.

Behind the small gray building in front of the pro shop is the lighted driving range that is corded off by a low white chain fence. Yardage is marked off on the range reaching out more than 250 yards, where a fence catches any balls propelled farther.

The course is open year-round (except when there is snow on the ground). The front nine on the popular course is very flat, and the back nine has gentle hills. The wide fairways are planted in Bermuda grass, while the medium-sized greens are of bent grass and well-maintained. A small creek bisects seven of the holes on the course, offering hazards for the golfer who chooses the wrong club or doesn't carry the ditch.

There are 27 holes at Ben Hawes State Park.

A few tables with seating are strategically located near the large practice green just west of the pro shop. Reservations for tee times are strongly advised.

Day-use areas: The entrance to the park is broad, flat and mowed. To the left are the golf course and driving range, to the right are some scattered day-use amenities that include a lighted ball field, basketball courts, play and climbing equipment (two in the shape of rockets!), toddler swings and a series of small wooded bridges that cross a tiny creek.

Informal picnic tables and grills are located around the open spaces and near parking. Some of the picnic sites are shaded by mature trees.

The picnic pavilion (shelter house) is one of the best in the parks system. Three modern shelters are connected. The gray-roofed buildings are partially cement block constructed and can be reserved in advance.

Electrical outlets at tabletop levels, grills, drinking fountains and rest rooms are at the buildings.

The park also maintains a one-mile hiking trail.

More golf jokes:

"How long can you go without drinking?"
"About six holes."

"Like my game, caddy?"
"Not bad, sir. But I still prefer golf."

Golf is backwards: Businessmen talk nothing but golf in the office, and nothing but business on the links.

Show me a sportsman who's a good loser, and I'll show you a man playing golf with his boss.

Nothing counts in a golf game like your opponent!

Special notes: Owensboro, on the Ohio River, is Kentucky's third biggest city and an interesting visitor destination. Three great annual festivals includes the International Bar-B-Q Festival, Owensboro Summer Festival, and the International Bluegrass Music Association (IBMA) Bluegrass FanFest. For more information about all of the things to do, call (800) 489-1131.

3 *Big Bone Lick State Park*

Land: 512 acres Water: 7.5-acre lake

In prehistoric times, great herds of giant mastodons, mammoths, bison, primitive horses and giant ground sloths lived in this area of north central Kentucky. These huge creatures were attracted to the warm salt springs that bubbled from the earth in this swampy land. Many of the massive beasts became mired in the ooze and died, leaving behind hundreds of skeletal remains and clues about life in ice age Kentucky. Over thousands of years, many of the bones have turned to stone and taught scientists a great deal about the history of the region.

These soft, wet swamplands were called "jelly ground" by pioneers and this area was the first widely-known collecting locality for ice age artifacts in North America. When Indian guides took French Canadian explorer de Longueil to Big Bone Lick in 1739, bones were literally lying on the surface of the marshy ground, virtually waiting to be picked up.

Five years later, Robert Smith, an Indian trader did just that, removing the first bones from the area. Other settlers and explorers, including Lewis and Clark, collected hundreds of bones, sending them to President Thomas Jefferson. By 1840, it was estimated that the bones of hundreds of mammals had been removed from the area.

These warm sulphur springs and salt licks attracted both animals and man. Indians and pioneers exploited the area, collecting salt that was used for food preservation and trading. Salt was an important commodity in those days and a small fort was erected in the vicinity to protect salt collecting expeditions.

The ancient salt licks are dried up now, and the sulphur springs are tiny. But in the 1800s a number of health spas were developed in the area for wealthy families to take advantage of their "curative qualities." In 1960 the Department of Parks began development of the park, constructing roads, shelters and day-use areas. Today, the park is a terrific family destination offering exciting information about "ice age mammals," great camping, fishing, game courts, an indoor and outdoor museum, gift shop, video program, picnicking and much more.

Children will be delighted to see life-sized models of prehistoric mast-odons and a herd of live bison at the park. Many of the park's amenities are open seasonally.

Information and Activities

Big Bone Lick State Park
3380 Beaver Road
Union, KY 41091-9627
(606) 384-3522

Directions: 22 miles southwest of Covington, south to KY exit 338 off I-75.

The Ice Age: Also called the Pleistocene epoch, it started 1.8 million years ago and ended about 10,000 years ago. The important part of the Pleistocene relating to the state park spanned an 8,000 year period 12,000 to 20,000 years ago. During this time tremendous sheets of ice covered the continent in a jagged pattern to just south of Cincinnati.

Scientists generally agree that many prehistoric mammals not previously found in Kentucky were driven southward by the ice. This factor and the salt swamps account for the many species and great numbers of remains found well-preserved in the area.

Many of these bones turned to stone by a process called mineralization, a slow natural process that may take anywhere from hundreds to thousands of years. Bones not exposed to the workings of sun, rain and changing temperatures were the best candidates for rockdom. Bones that sunk to the bottom of the bog or pond, or those scattered on cave floors, were often preserved.

Campground: Big Bone Lick has 62 sites with utility hookups. A small grocery store at the campground entrance stocks food items, camping supplies, T-shirts, firewood, cold drinks, souvenirs and newspapers, and there is a public telephone outside. The store is clean, and well-maintained.

Next to the campground store is an old root cellar that was built by slaves in the early 1800s. That was a pioneer substitution for the refrigerator and kept an average temperature of 50 degrees, year-round. It was built entirely of stone with no mortar. Kids will love to visit this dark and dusty walk-in pioneer refrigerator.

Big Bone Lick's campground is along a ridge that looks down into some semi-open valleys. Open year-round, no advanced reservations are taken for the camping area that is quite open and sunny. Each camping site has a fire ring, picnic table, nearby utility hookup and hard-surfaced pad.

Sites 16 and 17 are fairly shady, while sites 25-28 can accommodate large RV rigs and are at the end of a small, shady circular loop. The view from these sites is of rich agricultural lands and grazing pastures scattered across rolling hills that disappear at the horizon. Virtually all of the camping sites are flat and large enough for most camping rigs.

Behind site 43 is a small recreation area that includes a picnic shelter, portable bleacher seating and open spaces. Site 55 is one of the most private in the campground and also is close to the shower building and pool.

Campers will also enjoy the small swimming pool that is centrally located and next to the shower building. Although the pool is shallow, with a maximum depth of five feet, it is clean and colorful. An elevated wooden deck offers parents and sunbathers the perfect place to relax or work on a tan.

Museum: At the trailhead of the Big Bone Creek Trail, where huge life-sized models of prehistoric bison and mastodons stand really still, is the constantly improving block and wood museum that houses the gift shop, video viewing area and exhibit room (small fee).

From the elevated museum, visitors will have a nice overlook on to lands where both prehistoric animals and the modern American buffalo once roamed in large numbers. For many years bison roamed the lands that stretch from the Appalachian to the Rocky mountains with herds that numbered in the hundreds. They often moved great distances in search of prime grazing and mineral rich springs, which they found here at Bone Lick. These routes, called "traces," served as a wagon trail that aided in the development of the Commonwealth. Many of today's highways follow these traces.

The one-room exhibit's most dominant display is a huge mastodon skull that was collected in 1955. The skull has two huge tusks and is in about a 10-foot-long display case. Many other bone fragments, projectile points, skeleton parts, rib bones, jaw bones and a five minute video about the region offer background, insight and meaning to the history the park is so rich in.

Gift shop: The compact shop adjoins the museum and offers Kentucky crafts, many park-related objects, pottery and traditional souvenirs. The museum and gift shop are closed during January. Restrooms are inside, with soft drink machines outdoors against the building.

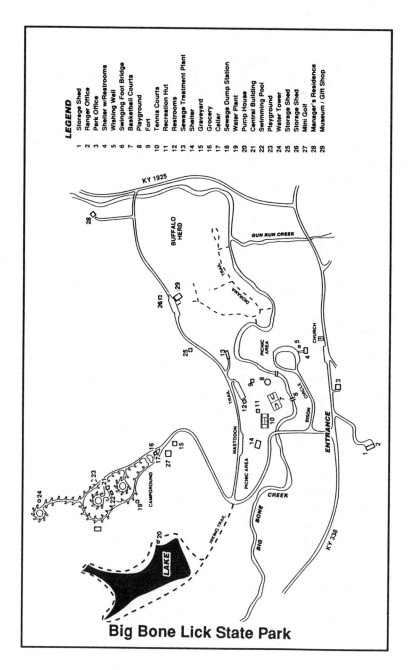

LEGEND

1 Storage Shed
2 Ranger Office
3 Park Office
4 Shelter w/Restrooms
5 Wishing Well
6 Swinging Foot Bridge
7 Basketball Courts
8 Playground
9 Fort
10 Tennis Courts
11 Recreation Hut
12 Restrooms
13 Sewage Treatment Plant
14 Shelter
15 Graveyard
16 Grocery
17 Cellar
18 Sewage Dump Station
19 Water Plant
20 Pump House
21 Central Building
22 Swimming Pool
23 Playground
24 Water Tower
25 Storage Shed
26 Storage Shed
27 Mini Golf
28 Manager's Residence
29 Museum / Gift Shop

Big Bone Lick State Park

Fishing: The small lake is sometimes stocked with bass, catfish and bluegill and bank fishing is the only method of angling. There is no public boat launching ramp on the small lake. Park staff suggested fishing in the spring using live bait.

Hiking: Big Bone Lick has 3.5 miles of trails, many of which are hard-surfaced and easy. The Big Bone Creek Trail is a six-foot-wide hard-surfaced trail that has life-size models in a couple of openings along with interesting interpretive signs placed at strategic locations (information on rivers, ice age, history, etc.).

One interesting point on the trail highlights the types of fossils found in the area. Some of the more important Cincinnatian series of the upper Ordovician strata, a rock unit dating back more than three million years, can be seen in the outcroppings of rock in the surrounding area of the park. The outlines of several marine invertebrates—animals without spinal columns—characteristic of that age when more than one-half of the North American mainland was under water are preserved in these rocks. Much information about the earth's history is gained by studying these extinct animals. Fossils can sometimes be seen in these rock outcroppings. Look, but don't collect.

From this gently rolling trail you can spot bison either at the feeding crib at the west end of the park or among the lightly wooded enclosed areas. The trail is shady and gentle with many wildflowers along the winding trail's edge.

The other maintained trail is an easy hike around the small lake.

Buffalo herd: Great herds of American buffalo, or bison, once roamed this area and provided food, clothing and shelter for Indians and pioneers. Bison nearly were wiped out by hunters, with the last wild buffalo seen in Kentucky around 1800. The park's small herd offers visitors a chance to see North America's largest land mammal. For a good view of the animals, plan an early morning visit and watch them at the feeding station. They can sometimes be seen rolling in sandy areas, especially in the morning or when the insects are thick.

Through hunting and settlement the bison were eventually pushed out of

Kentucky. By 1800, the American bison vanished from the blue grass. From the museum visitors can access the trail by the low wire fence that encloses the parks herd of buffalo.

The American bison is the largest land mammal in North America, reaching a length of 11 feet long, six feet tall and weighing as much as 2,000 pounds. Although their legs look small for such a large animal, they are actually very powerful. They can carry the bison up to speeds of 40 mph and jump objects up to six feet high. Both male and female bison have hollow horns which relate the woolly-looking creatures to common cattle and sheep. Once numbered in the millions, bison were brought to the brink of extinction. It is estimated that in 1900 only one thousand bison were left in the nation.

Protection and conservation efforts have brought the bison back to healthy numbers. The herds have returned and can once again be seen at Bone Lick.

Day-use areas: Nearly 40 acres of well-groomed day-use areas and picnic grounds for family and group outings are offered. There are many picnic tables and grills, a small playground, mini golf, tennis courts, softball field, basketball court, volleyball courts and horseshoe pits scattered around the park. Many of the picnic tables are located under shade trees and near open spaces. There are two shelter houses (one large, one small) with electrical service in the park that are available for rent. Advanced registration and a deposit are required.

The small cable wooden suspension bridge is a favorite of many visitors who cross Big Bone Creek.

Miniature golf: Small Indian, elephant and squirrel statues are positioned along the cement fairways of the 18-hole miniature golf course. Golfers will enjoy an excellent woodland view from the course. Next to the course is the historic Baker family cemetery.

Special notes: All cultural heritage items—bones and other archaeological remains—should be left in place. Do not collect fossils, bones or other materials from the park. The Big Bone Lick Salt Festival is held each October.

4 Blue Licks Battlefield State Park

Land: 148 acres Water: Licking River

The Battle of Blue Licks, known to generations of Kentuckians as "the last battle of the American Revolution," was fought Aug. 19, 1782, at a site just north of the Lower Blue Licks crossing of the Licking River, at modern day Blue Licks Battlefield State Park in what is now Robertson County

Actually, the battle was one of a series of frontier skirmishes between the 1781 defeat of the British army at Yorktown and the 1783 peace agreement. Fortunately, and sadly, for the United States, this remote encounter had no influence on the Revolutionary War's outcome, as it was one of the worst military disasters suffered on the Kentucky frontier.

The fierce battle, which took only 16 minutes, was a bitter defeat for the

182 Kentuckians trying to protect and defend their homes and country from about 300 Indians and 26 white British soldiers under the command of British Captain William Caldwell. On the site of the battle immediately upon entering the state park is a tall granite shaft bearing the names of those who fell on this site as well as a pioneer museum that houses many relics including a collection of prehistoric remains unearthed at the salt licks.

The British commander, after attacking Bryan Station, a fort in central Kentucky, became aware that Union reinforcements were on the way and moved north. His forces were overtaken by a much smaller band of Kentuckians, who—against the advice of Daniel Boone—crossed the Licking River and found themselves ambushed. Captain Caldwell had carefully concealed his army behind trees at the head of a deep ravine that furnished a natural and deadly trap.

Seven Kentuckians were taken prisoner and 60 were killed, including one of Daniel Boone's sons. The British and Indians resumed the retreat and escaped across the Ohio as more reinforcements joined the white survivors and prepared to renew the fight under General George Clark. This expedition succeeded in the Northwest Conquest, which ended the warfare in Kentucky.

Many years later the Blue Lick Springs region, famous from the battle which took place nearby, was a thriving health resort—or "watering place"—of the mid-19th century in Nickolas County on the south bank of the Licking River across from Robertson County. The salty water was first a "salt making" place in the 1770s, which lead to the bottling of the water for medicinal purposes and construction of Blue Lick Springs resort by William Bartlett. In the early 1840s John and L.P. Holladay bought the resort and built the much more luxurious, 300-room Arlington Hotel in 1845.

Only 21 miles from Maysville, along a major stage coach route between Ohio and Tennessee, the spa became the premier place for the rich to visit the "curative" springs and benefit from the "health giving" waters and resort. The mineral waters were said to benefit persons suffering from diseases of the stomach, liver and kidneys; asthma; gout; dyspepsia; rheumatism; neuralgia; "autumnal" fevers; and "general debility." The

670-foot hotel had a full-length gallery where guests could walk, socialize, and talk of their "cure."

Lavish banquets, balls and "cures" ended with the fire of 1862 that burnt the ornate hotel to the ground. By 1896 even the Lower Blue Licks Spring went dry. In an effort to locate the old spring, many ancient artifacts, including a mastodon tusk and two wagon loads of archaeological materials, were hauled from the site. The museum exhibits some of the remains from the more recent 1945 dig.

Information and Activities

Blue Licks Battlefield State Park
P.O. Box 66
Mount Olivet, KY 41064-0066
(606) 289-5507

Directions: 48 miles northeast of Lexington on U.S. 68 in Robertson County, which is only 101 square miles.

Campground: The campground is one loop with each site having asphalt pads, a table and fire grills. The shower building (three showers in each side) is adjacent to a sand volleyball court and timber play structures for children. The area is rolling and about 60 percent shady. Most of the camping sites have at least one tree that offers constantly moving shade from the branches and leaves. All sites have water and electrical hookups.

Site 11 is one of the nicer camping sites. Sites on the interior of the loop are not as shady as those along the perimeter that back up against wooded areas. Sites 23 and 25 have privacy and are somewhat notched out of the nature area; they are also near the shower building and its amenities, which include a public phone and laundry facilities. Sites 5, 7 and 9 are heavily shaded and next to the shower house. Site 31 is shady. Sites 39 and 41 are near a densely wooded ravine.

Families will like this campground, it allows parents a view of the entire play area and campground from any point along the small circular loop.

Cottages: Modern and clean, the two two-bedroom light-gray cottages rest on a ridge with a view of Licking River and wooded valleys. Each unit is air-conditioned and offers a comfortable balcony and seating for evening chats and chews. Cottages have a microwave oven, comfortable couches, dining table with six places, and tasteful decor. Many cottage guests are ancestors of the men fallen in the battle who are researching family lines and connecting to their past.

Meeting spaces: The two-level wooden Worthington Center can accommodate up to 400 people for meetings, conferences, dinners and special events. It is available for rent up to one calendar year in advance. A popular place for breakout meetings is the large deck that has an overview of the Licking River and pleasant natural areas.

Canoeing: The Middle Fork of the Licking River, which forms the western boundary of the state park, provides good canoeing south from the park all the way to its narrow origin in Magoffin County. But typically the very southern headwaters are too littered with logjams and too small to paddle. From KY 32 Bridge to the confluence of the North and South forks, which pass the park, canoeists can run year-round along hilly farmlands and wooded shorelines. Canoe camping trips that include a stay at the state park are recommended along these waters.

Fishing: Shoreline access to the Licking River is by foot trail only.

Hiking: The one-mile Licking River Trail starts at the small campground check-in station and takes walkers along the Licking River to the west. The trail is easy walking and likely traces some of the steps of Daniel Boone and near the site where he and his men were captured by Shawnee Indians on a salt making expedition (the museum has lots of information about salt making).

Day-use areas: Many picnic areas shaded by mixed deciduous trees are scattered along the park roadway, with some near the gravel sites of the Kentucky fighting men who died in the bloody Blue Licks battle. Two shelters (one with a restroom) are offered for rent to groups and families and includes tables, grills, small playgrounds and open spaces near parking.

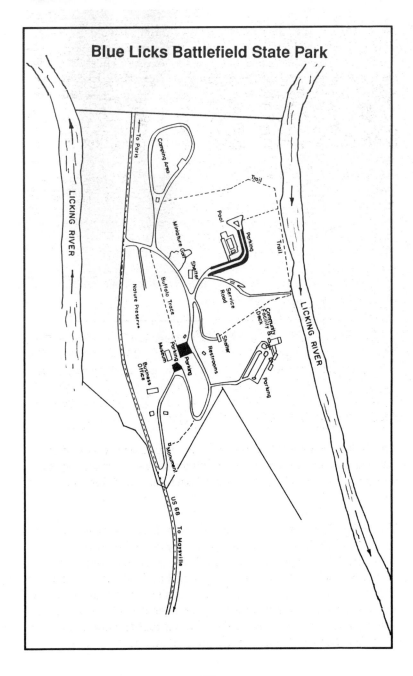

Blue Licks Battlefield State Park

The Pioneer Museum.

Swimming pool: The pool is open Memorial Day - Labor Day, Monday-Friday, 11 a.m. - 7 p.m.; weekends, 10 a.m. - 6 p.m. The bathhouse and concession are nearby. There is a small admission fee; campers swim free. A kiddies-size pool for youngsters 6 years and under is also operated at the complex. Mom and Dad can rest in deck-side lounge chairs as they watch the children swim.

The 18-hole miniature golf course along the main park road midway between the campground entrance and the swimming pool complex is open daily, Memorial Day - Labor Day (open during the fall on weekends only). There is a fee.

Museum: There is a small fee for admission (6 years and under are free) to the stately Pioneer Museum (open daily, 9 a.m. - 5 p.m., April - October) that is perched on a shaded hill overlooking the gift shop, parking lot and lightly wooded rolling grounds. Aside from a chance to hold a real tooth from a mastodon found on site (which is about the size of a football), there is also a wedding dress that has a 23-inch waist on display just outside the stone-walled room that features exhibits on cooking and ancient-looking housewares of the era.

Civil War artifacts, information about the area's salt making industry and the prehistoric animals that were attracted to the salt lick, trapped in the muddy bogs, and ultimately preserved by the salt and found by modern day archaeologists are on display in the high-ceiling museum.

Other artifacts on exhibit and interpreted are long rifles, glass bottles, Indian pottery and tools, dolls, high-wheeled bicycles and early American household items that included a biscuit kneader, hair curling irons, and coffee and sausage stuffers, all in basement display cases on the red brick floor.

The nearby gift shop is open weekdays, 9 a.m. - 5 p.m., and features Kentucky made crafts, souvenirs, mugs, paper and other items. The gift shop has a small sitting area in front of the building. Also in the area is a terrific timber and stone picnic shelter that can accommodate 25 tables.

Planned recreation: Scheduled programs are offered by the recreation staff from Memorial Day to Labor Day, primarily on weekends.

Nature: Short's goldenrod, named after Dr. Charles W. Short, an avid botanist and physician, is an endangered species found only along the route traveled by the buffalo in a 3.35-mile corridor (trace) some of which is in the park. The park's nature preserve is dedicated to the preservation of the rare plant. It is speculated that the buffalo might have been responsible for dispersing the seeds of this plant, and by grazing and trampling, they helped maintain the open habitat the plant needs to survive.

Between the museum and the gray-colored gift shop, the park's 15-acre nature preserve is carefully maintained. The preserve is jointly managed by the Kentucky Nature Preservation Commission and the Kentucky Department. of State Parks System. For more information about the Preservation Commission, call (502) 564-2886. There are limitations on visitor use of the nature preserve.

Special notes: A highlight is the Battle of Blue Licks Celebration, an annual reenactment held in mid-August featuring period costumes, 1782 battle reenactment, arts and crafts show, and other activities.

5 Buckhorn Lake State Resort Park

Land: 856 acres   Water: 1200-acre lake

Cradled in the rolling foothills of the Cumberland Plateau—part of the Appalachia Mountain Range—at the northern edge of the Daniel Boone National Forest, Buckhorn Lake is the only unit in the system to take its name after a local community.

Accounts vary as to how Buckhorn was named, however. Some say it was named after a small spring which was named for a foursnag buck killed there by the area's first settler, Jerry Smith. Another story claims that the unusual name derives from the discovery of a buck's horn at a neighboring salt lick.

Buckhorn Lake begins the Middle Fork of the Kentucky River, while the Middle Fork, South Fork and the North Fork merge at Beattyville to form the Kentucky River. The lake was formed after constructing a rock-filled dam on the Middle Fork by the Corps of Engineers in the early 1960s. The lodge and other amenities were opened for business in 1964.

In 1960, the voters of Kentucky approved a large bond issue which provided the Department of Parks the money to expand parks, upgrade facilities and open new units. On January 18, 1961, the Parks Board approved the area of Buckhorn Lake State Park for funding. An agreement was reached with the Corps of Engineers, and the clean and green park continues to improve today.

Information and Activities

Buckhorn Lake State Resort Park
HC 36, P.O. Box 1000
Buckhorn, KY 41721-9602
(606) 398-7510
(800) 325-0058 - toll-free reservations

Directions: Located 25 miles northwest of Hazard. KY 15 north to KY 28 west to KY 1833. 124 miles southeast of Lexington.

Lodge: The 36-room, medium-brown, bi-level lodge with teal-colored front entrance doors has a giant welcome mat on the porch that greets guests for a night's stay, a tour of the lodge, or a fine meal. The highly polished wood floors, tongue and groove ceiling and wood paneled walls enhance the terrific view of the lake and beach from the large lobby windows. Buckhorn is one of the smaller resort parks in the system and one of the best maintained. Facilities are down-sized from the larger parks, but that's good. The scale of the park matches the use, and offered a great weekend getaway.

The lodge is perched atop a low ridge line offering some of the most scenic countryside in Kentucky. The lodge has wonderful fireplaces, room balconies, accessibility to outdoor facilities, and great views of the pool, mountain, and lake from inside or from the long porch-like walkway that wraps around a large part of the building.

The park has three modern cottages.

Also in the lobby is a free-standing display case that shows information about the park's history and displays a variety of small artifacts, photographs, Bible and other effects. Also in the lobby is a gift shop that offers cards, T-shirts, caps, small souvenirs, film, dishware and other items of interest.

Cottages: Just east of the lodge, the newer cottages are off the main park road convenient to the Moonshiner's Hollow Trail and other recreational amenities. Shift into low gear to climb the hilly road that takes you to cottage 503, one of three cottages operated by the park. There are two two-bedroom and one three-bedroom models. Each of the cottages has a porch that overlooks the park.

Meeting facilities: A number of small meeting rooms are off the main lobby.

Fishing: Kentucky's most exciting predator fish, the muskie, is found in good numbers in the lake. And many serious anglers visit the mountain lake to try their hand at catching the vicious fish that hunts the shallows, breaklines and open water, often ripping schools of gizzard shad and other bait fish from their hiding places.

Muskies typically attack their prey from hiding. They are often found

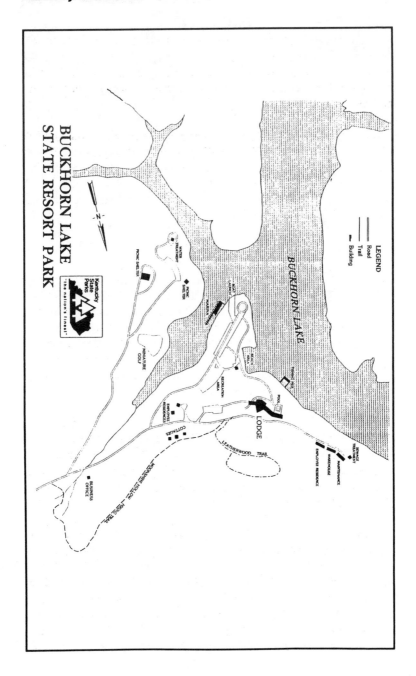

lurking among deadfalls, slinking around flooded timber and staying close to cover where they are not easily lured out by the angler's cast. Therefore, muskie anglers on the lake have adopted many techniques to catching the fiery denizens. A steady, fast retrieve is always preferred for muskie.

Or try casting bucktail spinners, topwater propeller baits, light-colored spinners and buzzbaits. When trolling many local anglers use flashy crankbaits that wobble, injured-minnow imitations, Hellbenders and other large shad-like lures connected to the line with a wire leader. Local anglers interviewed recommended white and silver patters, orange and black baits, or white and bright yellow lures.

Live bait and bobbers are recommend for shoreline panfishing.

Boating: A huge parking lot serves the many boaters who operate out of the marina. The marina has boat and slip rentals and some supplies including ice, live bait, snacks, soft drink machines, charcoal, inspect repellent and marine supplies. About half of the boats at the park are pontoons; the other half are large houseboats, with a few pleasure boats also buzzing about the lake's surface. The two-lane hard-surfaced launching ramp is free of charge and there is a convenient wooden mooring dock for temporary boat tie-ups.

Canoeists can find plenty of waters in the region to explore. A particularly placid stretch of the Middle Fork of the Kentucky River is the section from Hyden to Buckhorn Lake, offering only small riffles and waves. Closer to Hyden the river courses through green valleys to some exposed rock and gorge stretches. Quiet waters can also be found from the tailwaters of the Buckhorn Dam to Turkey Creek.

Hiking: The Leatherwood Trail is a moderately difficult trail that connects with the Moonshiner's Hollow Trail just east of the lodge.

Moonshiner's Hollow Interpretive Trail (1.5 miles) is a self-guided interpretive trail with 18 learning stations and a handy 12-page booklet that describes natural features and history of each numbered station. You'll learn about hardwoods, soils, ironwood trees, dogwoods, oaks, seeds, tulip poplar trees, coal, the forest floor, geology, stream ecology, insects and much more along the hilly path.

Along either of these trails you might see opossums, skunks, raccoons, rabbits, squirrels, white-tailed deer, woodchucks, foxes, raptors, waterfowl and songbirds.

Day-use areas: Near the marina is a sand volleyball court, one tennis court and some play apparatus for children. Bicycles can be rented at the lodge. Other amenities include horseshoes, a shuffleboard court and a basketball goal near Marina Road.

The older miniature golf layout across the small finger-like bay from the lodge and is near two large shady picnic shelters and day-use areas. Clubs and balls for the mini-golf can be obtained from the lodge.

Swimming pool: Lodge and cottage guests may use the lodge pool from 10 a.m. - 10 p.m. without charge. The pool is open seasonally and features a kiddies wading pool, two umbrella tables, sunning deck, lounge chairs and a good view of the surrounding environs.

Swimming beach: About 150 yards wide and sandy, the beach is in small cover close to the lodge across a peninsula at the busy marina. The beach and bathhouse open Memorial Day - Labor Day.

Nature: The park has a full-time recreation director during the summer who coordinates a host of activities including sporting programs, arts and crafts, supervised playground fun for the children, nature walks, ice cream socials, fishing, mini-golf outings, pool games and plenty more.

Many of the programs are nature-based learning experiences including owl prowl, bird watching, trail hikes, interpretive walks and outdoor crafts. One interesting avian event occurs when large turkey vultures stand along the beach drying out their wings. Pileated woodpeckers the size of crows are commonly seen, as are good numbers of waterfowl on the lake and songbirds in the upland terrains.

Special note: A favorite side trip for visitors is the Buckhorn Church, sometimes called the log cathedral, built in 1927. It was the largest log church east of the Mississippi River at the time of its construction.

6 Carter Caves State Resort Park

Land: 1,600 acres Water: 45-acre Smokey Valley Lake

There's a trace of mystery below ground at Carter Caves where more than 20 caverns—most chartered, others not explored—wind beneath the densely wooded terrain of this wildly interesting and awesome northeastern Kentucky park.

Through the sometimes narrow passages of caves like the X Cave, nature and a geological history offer visitors a glimpse of the earth's distant past, her most precious jewels—luminous fans, pipes and spirals in stone formed over millions of years—and a chance to view endangered bats.

Above ground you can play mountaintop golf, camp, fish, roam the gift shop or grounds, hike to a natural rock bridge, stay in a shady cottage, rent a boat, or take an exciting canoe ride down the Tygarts Creek through rugged, undisturbed country, only to return at the end of the day to modern luxury in the fieldstone lodge.

The park was a privately owned tourist attraction when the state purchased the forested area in 1946 and began operating it as a state park. Over the next few years Caveland Lodge, with a 114-seat dining room, gift shop and 15 cottages was opened to the public. Guests will also find more than 13 miles of nature trails, cave tours, miniature golf, nine holes of regulation golf, a swimming pool, two tennis courts, meeting rooms, horse back riding stables, planned recreation, picnic and playground areas and terrific apple cobbler in the dining room.

Even with all of these recreational activities, the biggest and best attraction is the caves. A visit to the Welcome Center offers visitors a chance to learn about the caves and purchase a ticket for the regular tours that are offered daily to three caves. For spelunkers with some experience, special tours can be arranged to some of the more remote caverns led by the park's interpretive staff. The park and tours are open year-round. The best part of Carter Caves Resort State Park is far underground. Take a tour as soon as you reach the park!

Information and Activities

Carter Caves State Resort Park
Route 5, P.O. Box 1120
Olive Hill, KY 41164-9032
(606) 286-4411

Directions: Off I-64 (exit 161, five miles north), 38 miles west of Ashland on KY 182 north. Eight miles north of Olive Hill, Ky.

Lodge: Built from rugged fieldstone and timber in 1962, Caveland Lodge has 28 modern rooms and full amenities for a night or a week-long stay. Once inside the glass door entrance to the lodge, you'll find a gift shop open Monday - Saturday 10 a.m. 6 p.m. and Sunday 9 a.m. - 5 p.m. Hours vary during the winter season. The dining room opens daily at 7 a.m. for breakfast.

The large fireplace and cozy furniture provide a warm place to rest after a tour of chilly and exciting underground caves. The eight-foot deep swimming pool (which is maintained exclusively for lodge and cottage guests) is near the lodge parking lot and looks down upon the brown and natural looking lodge building with a fieldstone facade. The pool has two umbrella tables, lounge chairs and a small sunning deck. There are two tennis courts nearby.

Meeting facilities: The William Jason Fields Meeting Facility, (606) 286-4411 or (800) 325-0059 offers a relaxing setting for meetings With seating capacity of 160 classroom style, 175 banquet and 190 theater, the facility is perfect for retreats, family reunions, dances, weddings, receptions and meetings.

Cottages: Perched along a shady ridgeline looking down a lush wooded valley across the road from the golf course, 15 cottages (one-and two-bedroom efficiency models) are busy places during the entire year at Carter Caves. Tableware, cooking supplies and linen are provided, and advanced registration is suggested.

The small, tan-colored cottages offer screened-in porches, privacy and shady retreats clustered between the golf course and nature trail, east of the lodge and boat docks. Cottage 237 is next to a small playground and on the golf course fairway, where you can hear and see golfers trudging along after bad shots, or walk briskly after good ones.

Cottage 249 is also on the golf course and has lots of hard-surfaced parking. If you want additional privacy, try cottage 244 nestled lower than the roadway grade and away from the other cabins. All of the cottages have grills and picnic tables. Staying in the snug cabins and playing golf daily would be many duffers' idea of heaven! Requests are taken, but sorry, specific numbers cannot be guaranteed.

Campground: The winding drive back to the high-quality, clean campground offers a couple of turnouts with picnic tables and plenty of shady open spaces. Like many Kentucky state parks, an often-busy miniature golf course is near the check-in station. A split-rail fence encloses the old mini-golf course that is open seasonally.

The popular and clean campground is often full on weekends.

There are two shower buildings in the campground. This is a popular park and campground, often full on weekends, and always full on holiday weekends. Pets must be on a leash and no hanging of lanterns on trees is allowed. Quiet hours begin at 11 p.m. No alcohol is allowed.

Many camping sites are carefully outlined by square pressure-treated wooden timbers that identify the space. Many of the pads are hard-surfaced and some back into shady private areas. Sites have tables, fire grills and nearby water and electrical hookups.

The tent camping area (or overflow area) is informal and located at the north end of the campground, protected by tall trees and understory cover. The sites are not marked for exactness; you may camp in the general area of the site marking post. Utilities are limited in this area.

Sites that are most popular are 3, 6, and 7, as well as sites near the bath

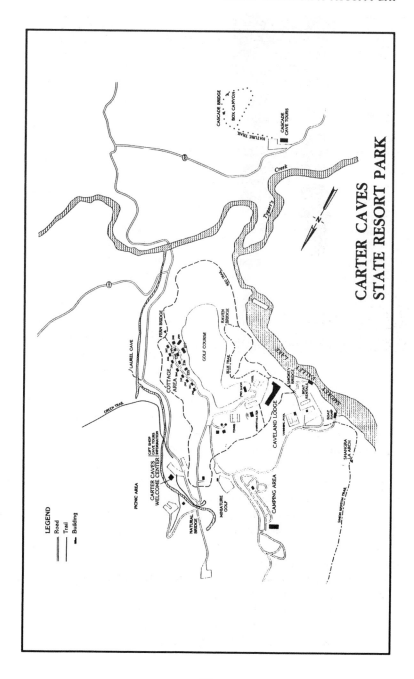

CARTER CAVES
STATE RESORT PARK

house and small play area that include 21, 24, 35, 39, 41, 44, 46 and 48. Other popular sites include 70, 72, 74, 75, 76, 78, 80, 82, 84, 86, 87, 88 and 89, which are all shady and great for use during the summer season. Behind the check-in building are a small game room, laundry area and three showers in each restroom area. Also there are ice and soft drink machines.

One caution about this campground is that some sites aren't completely flat. Sites are compacted and small, so choose your site carefully and be ready to adjust for slight pitched hard-surfaced pads.

Sites in the 50s are great for medium- to large-sized RV rigs, while sites 87, 88 and 89 offer good large hard-surfaced sites for big rigs. Many other sites are best for pop-up campers and small trailers. There are three pull-through sites in the campground near the registration office. There are 86 tent and RV camping sites at this nice campground. Reservations are not accepted, so try to arrive early.

Caves: Since the early 19th century settlers have been attracted to the area. For some the caves provided raw materials which improved daily life. Others entered for the pure pleasure of it and discovered the remarkable work of water cutting away caverns and channels far under-ground. Today, you can safely explore the caves and learn about how they were created and used in the past.

The ticket window located at the back is open weekdays, 9 a.m. - 5:00 p.m.; weekends, 9 a.m. - 5:30 p.m. All X Cave, Saltpetre and Bat Cave tours depart from the welcome center and are guided by trained leaders. All tours are gentle walking tours over prepared trails. The caves have been electrically lighted. Wear comfortable shoes and take a light jacket, especially if you are touring Saltpetre Cave, which is only 48 degrees. Caves are closed to the public except by organized tour and special activity permit, which may be obtained from the cave information window at the welcome center.

Cascade Cave: Is 3.1 miles from the ticket booth at the Welcome Center; you must drive in your own vehicle to the cave. Tickets are sold at Cascade Cave during the summer. Cascade, the largest of more than 200 caves in Carter County, is noted for its large chamber, many rock formations and underground lake. The highlight of the tour is the underground waterfall that is more than 30 feet high. There are tours daily and the total walking distance is about 3/4-mile or about 1 hour, 15 minutes. The cave remains at 50-60 degrees.

X Cave: A short, scenic tour. At the turn of the century a visit to X Cave would have been challenging. A 20-foot ladder made most people uneasy. Eventually an easier, safe way was prepared and today X Cave is one of the most popular tours. It gets its name from the configuration of its passages, which seem to cross in the center of the cave. The cave is noted for having some of the largest formations of any cave in the park. There are tours daily. Walking distance is about one-quarter-mile, or about a 45 minutes. Temperatures in the cave can vary from 40-60 degrees. There are about 75 stairs along the pathway through the cave.

Saltpetre Cave: This cave is historic and very much different from any other cave in the park. The dry dusty passages were once underground river beds. The dirt that water deposited was mined for "nitre," a major ingredient in gunpowder. Historic activities are a major part of the tour, including information about the Kentucky riflemen during the War of 1812. Indian graves have also been found in the cavern.

There are tours offered each day. The walking distance is about one-half mile and it takes about one hour. The temperature is always between 47-49 degrees. There are about 30 stairs leading to the cave; otherwise it's a flat walk, with some stooping.

Bat Cave: During the summer flashlight tours are offered and in the winter thousands of endangered Indiana bats hibernate in the cave. Check the parks schedule of events for tour dates and times. Bat Cave is closed to the public from Labor Day to Memorial Day weekend.

The Welcome Center is open 9 a.m. - 6 p.m. (with restrooms and soft drink machines and hours do vary during the winter season). In the center is a gift shop, ticket window where you can purchase tickets for the cave tours, and interpretive area with educational signs and information about the park and caverns. The modern gift shop has Kentucky crafts, rugs, handmade items, shirts, hats, chairs and so on.

Carter Cave's lodge has 28 rooms. The parks also has 15 cottages.

Fishing: Fishing is allowed during daylight hours only. Largemouth bass must be 20 inches in length and you may keep one of that size daily. Some muskie are taken in the quiet lake that has little boating and fishing pressure. If you catch a largemouth of legal size, please check it in by using a form available at the lodge. You may shoreline fish along open portions of the lake.

Boating: The Smokey Valley Boat Ramp is at the end of a narrow one-way road. Electric motors only are allowed on the 45-acre, tree-lined lake. Only small boats should be launched here. Paddle boats and small fishing boats are rented near the swimming pool in a day-use area down a series of steps to the shoreline, where a shady little area is operated seasonally.

Canoeing: There is some fine quality canoeing along Tygarts Creek from Olive Hill to the KY 182 bridge near the park. Guided trips are often offered by the park, or you can bring your own canoe and use the many public access points. The narrow stream in this area runs through a deep gorge with wooded blufftops and some pretty swift rapids. The best time to run this section is after rainfalls or from early spring to June. Farther downstream the creek flows through about five miles of scenic gorge before descending into a valley, where the water flattens out and the scenery become routine.

Hiking: The trails over three natural bridges are some of the most interesting natural features in the state parks system.

Carter Caves Cross Country Trail or THE 4Cs (7.2 miles) starts at the Welcome Center and follows a common path with the Simon Kenton Trrail for approximately two miles. The trail passes through the Shangra La Arch and runs parallel to Smokey Valley Lake, and crosses the Smokey Creek.

Natural Bridge Trail (.5 mile) starts at the welcome center and proceeds down the valley behind the building and past the picnic shelter to impressive on rock bridge. This rock bridge is the only one in Kentucky that is paved and supports vehicular traffic.

Red Trail (3.25 miles) is a loop that includes a close-up visit to the park's largest natural bridge, the 90-foot-high and 120-foot-wide Smokey Bridge. The winding and sometimes hilly trail also takes hikers to the Raven Bridge and Fern Bridge, near the lodge, cottages and camping area.

Simon Kenton Trail (9 miles) is a backpacking trail with a trailhead near the Welcome Center. It leads out of the park, through Tygart's State Forest and privately-owned lands to the 200-mile-long Jenny Wiley Trail. The rugged and steep trail is for the experienced backpacker and is not a loop trail.

Four smaller but equally interesting trails are also open to the public, including the scenic *Cascade Trail* (.75 mile) that travels by some unusual geologic formations such as the Cascade Natural Bridge, the 60-foot high sandstone Box Canyon, and a wind tunnel.

Day-use areas: Many small turnouts with tables and barrels are scattered along park roads and near amenities. The day-use area behind the welcome center is one of the largest in the park and is often used by group tours and families.

Community swimming pool: "Catch some rays," cool off, or spend the day with the family at the pool that has a small diving pool, kiddies pool, sun deck, chairs and wooden bathhouse. Next to the pool are a large picnic shelter, play area and plenty of parking.

Golf: The pro shop, (606) 286-4411 is lightly stocked with golfing supplies and has a television set and chairs. Outside, golfers can watch the action from a couple of picnic tables and sip soft drinks purchased from nearby vending machines. Golfers hanging about the ridgetop pro shop will also have a view of the pool and the lodge in the distance.

Allow two hours and fifteen minutes for your nine-hole round on the 2,849-yard hilly course that has dense, mature trees, but no water hazards. No. 2 is a dead straight 502-yard par five hole with a tree-lined fairway where three of my balls ricocheted among the hardwoods before dropping to the ground, never to be seen again. Fivesomes (and the author) are prohibited. Greens fees are reduced after 5:30 p.m.

Horseback riding: The little shed-like stable, complete with fern plants hanging from the gabled roof, is almost picture perfect and clean with a soft drink machine humming near the front entrance. The stable is open seasonally, daily 10 a.m. - 6 p.m. Rides are guided along the park's 2.5 miles of trails. Children must meet a height requirement to participate. The record riding day is 158 rides in an eight-hour period. Some small day-use areas are near the stable that can be a waiting place, if needed, at the busy equine rental center.

Planned recreation: Programs offered at the time of your visit might include cave walks, natural bridge walk, Saltpetre Cave crawling tour, Smokey Bridge walk, crafts, Bat Cave tour, nature at night, Tygart's Creek canoe tour, junior naturalist's program, caving for kids, pioneer games and lots more.

Special notes: About three miles from the park entrance are service stores, ice cream shop, bait and tackle stores, etc.

7 Columbus-Belmont State Park
Land: 156 acres Water: Mississippi River

Kentucky's most westerly state park played a fascinating role in the Civil War. The park is on the site of the northernmost fortified position occupied by the Confederate forces on the Mississippi River. The area was discovered in 1673 by French explorers Joliet and Marquette who named the area "Iron Banks" for the deposits of iron in the soils of the bluffs and shoreline banks.

The high bluffs overlooking the river made this strategic location a stronghold and marked the opening of the Union's Western Campaign led by General Ulysses S. Grant.

The site was occupied on September 3, 1861 by Confederate General Leonidas Polk, and through the autumn and winter of 1861-62 a garrison of 12,000-19,000 men labored incessantly on the earthworks (trenches) and other defenses. The almost impregnable site was called Fort DeRussey.

One hundred and forty heavy guns, most 32-and 64-pounders, were placed into position; a huge chain with 15-pound links was firmly anchored on the shore and stretched across the river on a series of wooden rafts to prevent gunboat traffic; and a floating battery and several river steamers, converted into gunboats, completed the carefully coordinated armament.

A second rebel camp was built in Belmont, on the Missouri side of the river. With all of this heavy defense, high bluffs and military strength, the position was dubbed the "Gibraltar of the West." At the time, this was the most heavily fortified area in the world.

Union General U.S. Grant, knowing the importance of the bluffs, launched the attack—his first active engagement of the Civil War— on Nov. 7, 1861 with artillery sounding from the blufftops and fighting taking place on the Missouri shore. The position was successfully defended by the South after a sharp skirmish when the Union were forced to retreat, and Grant turned his guns on the main stronghold in Columbus. A total of 1,000 lives were lost in the Belmont Battle.

Grant was overpowered and after burning the camp at Belmont, he withdrew upriver. His loss ended all Union ideas of taking Columbus by direct assault. So they proceeded to take up weaker positions around Columbus. In February 1862, the Confederates evacuated. One month later Union troops occupied the area and used it as a supply base and garrison during the remainder of the war, until 1870.

A portion of the huge chain which had been stretched across the Mississippi River, together with its massive anchor, is one of the major attractions in the small state park. In the late 1920s, a flood washed away much of the town of Columbus, forcing the community to move to higher ground. As the water receded, the almost forgotten chain was exposed in the Mississippi mud. Townspeople took up the challenge of preserving this bit of history and purchased the acreage of the former Fort DeRussey. In 1934, the state of Kentucky bought the area and developed the site into what is now Columbus-Belmont State Park.

An interesting bit of history about Columbus happened after a Washington, D.C. fire when Thomas Jefferson was president. According to legend, Jefferson proposed that Washington was too vulnerable, and that the town of Columbus would make a much better U.S. capital city. The provocative idea was defeated by one vote in the U.S. Senate. Jefferson felt that the central U.S. location of Columbus, Kentucky would make an ideal location for the nation's capital.

Information and Activities

Columbus-Belmont State Park
P.O. Box 8
Columbus, KY 42032-0008
(502) 677-2327

Directions: 36 miles southwest of Paducah on KY 80.

The Giant Chain: After the Civil War, the huge chain that was used by the South to span the Mississippi River to stop Union ship traffic was forgotten. Many years passed, until after heavy rains and landslides in 1925, a fisherman found a portion of the links and great anchor exposed. This portion of chain was about 60 feet in length.

According to historians, the chain was once about one mile long and was stretched across the river under the direction of generals Polk and Pillow in 1861. The object of the obstruction was to catch and hold federal gunboats, placing them at the mercy of Confederate batteries on the flats and blufftops.

After being found, the great chain was snaked down the bluff and displayed near Summer's Drugstore in the old town of Columbus. It remained there until the 1930s when the Civilian Conservation Corps built Columbus-Belmont State Park and made an attractive stone mounting for the chain with 11-inch links and broad anchor. The anchor, said to weigh four to six tons, was taken from the Washington Naval Yard and brought up the Mississippi River from Mobile Harbor, Alabama by southern sympathizers when the war broke out.

"Lady Polk:" The largest and by far the most famous Confederate cannon in Columbus, Kentucky, was named "Lady Polk" in honor of the wife of Episcopal Bishop and Confederate Major Gen. Leonidas Polk.

The experimental 6.4-inch Andersen rifle was made in 1861 at the Tredegar Iron Works in Richmond, Virginia. The cast iron "Lady Polk" weighed about 15,000 pounds, was more than 10 feet long, and nearly three feet across at the rear. She could throw her 128-pound, cone-shaped projectiles (nicknamed "lampposts") three miles. Throughout the Battle of Belmont, from high atop the river bluffs, the "Lady" pelted Grant's men with fire. About 140 other cannons did the same.

Each of the shots was hand-prepared for this thundering gun. The projectiles had copper saucers attached to the bottoms with carefully modified flanges to fit the rifles. She was the biggest cannon used at this time in the war.

Many thought the "Lady" helped win the battle, but this wasn't the reason it became so famous. During the Battle of Belmont, the huge cannon was fired time after time, super-heating the barrel, expanding the thick metal. After the battle the cannon was left loaded with unfired shot. Some two days later the Lady Polk was again fired. This time it exploded, breaking into three large pieces, killing 18 men—some were thrown into the river—and wounded 20 more. Although Gen. Polk stood near the cannon at the time, he was barely hurt, except for a slight facial burn and torn clothes.

The Yankees also memorialized the Lady Polk, saying in a northern newspaper, "...the reputation of the Columbus cannon is such that a person would be likely to consider himself as safe at one end as the other."

Museum: A white clapboard farmhouse with a wide porch was used as a Confederate dispensary during the Civil War and now looks down upon the park's day-use area. The only wartime building standing in the area, it was restored in 1935 by the Civilian Conservation Corps and is now used as a small museum. The museum is open April 1 - Oct. 31, seven day a week. There is a small fee.

A gift counter (mugs, books, caps, flags) is the first stopping point to pay the small fee to wander about in the creaking wooden structure that now houses a variety of relics of the Civil War, Indian artifacts and a video presentation.

The photographs and long guns under glass are interesting for all family members. Musket balls, grape shot and information about cannons and how they work are surrounded by some period-dressed mannequins. Other displays help the visitor understand the era.

Other bits of history include information about Mississippi shipping, 17th century medical care, soldier's equipment, the strategic importance of the area, cooking utensils, candle molds, cannon balls, broad axes, and many other tools and implements of the historic time.

Gift shop and concession: Open May 1 to September 30, and weekends only after Labor Day. Surrounded by picnic areas, monuments and open spaces, the gift shop offers a small assortment of books, souvenirs, Confederate caps and flags, refrigerator magnets and post-cards.

The concession stand offers simple sandwiches, soft drinks, snacks and ice cream. A strategically placed fan blows the inviting aroma of the snack bar toward the parking lot and gift shop.

Campground: Large oaks shade the tidy, 38-site loop that has the bath house (laundry, phones, rest rooms, etc.) situated in the center of the circular drive that outlines the camping area.

Sites 35-38 are pull-up sites (you don't back in). All of the sites are high and dry. The entire campground is near the jagged river bluffs. Virtually all of the sites are great in this sparkling clean campground, but you might want to take an extra look at sites 28, 29 and 31. They are very good places to spend a few days learning about the fascinating history and viewing the natural beauty of the area.

Sites 22-31 have a view of the Mississippi River in the distance. Firewood is sold, and each campsite has a fire box, picnic table and flat, hard-surfaced pad. The campground is typically full on holiday weekends.

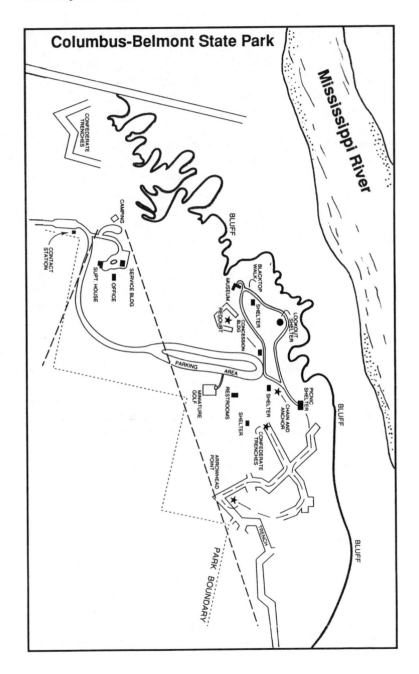

Columbus-Belmont State Park

Hiking: The trails that connect the museum and blufftops to the trenches and fields conjure up dramatic images of the bloody Civil War that split the country in half. The 2.5 miles of trails are easy walking and educational. The huge earthworks and deep trenching are impressive and easy to observe. Imagine what it must have been like to lie belly-down in these ditches as shots and cannons sounded and comrades fell.

Day-use areas: At the central day-use area in front of the gift shop and concession are a series of four interpretive signs that offers interesting historical and geological information about the region. Each of the professionally designed reader boards offer information about the history of Columbus, Kentucky; destruction of Columbus; Mississippi River; earthquake patterns and events (the February 1812 earthquake is the strongest known in North America!); Battle of Belmont; and more.

Also in this day-use area are traditional play equipment, cooking grills, activity area, four picnic shelters, other signage, and a great view of the Mississippi River from behind the low split rail fence that defines the area. From this vantage point, barge traffic might be seen, as well as wildlife, fishermen and pleasure boaters.

The timber picnic shelter and playground are open April 1 - Oct. 31.

Miniature golf: A small yellow windmill straddles one of the holes at the family-oriented golf layout. Carpeted fairways are open seasonally, May 1 - September 30. There is a small fee to play the course.

8 Constitution Square State Historic Site

Land: 3 acres

Constitution Square State Historic Site, in downtown Danville, was the birthplace of Kentucky's statehood. On the first day of June 1792, a constitution was executed—making Kentucky the 15th state to enter the Union. The highly manicured site was also the location for the 10 constitutional conventions it took to achieve the monumental task.

Thanks to many explorers like Daniel Boone, George Rogers Clark, James Harrod and Dr. Thomas Walker and many other early pioneers who immigrated through the Cumberland Gap and down the Ohio River, Kentucky's Wilderness Road soon was busy with settlers, traders and commerce. Kentucky is a bountiful state. Lush fields, abundant game and clear rivers quickly increased the popularity of the region.

As settlements grew, especially in the diamond-shaped area extending from Maysville to Crab Orchard on the east and Louisville to Crab Orchard on the west, the need for judicial courts and other administrative services increased. Danville's prominent location on Wilderness Road caused it to become a crossroads for early settlers and an increasing hotbed of political activity. By 1785, the Supreme Court of Kentucky moved into permanent quarters in Danville. Supplemental courts were set up in surrounding counties. Jails and courthouses were built, as well as other infrastructure to help administer law and order for the growing community. All of this was still under Virginia law.

The construction of all of these buildings and establishment of government services really didn't help much. When there was a problem in this far-reaching part of the territory, decisions often had to be made back in Virginia. Therefore the parties often had to travel to Virginia, sometimes more than once. It didn't take long for influential citizens of Danville to recognize the need for a formal convention to discuss statehood.

The road to statehood was as bumpy as the Wilderness Road, filled with turmoil and turf battles. Ten conventions were held from 1784-1792 in the courthouse on Constitution Square. In 1790, delegates from the area accepted Virginia's terms of separation, and the state constitution was drafted at the final convention in April 1792. Two months later Kentucky gained statehood and appointed Revolutionary War hero Isaac Shelby as its first governor.

Visitors can now take a self-guided tour of the historic structures and learn about the history of statehood, Isaac Shelby, and the Kentucky's first courthouse square.

Information and Activities

Constitution Square State Historic Site
134 S. Second Street
Danville, KY 40422-1880
(606) 236-5089; Fax (606) 236-4894

Directions: From Lexington, take U.S. 27 South to Ky. 34. From Louisville, take I-64 East to 127 South. In the heart of Danville, a very clean and scenic small town.

Hours: Constitution Square is open year-round, seven days a week, 9 a.m. to dark. There is no admission charge. Grayson's Tavern is available for weddings, luncheons, club meetings for a rental fee. Danville/Boyle Co. Historical Society Museum is open May 1 - October 30, Monday - Saturday, 10 a.m. - 4 p.m., Sundays 2 p.m. - 4 p.m. closed on Tuesdays. The Museum Store is open year-round, Monday - Friday 9:00 a.m. - 6:00 p.m., Saturday 9:00 a.m. - 5:00 p.m., Sunday 1:00 p.m. - 4 :00 p.m.

Constitution Square Buildings

A small park map offers visitors a full history and diagram of the square bordered by Walnut, Main and Second streets.

Alban Goldsmith House on the southwest corner of Constitution Square is a 1 1/2 story red brick building with attractive blue trim built about 1820. The owner was prominent physician Dr. Goldsmith. Goldsmith was a pupil of, and assistant to, Dr. Ephraim McDowell, whose home was across the street from Constitution Square on Second Street. Goldsmith assisted when McDowell performed the first ovariotomy on Jane Todd Crawford in 1809. The doctors pioneered abdominal surgery in Danville. In 1827 another physician by the name of Jefferson Polk purchased the house and also owned the Danville newspaper, the "Olive Branch." A museum store and tourist information center are located in the house.

Courthouse: In 1783, the Virginia Legislature organized the Kentucky territory into judicial districts. The original log courthouse was completed in 1785, housing the Supreme Court and 10 constitutional conventions which led to statehood. The courts ordered a jail "to be constructed of nine-inch-thick logs." The replicas of the jail and the courthouse were built in 1942. The old, rather rough tables—which acted as desks and conference tables—are equipped with quilled pens, wooden gavel and delicate-looking books.

Meeting house: The replica of the original meeting house that was built in 1784 is south of the post office. It was built under the direction of the

Rev. David Rice to house the first Presbyterian congregation in Kentucky. Interestingly, Rice originally came to Kentucky to farm, not to preach, but after being petitioned by 300 Presbyterians, including Caldwell, Cowan, Irvine, McDowell and Shelby, he moved to Danville and started the church.

Post office: Standing on the north side of Constitution Square, the structure was built before 1792 and served as the first post office east of the Alleghenies. On Aug. 20, 1792 Thomas Barbee was commissioned as postmaster and the first mail was received on Nov. 3, 1792. The small post office was moved to Constitution Square from its original site two blocks west on Walnut Street in downtown Danville. This original post office building was found when Danville workers were tearing down the historic-period post office, readying the site for a modern postal facility.

Fisher's Row: On the northeast corner of the Square, two two-story brick houses are joined by a common wall. Like the William Whitley historical house, the brick is laid in Flemish bond pattern. The row houses were built in 1817 by Jeremiah Fisher to be rented. They currently house the Art League and a gift shop.

Watts-Bell House: This was built in 1816 by William Watts for businessman David Bell. Joshua Fry Bell, a grandson to David, grew up to become a distinguished lawyer and statesman, serving as a member of the Kentucky Legislature, the U. S. Congress and as Secretary of State under Gov. Crittenden. The building now houses the Danville/Boyle County Historical Society Museum.

Schoolhouse: Along the east side of the Square, between Grayson's Tavern and the Watts Bell house, is the oldest brick schoolhouse east of the Alleghenies. The building, circa 1820, was originally only two rooms. The bricks are laid in common bond on a fieldstone foundation. The schoolhouse was renovated in 1975 and is now the park manager's residence. It is not open to the public.

Grayson's Tavern: On the southeast corner of the Square and built in 1785 by Benjamin Grayson, the tavern was often used as a meeting place—as it is today. It was the meeting place of the Political Club (early supporters of statehood) and the scene of many heated debates about issues concerning statehood. Delegates who visited Danville and the district court often stopped by the tavern during the struggles to shape a constitution and give birth to the state. The two-story, bell-shaped building has two entrances, one in the front and one on the side.

Governor's Circle: Memorial to Kentucky's Governors, located on the northwest corner of the park. The bronze statue depicts a statesman and a frontierman who are on the Kentucky Seal. The figures represent Kentucky's official motto, "United We Stand, Divided We Fall." The bronze plaques honor each Kentucky Governor.

Kentucky's First Governor:

Isaac Shelby, Kentucky's first governor, was actually a native of Maryland. He moved to West Virginia when he was 21 years old and learned surveying. His training served him well and he was hired by the Transylvania Company in 1774 to survey the new Virginia territory, which later became Kentucky.

In part, Shelby was paid in land, which he chose south of Danville where the rolling bluegrass country meets sharply defined knobs. After surveying in Kentucky for one year, Shelby returned to Virginia in 1775 to serve in the militia during the Revolutionary War. It was not until 1780 that Shelby again returned to Kentucky to secure lands which he had marked off five years before. It was during this time that Shelby visited Fort Boonesborough and met his future wife, Susanna Hart, daughter of Captain Nathaniel Hart. Hart was one of the owners of the Transylvania Company.

Not long after, the married couple constructed their new home, Traveller's Rest, on Isaac's original campsite. The two-story house is thought to be the first stone house in the state. The house burned in 1905, but a stone with Shelby's name carved on it was recovered. That was later set in the new house.

Shelby was a social climber. He quickly became well-known and active in the community with a wide range of interests in education, politics and farming. He was also on the board of directors of Centre College in Danville and active in the constitutional conventions. In fact, his skill and wide respect made him a virtual shoe-in for the first governor job. He was reputed to be honest and forthright, an experienced constitutional delegate, gracious, and a successful operator of the Traveller's Rest estate.

Isaac Shelby was a founding father of the Kentucky Society for Promoting Useful Arts, a group that advanced agricultural education and innovative farming methods. But maybe his most significant contribution to his elevation as Kentucky's first governor was his sterling military record. The governor fought in the Revolutionary War at the famous Battle of King's Mountain, and after being elected governor he also fought in the War of 1812, leading a regiment to the rescue of Kentucky troops during the Battle of Thames near Detroit. It was during these battles that Shelby became a well-known hero and leader.

Governor Shelby remained active in political affairs until his death at Traveller's Rest at the age of 76. The chair the governor died in is exhibited at Constitution Square.

The Isaac Shelby Cemetery State Historic Site is on Knob Lick Pike, 5.5 miles south of Danville on U.S. 127 and is open year-round.

Special note: On the third weekend of September the Constitution Square Festival is held. During Christmas the Square is decorated in period furnishings. Stop by Burke's Bakery, across the street from the Square, for some terrific donuts and other goodies and also enjoy the beautiful historic downtown area surrounding Constitution Square.

9 Cumberland Falls State Park

Lands: 1,657 Water: Cumberland River

Cumberland Falls State Park is Kentucky's most popular unit, deep within the handsome Daniel Boone National Forest. The park is known as the "Niagara of the South," where a wall of water plunges over the 68-foot-tall ledge into a boulder-strewn gorge below churning the waters into a mist that creates the magic of a moonbow—that is only visible on a clear nights during a full moon. This unique phenomenon appears nowhere else in the Western Hemisphere!

Sometimes tame, other times wild, the Cumberland River is formed by three small streams, Poor Fork, Clover Creek and Martins Fork, and meanders through the Cumberland Mountains for 80 miles upstream from the falls. The large river drains a 17,914-square-mile area and in places can offer very good fishing.

The falls is the result of millions of years of geologic activity. Ranging from the time when all of Kentucky was covered by a sea to when it dried up and sediments were deposited, eruptions happened, and now a long process of erosion is taking place.

As the Cumberland River came into contact with the hard, resistant rock type called rockcastle conglomerate, the downcutting action of the river that had cut many gorges and deep valleys was slowed down. Material under this hard rock was less resistant and has been eroded away by the water's action, and this is where the waterfall formed.

Interestingly the falls are actually moving upstream as more of the material under the resistant rock is eroded away and the sheer weight of the overhanging ledge causes it to break off. As a result, the falls is steadily—but not visibly—moving upstream.

Geologists predict that the 125-foot-wide falls probably originated nearly 40 miles downstream from the present location.

An average of 3,217 cubic feet of water per second pours over the falls.

Cumberland Falls is the third oldest state park in the Kentucky system and was a controversial subject for many years.

During the late 1920s a proposal to build a power dam above the falls was considered, until T. Coleman Dupont offered to buy the falls and the surrounding area and donate it to the Commonwealth of Kentucky. It was not until 1930, some three years later and after Dupont's death, that the Legislature voted to accept the offer.

The park was dedicated on Aug. 21, 1930, with considerable work beginning on roadways, cottages, shelters and trails by the Civilian Conservation Corps a short time later. Fifteen cabins were completed by 1933 and the Dupont Lodge, which was destroyed by a fire in 1940, was rebuilt and reopened in late 1941. In 1951, 40 rooms, a patio and a dining room was added.

Information and Activities

Cumberland Falls State Resort Park
7351 Highway 90
Corbin, KY 40701-8814
(606) 528-4121
(800) 325-0063 - toll-free reservations

Directions: 15 miles from I-75 at exit 25. About 20 miles southwest of Corbin, take U.S. 25W to KY 90.

Lodge: Dupont Lodge has 52 rooms offering beautiful river views and full amenities. From the fieldstone and wood-clad exterior to the solid hemlock beams and knotty pine paneling that compliment the large stone fireplace inside, guests will enjoy full services that include a 300-seat dining room and the Blair Museum.

The circular drive passes an almost courtyard-like area with a green-colored canopy entrance to the lodge. Once inside the lodge, built in 1952, the high-vaulted ceilings and wood parquet flooring offer guests a rustic but elegant experience that fits perfectly into the dramatic natural surroundings. The lobby's tasteful decor includes a stone fireplace, shinny brass lamps, large-screen television, books and comfortable furniture for leisurely evenings. Equally comfortable and offering a terrific view of the boulder-strewn river is the patio behind the lodge, where many sitting areas are strategically located for a cheery outdoor drink or chat with other guests.

The Robert A. Blair Museum, off the sitting room in the lodge lobby, is a small, 20-foot-square museum that is warmly lighted. That helps set the mood for slowly reading the interesting historical information and examining the many display items. One of the most impressive displays is that of the various types of tree species native to the area. Others include Indian artifacts, historical photographs, information about the formation of the Cumberland Falls.

Archaeology is also well-described in the small museum. telling the pre-historic story of the area. Some 12,000-14,000 years ago, the Cumberland forest was teeming with life. There were mammoths standing 14 feet tall at the shoulder, and slightly smaller mastodons. Super-sized bison and camels lived alongside deer, elk and beaver the size of grizzly bears. Strange creatures like glyptodon, which were actually huge armadillos, tapers, and giant ground sloths abounded. Among these plant-eaters stalked the predators, the ferocious dire wolf, the terrifying saber-tooth tiger, and the short-faced bear.

But the most cunning and skillful predator of all was man. The first in the area was the Paleo Indian, the hunter of game. His subsistence was based largely on his ability to stalk and kill the large animals with whom he shared the land. Their fur provided him with clothes, tools and food that filled their stomachs.

Some two thousand years later another culture began to emerge, called the Archaic. Archaic man was presented with a much different environment than his predecessors. He was by necessity forced to develop more diverse tools and weapons. As the Archaic period continued these tools along with his culture grew increasingly sophisticated. By the later stages of this period (2000-1000 B.C.) he had developed the first pottery, the first forms of horticulture and the first semi-permanent camps in eastern woodlands.

The Woodland culture began to develop at about 1000 B.C. and is marked by the first construction of burial mounds. For this reason the Woodland period is often broken into two sections, "Mound builders One and Two." Of the many woodland groups, two emerged to dominate these periods, the Adena, and later the Hopewell people. Of great significance during these years were the development of religion, permanent villages, increased development of agricultural practices, and trading networks that stretched from the Gulf of Mexico to the Great Lakes. Woven textiles were also made. These people were the forefathers of the Shawnee and Chippewa Indians.

Meeting facilities: An ideal location for conferences and meetings, the multi-purpose building behind Dupont Lodge can accommodate 350 people.

Cottages: Located near the campground grocery, a small loop with

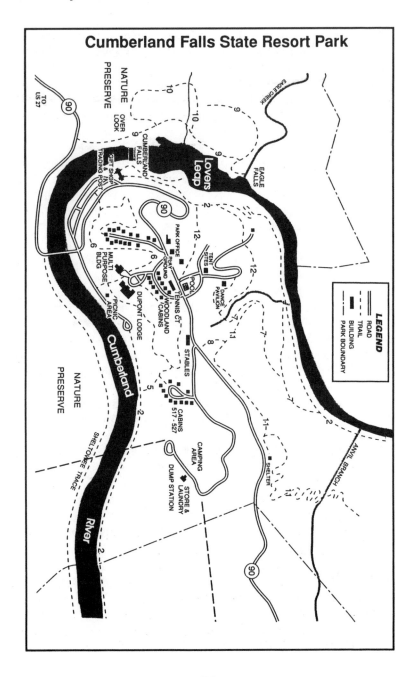

Cumberland Falls State Resort Park

wooden cottages 517-527 look down into wooded V-like valleys enjoying a shady quiet terrain. At the end of the loop is cottage 518, which is set back from the roadway and very private. Nearby is 523, perched on a hillside with a small porch that faces a deep ravine. For a rustic respite, try log cabin 524 with a fieldstone. Each of the cottages has cooking grills, tables and seating areas away from busy roads, making the cottages an excellent choice for families.

West of the lodge cottages 501-515 sit along a tree-lined ridge. This grouping of cottages is larger wooden clapboard and stone units. Cottages 507-511 are stationed at the end of the loop and look down into a densely wooded valley. Cottages 501-506 are older, 512-515 are newer offering two bedrooms, two bathrooms and full housekeeping facilities.

The Woodland Rooms, cottages 610-629, are a series of newer brown-colored cottages, all of which are duplex units with excellent private woodland views.

Campground: Early each morning along the roadway that serves the campground, a small herd of riding stable horses are run up the hill. Hooting cowboys keep them in line and vehicle traffic under control. The huffing and puffing horses are then groomed and saddled at the small stable, awaiting riders and sleepily swatting at flies for the remainder of the day. The open-air stable is open for business 10 a.m. - 6 p.m., May 15 - October 31, on KY 90, one-quarter-mile east of the lodge.

The campground is open April 1 - Oct. 31. There are 30 sites with electrical and water hookups, and 20 primitive camping sites. There is no advance reservation taken.

The showers are in the small store (open 8 a.m. - 10 p.m., April 1 - October 31) that sells light grocery items and other small supplies, including firewood.

Sites in loop 122-141 are the best sites in the park. Shady with hard-surfaced pads, these sites, however, are fairly narrow. At the end of the loop is a small set of play equipment.

Pull-through sites 143-148 are open and sunny. Each site is on a slight

Cottages are shady, private and popular at Cumberland Falls.

incline next to the campground store. Many other sites in the campground are for small to medium RV rigs only.

Tent campers will enjoy the shady area designated for their use. Sites 3-6 are excellent tent sites with fire rings and privacy. Many of the tent camping sites have nearby electrical hookups, elevated grills and gravel pads. Sites in the 20s are good rustic locations, with site 26 one of the best. One of the most popular features of the tent camping area is its proximity to the L-shaped swimming pool (small fee, free if an overnight guest).

Swimming pool: (Olympic-size) The pool is open during the summer Sunday-Thursday, 10 a.m. - 6 p.m. and Friday-Saturday, 10 a.m. - 8 p.m. There are also two basketball goals and a volleyball court near the park store for campground users. Near the pool are a picnic shelter and day-use area.

Rafters first paddle near the falls, then downstream.

Church services are offered in the park each Sunday at 9 a.m., in the summer.

The Falls: The large parking lot at the falls is outlined by a timber fence where you immediately hear the hiss of the falls in the distance. A small coffee (Trading Post Restaurant, open April 1- Oct. 31) and gift shop complex connected by a protective roof features lots of items to look at. The gift shop is one of the state park system's largest—and also has one of the best views— offering everything from spices and country decorations to Christmas items and jams and jellies.

Fishing: Far more sight-seers than anglers visit the park, even though the Cumberland River does offer a variety of game fish.

During the spring, striped bass migrate upriver from Lake Cumberland to spawn. Catfish can be taken in the pool below the falls, while smallmouth bass inhabit many of the pools above and below the falls. There are no trout in the Cumberland River.

Boating: Canoe rentals are offered by the park and rafting is available through the outfitter. The nearest marinas are at Grove Recreation Area on Laurel Lake and at Burnside on Lake Cumberland. The stretch of river below the Cumberland Falls is a popular run for canoeists familiar with white-water techniques. Put-in is at the beach below the falls and take-out is at the mouth of the Laurel River, 12 miles downstream.

Rafting: For many, a trip to Cumberland Falls complete without a raft ride. Rain or shine, call (800) 541-RAFT for details. The trip is a 4 1/2-mile ride that begins near the falls. Intrepid boaters are bused back to the starting point. (April 1 -October 31)

The skinny, hardy and muscled guides, who call themselves "river rats," generally take six rafts full of thrill seekers out at a time. Before everyone launches downstream from the waterfall, all are equipped with helmets, personal flotation devices, and a short witty lecture punctuated with wisdom and safety tips. There is also a warning about paddles—keeping them low—or you might end up with "summer teeth"—some are here, some are there! In short, the paddles are the most dangerous thing on the tours. The wild river also features some colorful names for rapids, including "Pinball" and "Screamin' Right."

Once in the sturdy air-filled rafts, the rubber boats are paddled down to the falls for a close-up look at the thundering wall of water and a spray of mist. After that exciting beginning, it's downriver for a couple very scenic and exciting hours.

Hiking: Cumberland Falls has excellent trails where even casual hikers will discover spectacular sandstone bluffs, the beauty of wildflowers tucked beneath towering hemlocks, and gentle river waters lapping against moss-covered rocks.

The park has 10 developed trails totaling about 18 miles.

Trail 2 is a seven-mile-long trail that begins at the far end of the picnic

Riding horses are run up to the public livery each morning.

area and follows the river for about two miles. Then it follows an old logging road. This is the longest trail in the park. Trail 4 is a self-guided nature trail that starts at the lodge and connects with Trail 5. The trail ends in the back parking lot of the lodge.

Although all of the trails are scenic, Trail 9 is an excellent one taking hikers to Eagle Falls and following a sometimes scary rugged cliffline. Children should be well-tended on this hike. The trail offers the best views of the main falls. Parts of the trail can be under water in the fall, and it has some rugged sections.

There are no backpacking trails at the park. However, the trail system connects with several trails in the Daniel Boone National Forest. Among these is Moonbow Trail, a 10-mile backpacking trail that runs from the park to the Laurel Recreation Area. The Sheltowee Trace also connects to the unit's trail system.

Day-use areas: Tennis courts are carefully located on a ridge that overlooks the pool. Other day-use amenities include two horseshoe courts and shuffleboard near the Woodland Cottages. Equipment can be checked out at the front desk at the lodge. Board games may also be checked out at the front desk. A picnic area, including a shelter, fireplace and picnic tables, is located beside the river upstream from the falls.

Moonbow: Over the years the famous Cumberland Falls has became popular as more people learned about its beauty and amazing "moonbow." Cumberland Falls is the only place in the Western Hemisphere where this phenomenon occurs. The only other moonbow happens at the Victoria Falls on the Zambezi River on the border of Zambia and Zimbabwe, in southern Africa. On a clear night with a full moon, one can stand at the observation point and see a moonbow that appears as an arch of white light stretching from the base of the falls and continues downstream. The best time to see the moonbow is during the fall and winter months, when you can see color like a rainbow.

There are several factors that must be present to see a moonbow. Not only is it necessary to have a full moon, but you must have enough mist rising from the falls to refract the light from the moon. Wind direction and velocity may also be important elements. Since there are many other rivers and waterfalls in which these conditions occur, no one really knows why there are only two places in the world where you can see a moonbow.

Planned recreation: Naturalist programs are popular at the unit. Environmental education program for junior naturalists, canoe trips, all about snakes programs, nature scavenger hunts, natural history-based slide shows, and many arts and crafts classes are offered. The recreation office is next to Blair Museum in the lodge.

Special notes: Square dancing is popular during the summer. Consider a side trip to the Yahoo Falls, a 125-foot-tall falls about 20 miles from the park in the South Fork National River and Recreation Area. Also in the area are the Beaver Creek Wilderness Area and Three Forks of Beaver Overlook in the Daniel Boone National Forest. For visitor information, call Cumberland Falls State Park at (800) 325-0063.

10 Dale Hollow Lake State Park
Land: 3,398 acres Water: 28,000 acres

Long before modern man transformed Dale Hollow Lake into a great fishing and water recreation area, the Wolf and Obey rivers ran through rugged, wild country, carving valleys and hillsides that exist today. The huge reservoir is 63 miles long (653 miles of shoreline) with a surface area of 48 miles, contained by a 1,717-foot-long dam that was built by the U.S. Army Corps of Engineers in the early 1940s.

The dam backs up the meandering Obey River for 51 miles and the East Fork River an additional 12 miles. Dale Hollow is a heavily used body of water that straddles the Kentucky-Tennessee line, offering clear waters for scuba diving, boating and swimming, and an excellent submerged habitat for many species of fish. In fact, the world record smallmouth bass—11 pounds, 15 ounces—was caught less then one-half mile from the state park.

The first human inhabitants of the Wolf River Valley were native Americans of the Paleo-Indian period.

Cindy Cave and the Wolf River Rockshelter, both in the park, were used as living quarters more than 10,000 years ago. Around 700 B.C.— the Early Woodland period—one or two small families lived in the Wolf River Rockshelter. These quiet people grew crops, stored food (including nuts and berries), fished and hunted in the bountiful region.

Many years later, about the time Christopher Columbus discovered the Americas, the Cherokee and Shawnee migrated through the area in hunting parties and used the rockshelters and other areas around the park as temporary camps. The first Europeans settled after the Revolutionary War. Veterans were given parcels of land west of the Appalachian range, and many farmsteads were developed. Some existed near the park until the 1970s. Remnants of these decaying home sites can still be seen along the park's hiking trails.

In 1971, the state leased 985 acres of land from the Corps of Engineers along the Wolf Creek tributary of Dale Hollow Lake. Throughout the 1970s additional lands were acquired, giving the park a total of 3,398 acres, with considerable frontage on the huge lake.

Dale Hollow is the state's second largest state park and many plans (including construction of a 36-room lodge with 156-seat dining room 300 feet above the water, golf course, etc.) for additional development on the property are being considered. The park officially opened in 1978.

Information and Activities

Dale Hollow Lake State Park
6371 State Park Road
Bow, KY 42714-9728
(502) 433-7431

Directions: From Cave City off I-65 and Glascow, take KY 90 east, then south on KY 449 to KY 1206. Twelve miles from Burkesville, Ky.

Visitor information: A small room adjacent to the park office and restaurant, near the marina, has small displays about daily history of the park, brochures, a tiny sales counter, and other information about the area. The room is open 7 a.m. - 4 p.m. Also in this building are a fish cleaning station, ice, information boards and small 48-seat restaurant, open 7 a.m. - 7 p.m. Fresh fish is the restaurant's specialty!

Campground: Dale Hollow has the best designed campground in the system. Eighteen small circles, each with eight campsites, are nestled along a ridge and various elevations. All of these sites have utility hookups. Three central service buildings offer showers, laundry facilities and rest rooms. Twenty-four of the unique camping sites are for horse campers, complete with horse tie-ups and adjoin riding trails. Reservations are taken for camping sites by mail-in form or in person; a small deposit is required.

Quiet hours begin at 11 p.m. Many of the loops have room for additional parking of horse or boat trailers. The campground check-in office has brochures and plenty of local knowledge about the best camping sites, fishing, day trip ideas and more.

The small loops are alphabetized. Generally speaking, the campground is open; most of the young trees are not large enough to offer significant shade. All of the pads are hard-surfaced and equipped with picnic tables and fire rings. Area B is very open. Area E has some shady sites and is next to a service building with laundry and telephone.

In the L area, sites 93 and 94 are quite shady, pleasant, and backed up against a natural area. On a ridge, overlooking the rest of the campground, loop O is near the small amphitheater and pleasant. Loops P, Q and R are equipped for horse camping, but anyone may stay in the ridgeline areas. These loops are shadier and more private than many of the other camping areas near the pool and beyond.

If you take the time to carefully choose your camping site, you can find the perfect site for a weekend or week-long stay in this water enthusiast's state park.

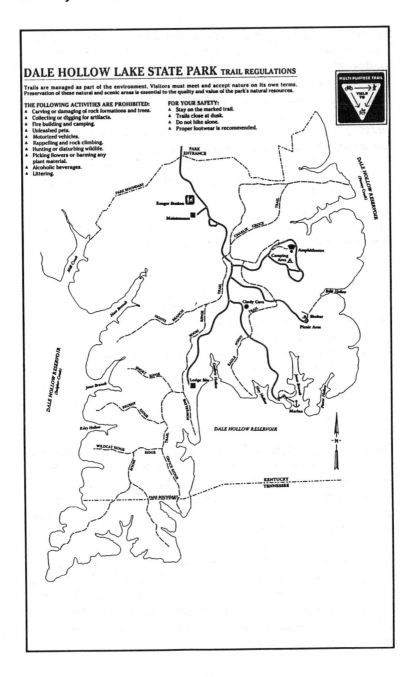

DALE HOLLOW LAKE STATE PARK TRAIL REGULATIONS

Trails are managed as part of the environment. Visitors must meet and accept nature on its own terms. Preservation of these natural and scenic areas is essential to the quality and value of the park's natural resources.

THE FOLLOWING ACTIVITIES ARE PROHIBITED:
- Carving or damaging of rock formations and trees.
- Collecting or digging for artifacts.
- Fire building and camping.
- Unleashed pets.
- Motorized vehicles.
- Rappelling and rock climbing.
- Hunting or disturbing wildlife.
- Picking flowers or harming any plant material.
- Alcoholic beverages.
- Littering.

FOR YOUR SAFETY:
- Stay on the marked trail.
- Trails close at dusk.
- Do not hike alone.
- Proper footwear is recommended.

Swimming pool: On a small hill, the five-foot-deep swimming pool is between areas H and K, and is open for park visitor's use. There is a small fee for non-campers to use the pool. Two umbrella tables and lounge seating are deckside. No lifeguard is on duty. Next to the pool are a small play area and basketball goal.

Fishing: On July 11, 1955, David Hayes landed a world record smallmouth bass near the confluence of Illwill Creek and Wolf River. The 11-pound, 15-pounce lunker is still an IGFA all-tackle world record. Another jumbo record fish—a 43-pound silver muskie—was caught in 1978 by Poter Hash.

Dale Hollow still has some great fish---but the fishing can be tough, especially during the summer months. The clear water, fishing pressure and sheer expanses of water can scare the average weekend fisherman. It shouldn't.

For the best bass action use very light line (four- to eight-pound test), sensitive graphite rod, and a pig and jig for year-round action. In the spring try crankbaits and floating minnow stick baits. Many top anglers learn to "swim" the pig and jig, while other anglers merely cast the lure and let it fall, hoping for a strike on the way down. Local anglers use a slightly larger jig (3/8-ounce) and bounce the pig and jig off the bottom along rock shelves and gravel substrate. Try twitching the lure as you bounce it, also.

The best fishing is often late February and early March behind embankments where the water warms up first. Minnow lures twitched along the surface can be deadly. Look for points, contours, and stained water areas at this time of the year, use long-cast crankbaits. Another good time to be on the water is overcast days that are windy, when the water is choppy. Fish the points on these days.

Other excellent places to fish in the early spring are Natty Branch, Pusley Creek, William's Branch of Sulphur Creek, Hogback Creek and others. Late spring is a good time to catch largemouth bass that are often found in willows or other cover. Worm rigs or rubber worms casted and retrieved with an irregular twitch can bring in many largemouth at this productive time of the year.

During the summer, the best fishing is at night. At this time of the year, anglers should fish parallel to the shore in at least 25 feet of water, working toward deeper water. Small spinners and jigs tipped with a plastic trailers or pork rind are standard lures for this type of fishing.

Good catches of white bass, spotted bass, walleye and rainbow trout are also taken each year at Dale Hollow. Trolling is the best technique for walleye and "stripes." Spinners and nightcrawler rigs are good in the summer for these species, while spring and fall call for crankbaits. Bluegill can be pulled from the submerged willow trees and in deep channels when the water is low.

Bass are to be caught, but not eaten. Release the bass you catch at Dale Hollow.

Boating: The park's staff says that the best boat ramp in the state is here, next to the small marina that has a long single dock with 36 open slips, overnight tie-ups, and fishing boat and pontoon boat rentals. At the end of the dock is a small fueling station that sells fishing licenses, lake maps, ice, soft drinks and other items. The lake view from the marina is tree-lined, with rolling hills becoming lost in the distance.

The long, two-to-three-lane launching ramp has a temporary mooring dock at its end. The ramp is next to the marina and all sizes of trailerable boats can be put in here.

Hiking: Dale Hollow has 13.4 miles of multipurpose trails where hikers, bikers and horsemen share the pathway, unless otherwise posted. The trails generally follow old logging roads along narrow ridge tops through the sprawling park. Most of the trails end at the tip of a peninsula into the lake, requiring a return trip on the same trail. Visitors are advised to avoid the steep hollows between the trails.

Cindy Cave: The ancient cavity is open to the public. Once inside the small entrance, the cave widens and careful visitors can explore the dark and cool orifice.

Eagle Point Trail: At the end of this 1.8-mile trail is the most scenic view of the lake, islands and rolling countryside. The trail meanders south from the campground check-in station.

Boom Ridge Trail System: Along the southern boundary of the park, this extensive ridge spreads into Tennessee. The rugged area is composed of finger and narrow ridges which lead out to the lake. Boom Ridge is the main artery of the trail system. Spur trails stem from Boom Ridge onto small ridges, each with its own name. Boom Ridge trail is four miles long with a trailhead at the campground check-in station. Smaller trails leading off Boom Ridge are Hoots Branch (1.2 mile), Brushy Ridge (.8 mile), Powerline Ridge (.4 mile), Groce Ridge (.6 mile), Short Ridge (.5 mile) and Wildcat Ridge (.4 mile).

Charlie Groce Ridge Trail is 3 miles long and turns north just past the campground check-in station, where it follows a tree line paralleling the park road.

Boles Hollow (.2 mile) is a foot trail that descends to Boles Hollow from the picnic area.

Campground Trail (.3 mile) is a foot trail that winds through a woodlot within the campground area.

Day-use areas: The park rents bikes, operates several small play areas, and features planned recreation and special events that might include a clogger's weekend, Fourth of July celebration, pet show, singing by the lake, kids camp, senior citizen's programs, quilt show, and if you ask, maybe a really neat chance to see the site superintendent's terrific collection of political buttons and memorabilia.

Nature: Aside from great hiking trails, excellent songbird watching and abundant flora, Dale Hollow is one of the best places in the country to see the American bald eagle between November and early March. Each year about 40 of the great raptors are counted in the mountainous regions of northern Tennessee and southern Kentucky.

The American bald eagle stands 30-40-inches in height, and has a wing span of six to seven feet, weighing 10-13 pounds. The bald eagle reaches maturity in four to five years when its head feathers turn white—hence the bald appearance and name. The bird also has white tail feathers,

There's all kinds of action on the lake.

yellow beak, and a dark brown to blackish body. The average life expectancy is 25-30 years, with some reported to reach 50 years of age.

Although Benjamin Franklin and James Audubon opposed the bald eagle as our national symbol, the Continental Congress adopted the majestic bird as our emblem in 1782. I'll bet Ben and Jim's hindsight is better than an eagles regular sight, which is eight times better than our normal vision. It's said that an eagle can see a duck swimming on a lake two miles away.

The Corps of Engineers conduct an eagle watch on one Saturday each January, when they take visitors into some remote habitats where eagles are seen hunting and feeding. Contact the Corps at Eagle Watch, Resources Manager's Office, Rt. 1, Celina, TN 38551.

Special note: The entire Dale Hollow region has many private marinas, lodging and visitor attractions.

11 Dr. Thomas Walker State Historical Site

Land: 12 acres

It was called "Kentucke" when Dr. Thomas Walker was engaged by the Loyal Land Grant Company to explore more than 800,000 acres. He discovered mountain gaps, including Cumberland Gap, named after the Duke of Cumberland, wild rivers, and vast expanses of forests. The Cumberland River was also named for the Duke on April 23, 1750.

Walker's party erected the first cabin in Kentucky in 1750. Today, a replica of the cabin at the park is surrounded by a fine day-use area, gift shop and miniature golf course.

Walker himself remained in the area for only a week, laying claim to the land, before heading back to his native Virginia. Nearly 20 years later Daniel Boone came through the Gap, and settlement of Kentucky began in earnest.

One of the fun things about the park is the series of Burma Shave-type signs placed along the road extolling the virtues of the park in rhyming one-liners on small white placards.

Information and Activities

Dr. Thomas Walker Historical Site
H. C. 83, P.O. Box 868
Barbourville, KY 40906-9693
(606) 546-4400

Directions: From Barbourville, take KY 459 off U.S. 23 E. The park is about six miles southwest of Barbourville. The park closes at 9:30 p.m. There is no camping at the small day-use park.

History: In 1750, when Virginia was a royal province of the British crown, the Loyal Land Company sent Dr. Walker with five associates across the Appalachian Mountains into the wilderness of Kentucky to locate land suitable for settlement. He left Castle Hill, Walker's hometown near Charlottesville, on March 6.

After struggling through the rugged mountains covered with primeval forests and dense undergrowth down through the southwestern part of the state and through eastern Tennessee, then a part of North Carolina, they observed a dip in the mountain range now known as the Cumberland Gap.

Through this gap the group came on down northwestward to the great gorge Pineville, naming the river Cumberland as they proceeded. Due to heavy rains they could not cross the ages-old Cumberland fjord and accordingly traveled on down the south side of the river. Ascending Brush Creek and Little Brush Creek on and over the Divide, they descended Swan Pond Creek to the river, again finding it too deep to fjord. So they made a bark canoe and successfully crossed on April 23.

After wading through the low marshland and on to the knoll, the group in the next seven days built a tiny house eight feet wide and 12 feet long, planted some corn and killed many bear, curing the meat for food for their further travels.

The Kentucky's first home replica is a faithful reproduction of the type of pioneer log hut of the period. Its roof poles hold oak clapboards in place, and the doors are made of rough wood slabs pegged together and hinged in the early pioneer fashion without iron. Other items added are the one-post bed, triple decked, hinge-wall table and three-legged stool.

Near the log house is a map board that details the zig-zag route the intrepid doctor took crossing the mountains, through valleys, building rough canoes and fjording large rivers as he went.

Amenities: Down the hill, behind the cabin, is a children's play area with swings, teeter-totter and nearby picnic tables. The mowed day-use areas are pleasant and well-equipped. The picnic shelter next to the cabin is great for family or group outings and includes restrooms and cooking grills.

If miniature golf is your game, the challenge of putting through a wishing well or a tiny schoolhouse is for you. The course is newer with cartoon-type characters watching over the carpeted mini-course layout. If golf isn't your game, try organizing a softball game, shoot some hoop, or bring a football to take advantage of the open spaces.

The park is well-manicured, freshly painted, and a clean day-use park that is outlined by a split-rail and stone fence. The gift shop and concession stand is lightly stocked with the usual items. The gift shop is open seven days seasonally.

12 E.P. "Tom" Sawyer State Park

Land: 370-acres

Rolling terrain and lots of housing subdivisions make up the attractive area where the 370-acre urban day-use park is located. The high-energy park on the outskirts of Louisville was once farmland, but now is the site of quality neighborhoods and a modern indoor and outdoor recreation facility.

Tom Sawyer is not your typical state park. There's no camping or lodge, fishing or boating, forests or mountains. But there is lots of fun for urban families and visitors.

E.P. "Tom" Sawyer a wonderful urban recreation center with the only gym in the entire state park system. It features a one-mile fitness trail with 10 exercise stations, a terrific aquatics program, BMX bike track, league sports (basketball, softball, volleyball, soccer, etc.), 12 tennis courts, gym rentals, innertube water polo, arts and crafts, archery, special events and a 1.25 mile nature trail. Many of the outdoor courts and playing fields are lighted for night play.

Information and Activities

E.P. "Tom" Sawyer State Park
3000 Freys Hills Road
Louisville, KY 40241-2172
(502) 426-8950

Directions: The park's main entrance is off of Freys Hill Road, which may be accessed from the La Grange Road side via Lakeland Road. If coming down Westport Road, Freys Hills Road is one-half mile west of the Gene Snyder Freeway, or one mile east of the White Castle on Hounze Lane.

Activity Center: Located next to a huge parking lot, the geometric-style recreation center's roof line swoops all the way to the turf, making the building both striking and useful. The angular facility has a gymnasium that can seat up to 600 people and also includes indoor basketball courts, volleyball, badminton, weight room, lockers and shower facilities. A wide variety of leagues and clinics are conducted throughout the year in the large gym with blue floors and great ventilation fans. The gym can be rented by the hour.

The business office, information rack, vending machines, meeting room and children's fun room are also located in the large building.

Swimming pool: There is a small fee to use the pool. Area residents may purchase seasonal passes. The pool is often scheduled for aquatic exercise classes, lap swimmers and water polo before or after public hours. Public swim hours are noon to 6:30 p.m. Swimming lessons are also offered in the mornings. The pool is a full Olympic-size, with a wide deck and bathhouse. A pool-side concession is open during the summer.

Outdoor facilities: The sprawling ground features athletic fields and game courts, a jogging trail, fifteen soccer fields, three lighted softball fields, archery range, 12 lighted tennis courts that are open until 10 p.m. daily, and one of the best motocross (BMX) tracks in the country. BMX races and clinics are held on a regular basis.

Picnic areas and a rental shelter are convenient to play fields and parking.

Special events: Three-on-three Tournament, BMX events, biathlon, storytelling festival, tennis tournaments, swim meets, concerts, Easter "Eggstravaganza" and much more are available.

13 Fort Boonesborough State Park

Land: 153 acres Water: Kentucky River

Welcome to Fort Boonesborough, the first fortified settlement in frontier Kentucky. Welcome to what many historians refer to as the "gateway to the Western frontier." The exploits of the early settlers here, especially those of Daniel Boone, have become legendary in American folklore and history.

No pioneer figure has been more revered and written about than superstar explorer and American frontiersman Daniel Boone. Ole Dan spent 70 of his 86 years settling and exploring the frontier, always on the cutting edge of the frontiers advance. He was born in 1734 in Berks County, Pa., and during his long life ventured as far south as Pensacola, Fla.—where he almost moved! He died in what was then the far west, St. Charles, Mo., when the Rocky Mountains were just beginning to be explored.

I bet Boone would have loved to explore the Rockies and beyond.

Boone was a thrill junkie. He craved excitement, he loved to explore, and he couldn't stay in one place very long. The wilderness frontier was his office and he loved it.

The sixth child of Squire and Sarah Boone was known as a prankster, never keeping still for long. He didn't get much of a formal education, even through he was raised with a strong Quaker influence. In the late winter of 1752, the Boone family moved to the Yadkin Valley of North Carolina, which at the time was the western edge of the frontier. It was about then that Daniel started to develop his talents and hone his skills as a marksman, hunter, woodsman and explorer. He was known to have killed as many as 30 deer in a day.

Boone's life took a radical change in 1775 when he signed up as a wagoneer, along with John Findley, with Major General Edward Braddock's forces during the French and Indian War. During these months Findley described to Boone the beauty, richness and adventure of the wild lands beyond the Cumberland Mountains. Findley showed Boone the way through the Cumberland Gap to Warrior's Path and the Ohio River.

Eventually Boone returned home to Yadkin where he married Rebecca Bryan and settled on Sugar Tree Creek. They lived there for 10 years. Six of their 12 children were born there proving Boone was home at least some of the time.

Boone set about exploring Kentucky in earnest in the autumn of 1767 with his brother Squire Jr. and William Hill. The intrepid threesome followed the banks of the Big Sandy River that flowed west of Cumberland when they ran into snowstorms and were forced to build camp for the winter near a salt spring 10 miles west of the present town of Prestonburg, Ky. Although this trip was a failure, it taught them much, and upon returning home, where his old pal John Findley had spent the winter, Boone learned from him the way down Warrior's Path through the Cumberland Gap westward.

In the spring of 1769, Boone tried again with John Stuart, his brother-in-law Joseph Holden, James Mooney and William Cooley. This business trip was partly financed by Richard Henderson and the Transylvania Company. After straying from the path, then rediscovering the route through the Gap, Boone's party climbed a tall summit from where they saw the rolling land of Garrard and Madison counties and beyond. This was the Kentucky he was looking for.

This is also just the beginning of Boone's often heroic exploits and colorful history. To learn more about this fascinating American hero and pioneer life, plan a visit to the fort and museum soon.

Information and Activities

Fort Boonesborough State Park
4375 Boonesboro Road
Richmond, KY 40475-9316
(606) 527-3131

Directions: Ten miles from Winchester. From I-75, take Exit 95. On I-64, exit at Winchester. The park closes at 10 p.m. The fort entrance is off of South 627, about 2,000 feet from the campground.

Fort/museum: The fort is the major focal point of the state park. With plenty of parking at the fort, visitors will first see the square gray, granite memorial and flag pole near the entrance. It was erected in 1981 and dedicated to the sacred memory of the brave pioneers who entered the wilderness of what later became Kentucky and formed the settlement known as Boonesborough, the first fortified settlement in Kentucky. Carved into the face of the stone are the names of many, including many members of the Boone family.

Reconstructed and moved from the original site, the logs of the rectangular walled fort are now chinked with modern gray material to better fight the ravages of the weather, its only modern enemy.

Established on April 1, 1775, the first construction was of several small log huts about 60 yards from the river and about 200 yards from the salt lick. Within months the fort expanded to include 26 log cabins and four blockhouses arranged in a square. During the flurry of development and construction, the fort began to suffer a series of Indian attacks, the most famous of which was known as "The Great Siege of Boonesborough." The siege is well documented in the museum.

Fort Boonesborough was a stopping point for many settlers from 1779-1790, but the population of the fort steadily declined after the Revolutionary War ended and the fort was not needed for defense. Today, visitors will witness a wonderfully reconstructed fort with blockhouses, cabins and period furnishings. But most interesting are the friendly artisans who perform pioneer craft demonstrations and carefully relate 18th century lifestyles and pioneer experiences to modern-day visitors.

The fort was to be the hub of a great colony—but was really short-lived, about 50 years—before a swift decline when it was no longer needed after the Revolutionary War ended. When you visit the fort, you will see a snapshot in time, a period when the fort was full of activity and skilled pioneers, a time when it was indeed a gateway to the west.

In its heyday the fort contained about 30 buildings—26 cabins, two to four blockhouses, and two houses inside the enclosure. Cabins were outside the fort walls. The fort, about 200 yards from the river, measured 180 feet wide by 280 feet long. The blockhouses, with their projecting second stories, formed the angles or bastions of the fort, and the roofs of the cabins sloped inward for additional protection. There are two gates, front and back.

Inside the fort, the best way to start the experience is to watch the 23-minute orientation video shown in a cool, dark log cabin with theater-style seating, brochure rack, and an expert staff to answer questions and start you on the tour.

In the neighboring Stoner cabin you will immediately see and feel how tiny the cabin spaces were and, frankly, how small the beds, furnishings and kitchens were. Inside the Transylvania Store are examples of commodities once traded and sold, such as simple items we take for granted like sugar, salt and simple metal tools. From the blockhouse you can look out the small ports cut through the logs to accommodate rifles.

Along the courtyard like area, where herb and vegetable gardens grow, are rows of small cabins that now house a wide variety of artisans who will interpret and demonstrate activities like candle making, broom making, a weaver who will show you how to make thread, potter's shops, quilt makers who demonstrate all of the many patterns and techniques, soap making, blacksmithing in the outdoor shop filled with smoke when the bellows blows, and many other living history activities.

Inside the fort's museum you are greeted by a huge oil painting that depicts the treaty of Sycamore Shoals and an oil of Daniel Boone at Pilots Knob. Another terrific painting is of Daniel Boone "Blazing the Trails," showing Daniel recruiting road builders and blazing a trail through the Cane Break.

The wooden floors of the museum creak underfoot and the walls are often filled with interpretive paintings, photographs and exhibits of pioneer history. In fact, above the fireplace is one of the best oil paintings of, you guessed it, Daniel Boone. There's also a seating where you can almost lean against a large log that holds a larger-then-life bust of Daniel gazing into the distance.

A favorite display, although not terribly historical, is the sample of Kentucky wood, shaped as canoe paddles, where you can see the wood-grain and color of labeled specimens.

The next building along the square pattern of the fort is the two-story, fully-stocked gift shop that specializes in the wares of the fort's artisans. Yarns, stools, candles, brooms, dolls and pottery are offered for sale that have been made at the fort. You can also buy small reproductions of the oil painting of Daniel Boone for your fireplace!

Small kiddie-type items, Kentucky crafts, and many other interesting handcrafts are also sold at the shop that closes at 5 p.m. daily.

The fort is open 9 a.m. - 5:30 p.m. April 1 - Oct. 31; it is closed Mondays and Tuesdays after Labor Day.

Museum tours: For even more history about the Richmond area, a combination museum tour includes a visit to Fort Boonesborough and

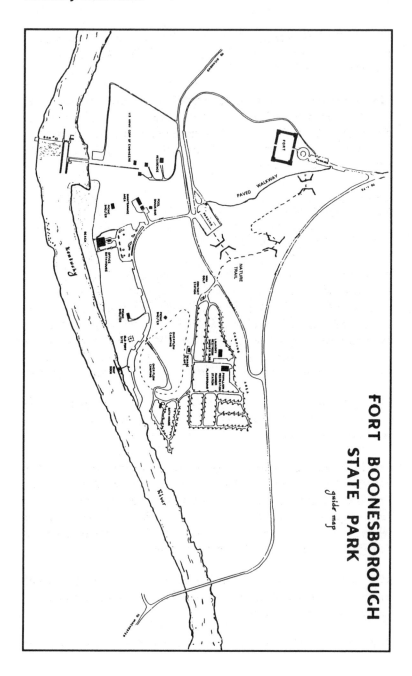

FORT BOONESBOROUGH STATE PARK

guide map

White Hall State Historic Site, the home of abolitionist Cassius Clay. Tour are offered April 1 - Oct. 31, except for Mondays and Tuesdays after Labor Day, there is a fee.

Gift shops: Everything from clay dishware to slightly corny souvenirs like rubber hatchets and tom-tom drums is offered at the shop in the large modern building that houses the park office/beach house. In a small room adjacent to the gift shop is a small grocery store that offers camping supplies, ice and snack foods.

The fort gift shop—as already mentioned—is one of the finest in the state parks system, featuring delightful handcrafts made by fort artisans and many Kentucky craft items. The shop is open seasonally, April 1 - Oct. 31, and is closed Mondays and Tuesdays after Labor Day.

Campground: Sites at the campground are generally large enough for any size RV rig. Most sites have adequate shade, a picnic table, fire rings, and proximity to utility hookups. A favorite play area for the children has an old stage coach-style wagon with tiny horses pretending to pull it over the terrain near a small play log cabin. There's also other traditional play apparatus in this large campground. Also for campers are court game areas and open spaces for day-use. Firewood is sold in the campground.

Next to the flagstone-and-wood shower building and laundry is the recreation pavilion, formerly the park store, that now has a variety of video and other games.

Sites in the 60s and 70s are backed up against a wooded area. Sites 158 and 159 (160 is also excellent in this area) face each other in a shady area for two families on a long weekend. Site 154 is a great tent site where you can pitch your tent on a small berm. Sites 140 and 144-147 are tucked along the river and have a view of the slow-moving waterway. Campers have good river access from these camping sites.

Many large RV rigs use the Fort Boonesborough campground because of its large size and overall quality. Overflow parking is also available for campers with boats or other needs.

At the entrance to the primary tent camping area (sometimes called overflow area) is a wooden shower building along a small gravel road that winds through a rustic area shaded by some super-sized hardwoods, especially sycamores. Located on the east end of the main campground, the valley-like area is cool and flat, often filled with family campers who like to set up near the small creek that bisects the terrain. At the far end of the tent camping area is a porta-john. Many of the rustic sites have fire rings and picnic tables.

Meeting facilities: The multi-purpose building near the recreation building can be used for meeting and activities, accommodating up to 150 people. Rentals are available during the off-season.

Fishing: This stretch of the Kentucky River near the dam is often slow moving and muddy. Rough fish anglers often use stink baits and crawlers to bring up catfish and carp. Bluegill and bass are also taken in reasonable numbers during the spring and fall. The best fishing is usually near the dam.

Boating: A one-lane hard-surfaced boat launching ramp is located east of the park office. The tiny ramp can accommodate fishing-sized boats for an effort on the often murky Kentucky River. The privately operated Riverview Marina is nearby.

Walking tour: A handy and informative Fort Boonesborough Historic Site Walking Tour self-guided brochure is published by the park and available at the various offices around the unit. The tour has 14 markers scattered around the park that correspond to sites on the brochure's map.

The tour will guide you through sites where the actual events behind the legends took place. Each stop is marked by a post-type marker bearing its number in the tour sequence. Go to each marker in order, if possible, and face the number on the post while you read the text in the handout. The tour starts and ends at the office building overlooking the beach.

Walking tour participants will learn about the importance of the Wilderness Road, factoids about fort life, "The Divine Elm," the 1778 siege, a sulfur well, "Lick Spring," Hackberry Ridge, a trail to New Fort, Canoe Ridge and the Tobacco Warehouses. The tour can take up to one-half day, if you include the fort tour.

Artisans in period costumes demonstrate many pioneer crafts.

The Pioneer Forage Trail is a one-half-mile self-guided trail that is nature-oriented. Interpretive points detail interesting flora and fauna. You will learn about vegetation that was documented by explorers Lewis and Clark and Daniel Boone. This trail also connects to other short park trails.

Day-use areas: "The family that plays together, stays together" is the motto at the shady, older miniature golf layout near the campground entrance. Eighteen holes with wide curb-like roughs are surrounded by a low wooden fence. Golfing is open April 1 - Oct. 31 for a small fee.

An interesting plaque adjacent to the putty golf course commemorates the first ferry licensed in the Commonwealth in 1779. A man and a horse cost 50-cents per ride across the Kentucky River. The ferry discontinued operation in 1931.

Fort Boonesborough has three picnic shelters (one with restrooms), tables, cooking grills and a playground. There are plenty of picnic and open spaces in the mowed rolling terrain spreading in each direction from the swimming pool/park office area. Many interesting historical markers are also situated around the park, detailing events and sites where battles took place and brave men died. The Divine Elm is one such place.

Swimming pool: The junior Olympic-size swimming pool and water slide opened in 1993 and is sparkling clean and exciting. Open Memorial Day - Labor Day, you can enjoy a treat from the concession stand, lounge around 12 umbrella tables, sun on the wide deck and watch children play among the water-based play apparatus. The bathhouse has a grand entrance with a tongue and groove ceiling and exposed wooded beams. All riders of the bright yellow water slide must be 48 inches inches tall. The pool is open Monday - Thursday, 10:30 a.m. - 6 p.m. and Friday - Sunday, 10:30 a.m. - 8 p.m., weather permitting.

Swimming beach: Behind the beach house and park office with the ramp-like entrance, the beach is open for sunbathing only. The sandy, riverside beach is at least 400 yards long. The beach house has a balcony offering a view of the beach and slow-moving river. No swimming is allowed at the beach.

Planned recreation: Fort Boonesborough's campground is a busy one. Flat and 50 percent shady, many families and long-distance travelers pack the facility during the summer. A variety of fun recreational activities are planned and posted for campground guests.

Special notes: Annual Admiral's Day in September and Greaser's Car Show in October are popular.

14 General Burnside State Park

**Land: 430 acres Water: On Lake Cumberland,
1,255 miles of shoreline**

The 430-acre state park on an island surrounded by the glistening 50,250-acre Lake Cumberland offers rural charm with city conveniences. The only island state park in the system, General Burnside is centrally located in this busy vacation region of Kentucky. Within an hour's drive you can visit Kentucky's busiest state park, Cumberland Falls, shop for antiques, hike endless trails on state or Corps of Engineers lands, and visit quaint communities or bustling towns with shops and fine restaurants.

The park and nearby town were named for General Ambrose Everett Burnside (1824-1881). Burnside, a gallant Union officer, tasted victory early in the Civil War, and bitter defeat at the battle of Fredericksburg. After another disastrous defeat at the siege of Petersburg, Va., Burnside resigned from the Army.

The General did better in civilian life as he became governor of Rhode Island, serving three terms from 1866 to 1869. In 1875 he became a Republican member of Congress and served faithfully in that House until his death in September 1881.

Burnside also furnished the name for the style of wearing bushy side whiskers with a clean shaven chin. They were called burnsides, better known today as sideburns. Inside the pro shop is a tiny glass display with some interesting memorabilia about General Burnside.

The park was dedicated for the rest and recreation of Kentuckians and guests in 1958.

Information & Activities

General Burnside State Park
P.O. Box 488
Burnside, KY 42519-0488
(606) 561-4104
(606) 561-4192

Directions: Eight miles south of Somerset on U.S. 27. One mile south of Burnside, Ky.

Campground: Soft drink and ice machines are at the small brown check-in station that manages the activity of the 94-site campground. Each site has utility hook-ups. The park also operates a number of primitive camping sites. The rolling campground is mostly shady and open April 1 - Oct. 31.

Staff reports that sites 30 and 31 (pull-through) are the most popular in the park. 36-38 and 42-47 are also popular due to their proximity to the shower house. The campground has two shower houses with restrooms, one with laundry facilities. All 94 main camping sites are hard-surfaced and furnished with picnic tables and grills or fire boxes. Site 88 has the longest camping pad in the park, more than 40 feet in length, cut into a natural area.

Other excellent sites are 32, 33, 35, 60, 69 and many others. The campground play area near the entrance features a full selection of play equipment for the kids.

For big RV rigs, try site 35 on a knoll above the lake. Sites 22 and 23 are also large and have easy access for larger camping rigs. The park maintains a group camping area that is heavily used by scouts and other groups.

Boating: The six-lane launch is the best on the lake. The gentle slope of the ramp helps boaters carefully dip their craft into the waters. More than 120 cars and trailers can park at the ramp. A restroom building and fish cleaning station with screen doors and sinks is at the ramp. Because of the perfect ramp angle, many large pleasure boats put in here. A temporary mooring dock is at the base of the grooved launching ramp. Nearby, privately owned, Burnside Marina rents houseboats and other watercraft.

Fishing: For more information about Lake Cumberland fishing, turn to the Lake Cumberland State Resort Park entry. Also stop at one of the area bait and tackle shops for the latest local fishing information and hot spots. Lake maps are sold at most sporting goods outlets. Shorelines fishing is possible at some sites around the island park. The lake waters have a variety of fish including rockfish, largemouth, smallmouth, Kentucky bass, walleye and crappie.

Day-use areas: On a knoll above the community pool is a day-use area outfitted with picnic tables, grills and a large shelter. Two picnic shelters (one with restrooms) are reservable. Campers may check out various sporting equipment (shuffleboard, etc.).

Golf: The park superintendent's office in the modern pro shop is nestled in a grove of trees. The 18-hole, par 71 course is challenging, with some blind shots and water on the 18th hole. From the blue tee the course measures 5,905 yards, with average-sized Bermuda greens and rolling fairways. Many fairways are wooded with evergreen trees and short

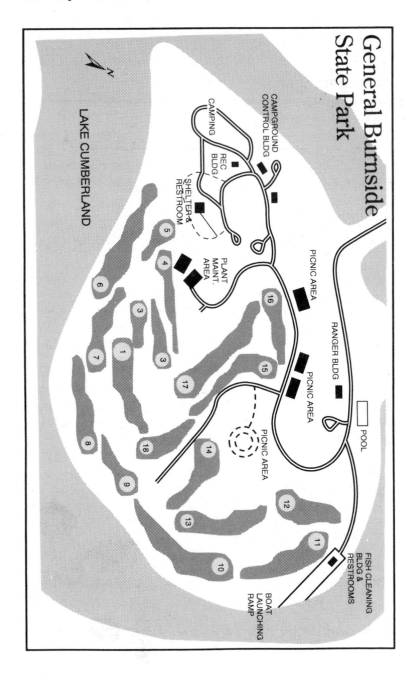

General Burnside State Park

LAKE CUMBERLAND

N

CAMPGROUND CONTROL BLDG

CAMPING

REC BLDG

SHELTER & RESTROOM

PLANT MAINT. AREA

PICNIC AREA

RANGER BLDG

PICNIC AREA

PICNIC AREA

POOL

FISH CLEANING BLDG & RESTROOMS

BOAT LAUNCHING RAMP

Play golf, go boating, take a swim or just relax at General Burnside.

roughs. Tee times are required on holidays and weekends during the prime part of the season. The golf course is open year-round, except when there is heavy frost or snow. The 15th hole maybe the most scenic on the layout.

Swimming pool: Burnside's community pool is a refreshing destination on a hot summer day. A diving pool, Olympic-sized pool and kiddies wading pool are open seasonally and boarded by a wide, sometimes grassy deck and seating area.

The diving pool has two diving boards of different heights. The bathhouse and small concession stand are at one end of the pool, with an elevated wood deck at the other end that is open for sunning and relaxing. There is a small admission fee to the public pool. Hours vary by the season; it is open Memorial Day to Labor Day.

Special notes: Tourist information on the region, call (800) OH-BOATS. Christmas Island: Each holiday season thousands of animated light displays (flying reindeer, jack-in-the-box, penguins, etc.) are set up by the local tourism board for the general public to enjoy. From about mid-November to Jan. 1, the park is transformed into Christmas Island. There is an admission fee. For more information call (800) 642-6287.

15 *General Butler State Resort Park*

Land: 809 acres   Water: 30-acre lake

General Butler State Resort Park has it all! Named for William Orlando Butler, the famous War of 1812 hero and staffer to Gen. Andrew Jackson, the sprawling park has an interesting history, a 19th century house, beach, golf course, tennis courts, lodge, meeting rooms, scenic vistas, hiking and biking, and snow skiing.

Butler, soldier and statesman, poet and politician, was born on April 19, 1791 in Jessamine County, Ky. to Mildred and Percival Butler, the first adjutant general of Kentucky. On Sept. 4, 1933, the park, then named Butler Memorial State Park, was dedicated. Gov. Ruby Laffoon made the dedication speech and guests were treated to an open pit barbecue and burgoo. The ceremony honored years of work by CCC and WPA workers and the Kentucky State Parks Commission. It was the sixth state park in the system.

General Butler State Resort Park is a focal point of Carrollton County, an area that offers a unique historic setting of home and buildings which span two centuries.

The popular destination area has four 18-hole golf courses near the state park, proximity to I-71, an attractive downtown area with 19th century facades, outlet shopping, hunting, and some of the best antique stores in the state.

Information and Activities

General Butler State Resort Park
P.O. Box 325
Carrollton, KY 41008-0325
(502) 732-4384
(800) 325-0078 - lodge reservations

Directions: 45 miles northeast of Louisville, take I-71 to Carrollton, on the west side of KY 36. The beautiful stone wall entrance is one of the most impressive in the park's system. The park is two miles long from entrance to entrance.

Lodge: The sweeping views of the broad Ohio Valley from the hilltop lodge are spectacular every month of the year. The vaulted ceiling, pine paneling and brilliantly polished floors are framed by arched windows that offer wonderful views of the surrounding terrain and two small swimming pools that are open for guests use. The angular lodge has that wonderful warm feeling of a backwoods resort. There are 57 rooms in the lodge, each with a balcony or patio for a scenic view.

The big-screen television in the upper lobby is surrounded by comfortable couches and easy chairs. In places on the floor you can see tiny spike marks from golfers who have clomped around the lobby. The stone fireplace is also nearby and comfortable seating is situated in front of its hearth.

The gift shop across from the front desk offers Kentucky crafts, glass-ware, quilts, framed photographs, T-shirts, clever game-like souvenirs, postcards, stationary and limited toiletry items.

Down a few steps from the main lobby is the pleasant triangular-shaped dining room with tasteful natural colors underfoot and throughout the decor. The 176-seat eating space opens daily for breakfast at 7 a.m. and offers a view of the beautiful Ohio River Valley. There is a Sunday buffet from noon-4 p.m. Try the Derby Pie, only, of course, after a Cajun Chicken dinner. It's great!

A small recreation room features a selection of flashing video games, checker boards, and a well-used ping pong table. This room is also used as a meeting space.

Meeting facilities: The park manages a private dining room with seating for 43 people and the above mentioned recreation room in the lodge that can also accommodate 43 people. Next door to the lodge is a small brown conference center with fireplace that can handle groups of up to 100 people.

Cottages: General Butlers has some very nice cottages. Some are angular and modern, while others are more rustic and blend cleanly into the wooden surroundings. There are a total of 23 cottages and each is equipped with tableware, cooking utensils and linens provided fresh daily. All of the units have balconies or patios with seating. There are one, two, and three-bedroom models available with one- and two-baths.

Cottages 533-534 are extra shady at the end of a narrow loop-like drive. For a more rustic cottage, try 529 at the end of a loop. Complete with grills and picnic tables, some of the cottages are light and dainty looking, with small wooden walkways leading from the car parking area to the attractive front door.

If you are vacationing with small children, cottages 518-520 are excellent choices due to their closeness to a small playground and quiet roadways. Frankly, every one of the cottages at General Butler is great!

Many Kentucky state parks offer excellent conference facilities.

Campground: At the check-in station, campers can purchase ice and pick up camping and park information from the attendant. There are 111 camping sites, with utility hook-ups and grills, on several loops. The campground is busy. Two shower buildings with laundry facilities and restrooms serve fun-seeking campers. No advance registration is taken at the campground.

The first loop, sites 1-19 are in a grove of mature trees. Several pull-through sites are available. The pull-through sites are large, and can accommodate campers with a boat and trailer to park. All of the sites in the terrific area have hard-surfaced pads. The most private sites in this popular loop are 10 and 11, at the very end of the loop. Sites 18 and 19 are near the newer, green-and-brown shower building.

Loop 20-31 is heavily shaded, with a handful of sites having a slight incline. Chose your site carefully if you don't have a leveling device for

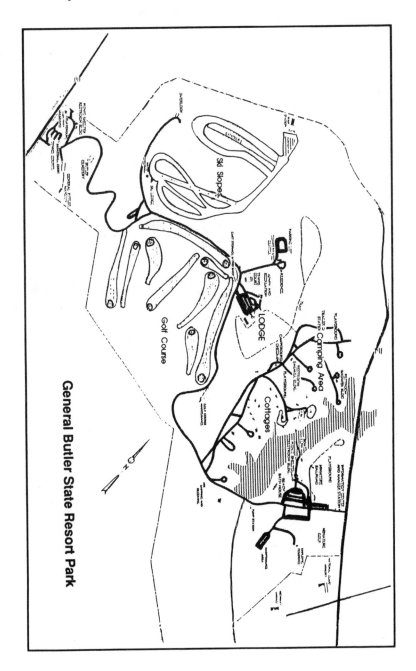

large RV rigs. Site 23, for example, is not flat. Sites 24-26 are terrific for smaller RV rigs. Sites in the loop are also a little close together, lacking much privacy. But the nearness to the modern shower building is a great advantage.

Loop 35-71, a heavily used area is a favorite with big RV drivers. The shower building is about halfway down the loop. There are two coin-operated washing machines and two clothes dryers at the newer shower building. In front of this service building is a bulletin board where you can post notices and items for sale. Shady, and a bit tight, this loop often fills up early.

Sites 75-84 are on a tiny loop, with site 79 being the best choice.

Camping sites 88-111 are a more spread-out loop. Sites 90 and 91 are terrific if you need parking for an extra car. Sites in this segment of the loop have a view of a wooded ravine and are close to a small playground and open spaces. The wooden cabin-like play structure is a popular climbing object for youngsters staying in the campground.

A sand volley ball court is also across from sites in the 90s. Site 102 is elevated, on a small ridge, offering a unique perspective—a great place for pitching a tent.

Butler-Turpin House: The Butler home on the park grounds was the home of Mary Eleanor Butler-Turpin and Philip Turpin. The beautiful red brick 1859 farmhouse is a three-bay, two-story brick structure of Kentucky Vernacular style with Italian and Greek Revival influences. The house overlooks the stately grounds once used for picnics, political rallies and encampments along the Butler family cemetery.

In 1797, Revoluntary War soldier Percival Butler purchased the land that is now General Butler State Resort Park. After his death the extensive holdings were divided among his children and consolidated by one of his sons, William O. Butler, for whom the park was named. Gen. Butler later sold 124 acres of his estate to Philip Turpin, son-in-law of his brother, Thomas Butler.

The Butler-Turpin House was built in 1859 by Philip Turpin and his wife,

Mary Eleanor Turpin, and is a fine example of mid-19th century farmhouses in Kentucky. Two rooms extended off each side of the central hallway on both floors. The one and 1 1/2-story stone kitchen south of the main house is connected by a roofed porch.

The house has eight rooms. Tours are offered of the period furnishings, and visitors will enjoy the view of the Kentucky River valley. The house is on the west side of the park property, due west of the family cemetery. The brick walkway that circles the house gives a good view of the restored home's exterior and manicured grounds.

Tours (small fee) are typically offered seven days a week: Monday - Saturday at 10 a.m., 2 p.m., 3 p.m. and 4 p.m. and on Sundays at 2 p.m., 3 p.m. and 4 p.m. Public restrooms in the basement of the house are accessed from the outside.

Fishing: The fishing is considered fair at the 30-acre lake that is sometimes stocked. Anglers often catch catfish, crappies and some bass, especially during the spring and fall. There are shoreline access points around the pond.

Boating: Paddle boats, canoes and rowboats are rented for use on the lake.

Hiking: The nature trail head is located near the lodge, and the pathway circles around the campground.

Biking: Whistling through the woods, up hills and down ravines on a mountain bike, is increasingly popular at nearby Ski Butler. The ski area, at the summit of General Butler State Resort Park, has made its 25 acres of ski slopes, 55 acres of forest, and its lodge available to mountain bikers for many years. A variety of mountain biking events are held each summer. For more information about mountain biking at Ski Butler, call (502) 484-2998 or write Bike Butler, 4770 Squireville Road, Owenton, KY 41008.

Skiing: A natural area and place to hike in the summer, Ski Butler is very busy in the winter when the "Snow Gods" bless the area with lots of the white stuff. This is Kentucky's only downhill ski resort, just minutes from

The miniature train operates on weekends.

I-71 at Exit 44 and a short drive from many several metro areas (one hour from Louisville and Cincinnati). The terrain is managed for beginners, intermediates and experts skiers for some really exhilarating winter fun.

Ski Butler is equipped with snowmaking machines, plenty of lodging at the park and nearby inns, and offers a complete menu of ski schools and lessons on the slopes. The longest run is 3,300 feet with a 300-foot vertical drop. There are two double and one triple chairlifts, two double and one pony rope tows, 1,300 sets of rental skis, snowboard rentals, new beginner area, night skiing and trails. For a snow report, call (800) 456-3284 or the office at (502) 732-4231.

Day-use areas: Large expanses of mowed areas with significant day-use amenities are just inside the main entrance. A 24-inch-gage railroad train, called the Kentucky Flyer, is near parking and other day-use facilities, including a mini-golf course. The train is open on weekends and there is a small fee for each ride.

Atop a low ridge line near the entrance is a wonderful stone block shelter that looks down into a wooded valley. The building is classic in design and workmanship with huge fireplaces offering an excellent location for group picnics. There are soft drink vending machines, restrooms and a large grill at the building. The stately shelter is near the small lake where paddleboats are rented during the summer season. The small sandy beach and bath house are also in this area, and there are two lifeguard chairs in the controlled area. The beach (open seasonally for a fee) is about 125 yards long and 20 yards wide. The view from the beach is of tree-lined shores and rolling hills with occasional boat traffic moving past.

Horseshoe courts, water fountains and many shady sites for picnics make this one of the finer day-use areas in the park system. The miniature golf course is surrounded by a split-rail fence and is open Monday-Friday, 2 p.m. - 10 p.m., and weekends, 10 a.m. - 10 p.m., for a small fee. The lighted course has been updated in recent years and from it you can see through the trees to the beach and hear happy children playing and splashing.

There are two basketball courts in the park, one at the west end and one at the east. The park has three well-maintained tennis courts, one next to the lodge. There are also many open spaces and day-use areas near the Butler-Turpin House.

Golf: The nine-hole course and the pro shop are across from the lodge. The public course is hilly, with wooded terrain and wide fairways. The course from the blue tees is 2,820 yards. The first and ninth holes are 480 yards long. There are no water hazards and few sand traps on the course. The small pro shop has limited supplies and a practice green. Carts are available to rent and you do not need to schedule a tee time.

Special notes: Each 4th of July, the park hosts a fireworks display over the lake. The park hosts other special events including Heritage Days in August, Kentucky Scottish Games and historic baseball games with authentic uniforms and equipment, peanuts and lemonade.

The Old Stone Jail is a fun tour in Carrollton. For more information about the many things to see and do in Carrollton County, call (800) 325-4290. Madison State Park in Indiana, about 15 miles from General Butler, is one of the finest park facilities in the region.

16   Grayson Lake State Park

Land: 1,200 acres Water: 1,512-acre lake

Boaters at Grayson Lake can glide past bluffs where Shawnee and Cherokee Indians camped under cliffs as they hunted the rich area. Pick a camp spot under the stars. Cool off at the beach and wiggle your toes in the sand, or catch a bass, hike a trail and take in a play at the outdoor summer theater. Grayson Lake is a fine family-oriented park with many amenities for a long weekend stay in northeastern Kentucky.

In 1964 the U.S. Army Corps of Engineers started construction of a random-rock and earth dam on the Little Sandy River in an effort to better control flood waters, create recreation, improve water quality, and enhance the fish and wildlife resources of the area. Grayson Lake is the beautiful result of this "hand of man" effort to improve nature.

From the upstream dam to Bruin Creek, the typography is wonderfully rolling and sloping in each direction, with uplifting small cliffs and tree-lined shores and ravines. Beyond Bruin Creek, the cliffs start to tower. Sheer sandstone canyons reaching 50 to 150 feet in height offer graceful vistas and spectacular splashes of reds, crimsons and golds during the autumn.

The lake has more than 70 miles of tree-lined shores where anglers play, canoeists cruise, and pleasure boaters delight in the shade on hot summer days, or bask in the sun during early spring or late fall. The park was built and opened along these rugged banks in 1970, and the popular 71-site campground above the lake has been busy since.

Information and Activities

Grayson Lake State Park
Rt. 3, P. O. Box 800
Olive Hill, KY 41164-9213
(606) 474-9727

Directions: 25 miles southwest of Ashland on the east side of Grayson Lake. From Ashland, take I-64 west to KY 7 south. Six miles south of Grayson, the county seat has a fine brick courthouse of classical beaux-arts influence.

Campground: Climbing a small hill, along a ridge line off KY 7, is the entrance to the campground. Quiet hours begin at 11 p.m. The campground is open April 1 - Oct. 31. The camping area is a loop configuration and has two shower buildings. There is no advance registration taken at Grayson Lake campground. Firewood and ice are sold at the check-in station and all sites have hard-surfaced pads.

Sites on the outside of the loop are usually backed up against a natural area, while camping sites on the interior of the loop are more open.

Some of the more shady and private sites include 13, 14, 15, 16, 19 and 52. All camping sites have fire rings or grills, picnic tables, and nearby water and electrical hookups. Sites 26, 27 and 28 are very private and located at the end of a small loop.

If you like more open sites consider 29, 30 and 31, which are sunny, but fairly private. Camping sites 37, 39, 41 and 43 are terrific open sites large enough for any sized RV rig.

Other excellent camping sites include 44, 46, 48, 49, 61 and 63, which are lightly shady, flat and large enough for medium to large camping units. Site 57 is a pull-though with two picnic tables.

Behind the newer shower building is a small kiddies play area that includes swings and climbing apparatus. There are lots of mowed areas in the campground. Rolling surroundings give a feeling of open space.

Emergency numbers: sheriff, 911 or 474-5616; fire department, 911 or 474-5444; boating officer, (800) 828-2628.

Fishing: Grayson Lake is considered a good to very good fishing lake. Largemouth bass, bluegill and catfish are the star denizens sought by boat anglers. Smallmouth bass, crappies and Kentucky bass are also taken in the waters.

The lake has a good forage fish base, which accounts for the populations of largemouth bass. Because these bucketmouths are taken with a greater variety of techniques and tackle than any other freshwater fish. Local experts vary on what's the best lure or bait. The fish are most active and surface feeding in the springtime when you can try popping bugs, topwater and crankbaits and jigging the structure; summertime anglers may want to try jig combinations, plastic worms, vertical jigging spoons/jigs or spinnerbaits. In the winter the best bet is pig n' jigs that are black crawled along the bottom and across any submerged structure.

Catfish are best taken at night on the narrow lake using cut baits, sponge cheese, shad viscera or chicken livers. You can also jig fish shallow flats at night. This is especially fun on moon-lit summer evenings.

Local experts say good populations of crappies can be found in the Greenbrier Branch, and bass in the Little Gimlet area. In the coves near Deer Creek anglers should try buzzbaits for large- and smallmouth bass.

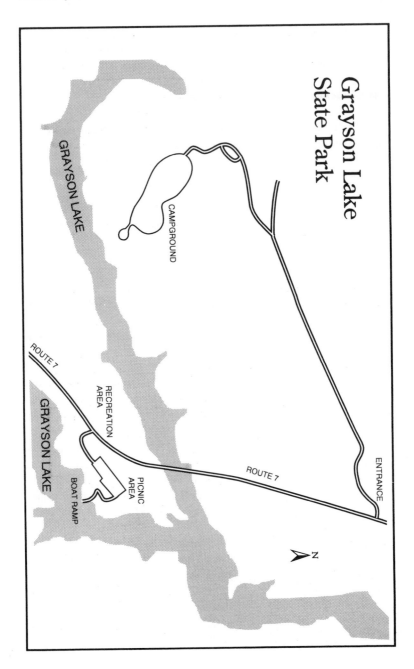

In the springtime, trout can be taken in the dam spillway. Weekdays are the best times to fish during the summer due to considerable pleasure boat traffic each weekend.

Fishing rules: Bass has a 15-inch minimum size limit.

Boating: The launching ramp and beach are south of the campground. The boat ramp parking area can accommodate 100 vehicles and trailers, and is located above the small cove where the ramp gently meets the water's edge. The two-lane, hard-surfaced ramp is busy and has nearby parking for the disabled and a vault toilet.

A small wooden mooring dock for temporary tie-ups is next to the ramp outlet. Also in the area are a small playground with colorful apparatus, plenty of trash barrels and picnic tables, where launching ramp spectators and weary anglers sometimes gather.

Canoeing: Aside from plenty of gimlets, creeks and branches off the main lake, canoeists can find good paddling on the river from the Dehart Road Bridge downstream to the lake virtually all year. From the tailwaters of the dam to Leon, Ky., the river is 25-40 feet wide and flows beneath steep rock walls and overhangs on the west and forests on the east. Downstream of the KY 7 bridge to Grayson the river is flat and wide, offering pleasant paddling through pastoral settings. Canoeists may also want to travel to the historic covered bridge in nearby Greenup County that spans a stream near Oldtown.

Hiking: Beech-hemlock forests surrounding the lake offer hikers an interesting habitat filled with several species of ferns, mosses, lichens and flowering rhododendrons. The short, .8-mile Beech-Hemlock Trail passes many rock formations and shady woods, and offers a prime opportunity to view wildlife and other flora. The trail head is near the theater.

Day-use areas: The narrow fingers of Grayson Lake project along valleys that were once wooded and are now flooded, but the Corps and state park managers have taken considerable time designing prime day-use areas with amenities along the lake and on ridges that offer wonderful views and pleasant places for family outings, field games and activities.

Planned recreation is also offered for campground guests.

Grayson Lake is the stage for outdoor plays, most notably *"Someday,"* a drama and poignant tale of love and war, divided loyalties and family conflict, set against the backdrop of life in eastern Kentucky. For more information call, (606) 286-4522.

Swimming beach: About 100 yards long and 30 yards wide, the swimming beach is open seasonally and when staffed. Two lifeguards staff the beach most days between Memorial Day and Labor Day. Children under 16 must be accompanied by a responsible adult to enjoy the corded-off beach. You must have permission for any floating objects, such as inner tubes.

Special note: Also in Carter County are Carter Caves State Park and neighboring 14,700-acre Grayson Lake Public Wildlife Area. In the northwestern part of the county is Tygarts State Forest. Cliffy Boat Launching Ramp (two lanes), a large marina (seasonal slips, small boat rental, for more information call (606) 474-8515), and handicapped accessible fishing pier are nearby on KY 7, as are many other Corps facilities. The Corps of Engineers office features some small displays and animal mounts, and plenty of literature on the area.

17 Greenbo Lake State Resort Park

Land: 3,300 acres Water: 192-acre lake

Greenup County, the 45th formed in Kentucky in 1803, occupies 350 square miles of Cumberland plateau and is comprised of narrow hills and hardwood forests that were the home of the first white settlement in Kentucky in 1753. All traces of the village, near the mouth of the Scioto River, disappeared before 1800.

Mineral deposits and ready supplies of coal and iron ore made the area a center of smelting iron in the 19th century, when river transportation was an important consideration. The Little Sandy River and Tygart's Creek flow northward into the Ohio River, dividing the county into three almost equal parts.

Production of iron began in Kentucky in 1791, and during the 1830s

Kentucky ranked third in production in the U.S. The remains of old furnaces can still be seen throughout the county, including Buffalo Furnace (built in the early 1880s) in the state park and Argillite, east of Greenbo Lake.

Greenbo Lake was originally a local park governed by a group of citizens known as the Greenbo Recreation Association. The name "greenbo" came from the combination of the names of the two area counties of Greenup and Boyd.

The park became part of the state parks system in 1955, and the lake, which is fed by three streams, Claylick Creek, Buffalo Branch and Pruitt Fork, opened in 1958 for fishing.

Early settlers came down the Ohio River from the eastern states to settle in the broad valleys formed by the Ohio and Little Sandy rivers. These hardy settlers scratched out a living farming and trading, and shipping products back up the Ohio River to Pittsburgh and other eastern population centers. One of these products was iron, mined and partially refined in the county during the 1800s. By 1850 there were 19 blast furnaces in the immediate area.

The Buffalo Furnace, one of the earlier furnaces in Greenup County, can be seen upon entrance to the park. This furnace operated from 1818 to 1856. After the Civil War, the iron industry began to decline and the last furnace in the county ceased operation in 1881.

Greenbo, the second largest unit in the state parks system, features a one-room schoolhouse and a beautiful clifftop lodge named for famous Kentucky poet and author Jesse Stuart (*Taps for Private Tussie* and *The Thread That Runs So True,* among other novels) who lived his entire life in Greenup County. His home is just outside the park boundary in W-Hollow.

For avid hikers, Greenbo Lake State Park is your gateway to the 25-mile Michael Tygart Trail that connects the park with the Jenny Wiley National Recreational Area.

Information and Activities

Greenbo Lake State Resort Park
HC 60, P.O. Box 562
Greenup, KY 41144-9517
(606) 473-7324
(800) 325-0083 reservations

Directions: Eight miles southeast of Greenup on KY 1. Exit I-64 at Grayson, 18 miles north on KY 1. 107 miles east of Lexington.

Lodge: The secluded resort, named after Jesse Stuart, is perched on a tall cliff looking down to the shimmering waters of the lake, with boaters and fishermen plying in the distance. The lodge, made entirely from Kentucky materials, has 36 rooms. The rooms have private balconies or patios overlooking the lake. A 232-seat dining room is open year round, as are meeting rooms and a gift shop that sells T-shirts, dolls, posters, craft items, souvenirs, books, glassware and Kentucky-made items.

Hummingbird feeders suspended from the lodge porch are busy with the tiny birds, especially in the evening as they tank up on red nectar water. If you stand very still, the incredibly fast little birds act like they don't even see you. Some experts say hummingbirds, by virtue of their rapid wing beat and high metabolism, almost live in a different time dimension. They move so fast, they barely see us slow moving humans.

Off the lobby that has a huge stone fireplace and piano is a diorama of the Buffalo Iron Furnace (remains of the huge furnace are located near the entrance of the park). This furnace was built on Buffalo Fork of the Claylick Creek and was one of 94 furnaces that once operated in northern Kentucky and southern Ohio. The Buffalo Furnace was built by John Sperry in 1851 and was blasting in 1852 with H. Hollister & Co. as proprietors. The first blast produced 2,400 tons of pig iron.

The Greenup & Little Sandy Railroad (later known as the Eastern Kentucky Railway) operated a run served the growing furnace community that employed 80 men with their families totaling about 400 people in the area. The tiny rail line annually steamed in 75,000 pounds of meat,

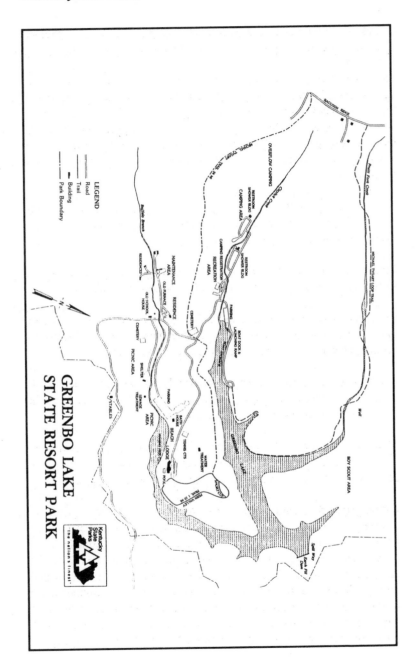

GREENBO LAKE
STATE RESORT PARK

LEGEND

Road
Trail
Building
Park Boundary

600 barrels of flour and 15,000 bushels of corn to feed the townspeople. Of course, pig iron was also transported by rail to river barges.

Those were the successful years for the iron smelting furnace. After the Civil War the facility remained idle until 1869 when it was sold. Furnace blasts by the new owners were a failure. In fact, a bit later, a new hearth was installed. A final blast was made in 1875 when yet another hearth blew out, dumping a full burden into the slag pit. A short time later the whole operation was sold to a scrap metal dealer and the facility has laid quiet since.

Also in the high-ceiling lodge is the Jesse Stuart Library that has eight comfortable stuffed chairs and lamps, book shelves and personal mementos of the famous Kentucky author.

From behind the lodge you may walk a concrete path to docks and a fishing pier, where ducks often quack for morsels of food.

The game room has two pool tables, a bumper pool table, two fooseball tables, ping pong and a half-dozen video games flashing and lined up against the wall. The game room closes at 11 p.m. nightly.

A short evening stroll after dinner can be taken to the beach via a hard-surfaced walkway beginning under and behind the lodge. The gentle walk is the perfect ending to an evening at the lodge.

Meeting facilities: Banquet, meeting and breakout rooms are on the lower level of the lodge. The Greenup, Carter and Boyd rooms can each seat 100 guests and the main meeting room can accommodate 300.

Campground: Open seasonally from April 1 - Oct. 31, the 30 primitive camping sites that have water and electrical hookups are not offered for advance registration. Thirty primitive sites are also available. Two shower buildings with laundry facilities service the shady area. Near the campground entrance is a miniature golf course, basketball goal and volley ball court. Some sites are next to sheer rock walls. Conveniently near the campground entrance is a single basketball goal, miniature golf course and a volley ball court. The campground is long and linear with plenty of shade and a small creek running through it, and has a campers-only picnic shelter. Each camping site has a hard-surfaced pad and fire ring, and there is additional parking for boat trailers near the large shower building. The primitive camping area is past the second shower building (there is a terrific little play area here with a snail-like climbing structure the children will love!) The best sites in this section for tent campers are 13, 15 and 17, since they are level and dry.

In the main campground, sites in the 50s are somewhat small, suited for small RV rigs. If you like sunny and open camping, try sites 63 and 64. Shade-loving campers will appreciate sites 25 and 26 along a tiny creek that runs full after rainstorms.

You can play miniature golf and buy firewood or other small items at the camp store.

Fishing: Greenbo Lake is the home of plenty of lunker largemouth bass. In fact, the small lake has yielded two state record largemouth bass over the years. A record 11-pound, 8-ounce bass was taken on Sept. 21, 1965. Only a few months later this record was broken on the narrow lake.

Trophy hunting bass anglers arm themselves with six-inch rubber worms that are wine, black or purple in color. Simply cast the unweighted plastic worms at the bank and retrieve slowly. Other proven lures include floating minnows-type surface lures in shad colors or pig n' jigs in the fall. The best patterns are typically fishing the shallows near dropoffs, near points, and at the front of coves and embankments, and in any deep underwater vegetation beds.

During the summer, fish at night and try casting parallel to the shoreline with shad-colored or red and silver crankbaits. You can also try some shoreline fishing near the boat launch or the beach. Rental of pontoon boats, fishing and rowboats, pedal boats and canoes can also be rented from the marina operator. There are soft drinks, gasoline, snacks, bait, picnic and camping supplies offered for sale at the marina grocery store.

Boating: No motor limit. Boaters must observe No Wake/Idle speed.

The feeder creeks (Pruitt Fork Creek, Claylick Creek and Buffalo Branch)offer canoeists narrow waterways to explore during high water

Hummingbird feeders hang from the lodge porch.

times. The lake is also generally quiet and offers many smaller coves to explore. Canoeists may also consider a run down the narrow Tygarts Creek that flows northeast through Carter and Greenup counties and empties into the Ohio River. Parts of the creek are scenic while other sections are filled with logjams.

For a better run, try the Little Sandy River (see Grayson Lake State Park for more details). Sections of this river can be very scenic, free from navigational hazards, and fun.

Hiking: Greenbo Lake has nine miles of hiking trails. At the end of the lodge parking lot is a large kiosk with information on hiking trails, and this is the trailhead for two of the park's moderately difficult trails.

The Fern Valley Self-Guided Interpretive Trail (1.1 mile) follows a hillside maintenance trail and then winds through a valley, passing flora and habitats where quiet hikers might see deer, grouse, songbirds or chattering squirrels squinting down from treetops. There are 16 learning stations along the easy trail that correspond to a guide booklet that describes a variety of natural features along the way. The booklet is available at the front desk. Marked in yellow paint blazes, the Michael Tygart Trail also begins at this bulletin board and continue 24 miles out to the 200-mile Jenny Wiley Trail system. The Wiley Trail connects the Ohio River at South Portsmouth, Ky., and stretches to the Jenny Wiley State Resort Park and Carter Caves Resort State Park. It also connects to the Simon Kenton Trail. It is 56.6 miles from Carter Caves to Greenbo Lake using these trailways.

The Michael Tygart Trail is marked with blazes of orange paint and starts hikers down a gravel road past the boat dock. It follows the lakeshore into Pruitt Valley. Walkers will pass old abandoned homes of the 1800s and a variety of wildlife and flora habitats. At the end of the valley you will ascend a short moderate hill, follow the edge of a pasture, and enter a gravel road. Turn left for 1/4 mile, where you will junction with the actual Michael Tygart Trail (second gravel road to the left). There you will make a sharp left and follow the yellow markings across mostly forested ridge tops, back into the park. This is about a seven-mile hike.

Day-use areas: Tennis courts and bicycles are rented at the lodge. Other features are an old unused beach, miniature golf, basketball, sports equipment checkout and a privately owned golf course five minutes away that is open to the public. The playgrounds at Greenbo are fun. From the daisy and snail-shaped climbing apparatus to swing and spinning equipment, children will love the brightly painted day-use areas.

Swimming pool: Next to the lodge, the swimming area includes a large pool and a shallow kiddies pool. The larger pool features a sun deck and a distance view of the lake. The pool is open 10 a.m. - 10 p.m. seasonally.

Nature: White-tailed deer abound in the park. Many are seen along the main park road near the lodge, where salt licks and hand feeding have tamed the finicky animals. Look for them in the early evening. Wading birds picking about the shoreline searching for food are often seen near the old beach and along the shallows of the creeks and coves.

Special notes: While in the area, plan a trip to the 1880 Oldtown Covered Bridge, nine miles south of KY 1 and the 1855 Bennett's Mill Covered Bridge, north on KY 7 about 12 miles from the park.

18 Green River Lake State Park

Land: 1,331 acres Water: 8,200 acres

The Green River winds through lush valleys, and small picturesque streams meander at the foot of the mountains in south central Kentucky's cave country. At the state park—behind the Corps of Engineers' earth and rock dam that was opened in 1969—the Green River spreads out into an 8,200-acre lake offering all types of water-based recreation. The lake has 147 miles of shoreline and is surrounded by rolling hills as high as 940 feet. The dam is 141 feet tall and drains 682 square miles.

Green River is in a section of central Kentucky known as the Highland Rim. More specifically, this is the Eastern Pennyroyal, which is higher than the rest of the region with greater mountain relief. Generally the terrain is made up of low rolling hills, although some section may be very hilly with sinkholes and depressions. Terrain near the park may be rough and precipitous.

During the construction of the dam, rock strata ranging in age from 300 million to 350 million years old was found. The lowest strata, Devonian New Albany Shale, underlies the dam, lake and the immediate area. At the spillway visitors can see three other distinctive rock types: Mississippian New Providence Siltstone, Mississippian Broadhead Siltstone, and Mississippian Muldraugh Limestone.

The lush Green River Valley was dotted by buffalo herds and other game, which attracted early visitors like Daniel Boone. The river was the main source of transportation for mail boats. Settlement grew in the region. In Green County, one of the world's first oil wells, on the north bank of the river, caught fire and burned for months. This part of the state has long been known for its oil reserves and other natural resources.

Today, 600,000 people annually visit the greater area, and the lakeside campground is one of the most popular in the state. The facilities at the park are new and well-maintained.

Information and Activities

Green River Lake State Park
179 Park Office Road
Campbellsville, KY 42718-9351
(502) 465-8255

Directions: The park is south of Campbellsville on KY 55, 26 miles from Greensburg. The park is 80 miles southwest of Lexington.

Campground: The flat, shaded, lakeside, 156-site campground is one of the busiest in the region. Three service buildings with showers and restrooms, soft drink machines and laundry facility are in the campground. The campground is open year-round, reservations are not taken. Green River Lake's camping sites are small and tightly packed—a little bit like ducks in a row.

All of the camping pads are hard-surfaced and furnished with ground-level cooking grills and picnic tables.

One of the big advantages of this campground is the chance to camp near the lake and tie your boat up only a few hundred feet away from your tent or RV rig. In the parkway, between the campground road and the lake shore, are a playground, fish cleaning station and open spaces for leisurely walking or watching the boats on the lake. Also horsehoe pits and volleyball court.

The gray-colored campground store (open April through October) is a long cabin-like structure with a wide porch and simple grocery items, snacks and basic camping supplies.

Fishing: Over the years, Green River Lake has been an excellent smallmouth bass fishery. There are reports that a nine-pound smallmouth has been taken from the lake. Springtime is the best time—especially April—for good to excellent smallmouth action. Try fishing the southern exposed banks with jig and pigs or pork rind combinations. Also look for points and use crayfish-patterned crankbaits. Small spinners can also be the effect at this time of the year.

Flipping and casting along stump lines, weedbeds, brush piles or just about any other structure is always a good strategy. During the early summer bass often go on the bite on rainy or overcast windy days. Later in the summer, when the weather and water temperatures heat up, stick with night fishing along the drops and near the dam with rubber worms. One local angler swears by spray-on scents during this tough fishing season. Nighttime anglers should also explore the shallows, in four to six feet of water, using noisy topwater lures.

From fall to winter, start with crankbaits on days when no one else is on the water. As colder temperatures come in, bring back the pork rind tipped jigs for a try.

The springtime white bass run can be substantial. Muskie are often taken, while catfish and panfish offer fair to good action most of the year.

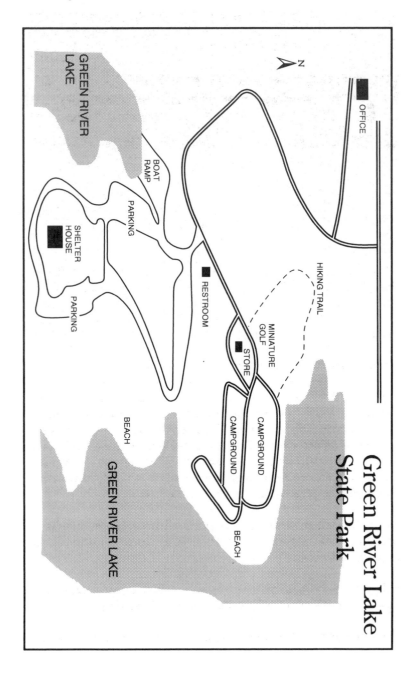

Green River Lake State Park

Day-use areas are great at Green River Lake State Park.

Boating: The main park road passes the launching ramp at the base of a small, sheltered cove near a large day-use area. The parking lot is shared by boaters and day-use visitors. The launching ramp is six lanes wide, grooved, hard-surfaced and busy on summer weekends and holidays. A low ridge above the ramp is a great place to sit, rest and watch the comical activity as nautical novices wrench their trailers back and forth, desperately trying to get the boat retrieved or launched.

At the north end of the campground is a small one-lane launching ramp, open for use by smaller trailer or cartop boats. Boating is very popular at Green River Lake.

Hiking: The 1.5-mile trail is a loop that winds north of the camp store, along the shoreline and into the campground. It is an easy, flat hike.

Day-use areas: The Whitley Airfield, for remote-controlled aircraft, is a hard-surfaced runway with parking and plenty of open spaces near the main park entrance. A stone picnic shelter, play equipment, picnic tables and grills are scattered in the vicinity. The rocky shorelines here, and throughout the park, are open for bank fishing. Volleyballs, basketballs, croquet equipment and horseshoes may be checked out with a small deposit and identification.

Planned recreation: Offered during the summer, planned family recreation activities include tree identification hikes, court game tournaments, arts and crafts, compass reading, movies, mini-golf, fossil hunt, nature walks, sack races, and so on.

Swimming beaches: Two swimming beaches service park goers at Green River. One is at the campground, the other on the east side of the main day-use area on a large peninsula south of the campground. Both beaches are sandy.

Miniature golf: If mini-golf can be cute, this one is. Behind the grocery store, near the heavily used campground, small statues of animals guard the putt-putt golf fairways. A totem pole, Indian chief, chipmunk and others figures are brightly painted on the 18-hole layout.

Special note: Hodgenville, Ky., Abraham Lincoln's birthplace, is nearby. There are many RV dealers, private marinas and bait and tackle shops near the park entrance.

A view from the monument down upon the birthplace of Jefferson Davis.

19 Jefferson Davis Monument State Historical Site

Land: 19 acres

The Jefferson Davis Monument in Fairview marks the birthplace of Jefferson Davis (1808-1889) West Point graduate, U.S. senator, Kentuckian, American hero, secretary of war and the only president of the Confederate States of America from 1861 to 1865.

Perhaps no other American hero has been so misunderstood and unobjectively remembered than Jefferson Davis. Although, no one can agree with his insistence that slavery was constitutional, in the end, it was his basic conviction that states should rule their own destiny that caused him to be such a controversial figure. He was a reluctant secessionist.

Early on, he was known for his interest in approving a North-South compromise in lieu of plunging the American people into a military bloodbath, the Civil War.

Davis was considered to be a highly honorable civil servant, devoted to his family, and a genuine patriot. He loved the Union as it had been in the days of Washington and Thomas Jefferson (he was named for Jefferson), but he believed that the principles of his beloved Constitution had been altered by the Northern majority. Not surprisingly, Davis' greatest imprint on the country was not in areas of war.

He was in many ways a forward looking politician, keenly aware of foreign affairs and international matters. While in Congress, Davis advocated the purchase of Cuba—that sure would have solved many problems years later!—and he envisioned a canal connecting the Atlantic and Pacific oceans. As secretary of war he began a pension system, founded the Army Medical Corps, introduced the light infantry, made improvements at West Point, and was instrumental in the development of the rifle musket.

About 3,500 people monthly take the elevator ride to the top of the obelisk monument to enjoy the view of the surrounding countryside.

Information and Activities

Jefferson Davis Monument State Historical Site
P.O. Box 157
Fairview, KY 42221-0010
(502) 886-1765

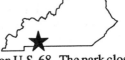

Directions: Ten miles east of Hopkinsville on U.S. 68. The park closes at 10 p.m. daily. The facilities are seasonal open from May 1 to October 31.

Jefferson Davis: Born where Bethel Baptist Church now stands near the monument, on June 3, 1808, to Samuel (a captain in the Revolutionary War) and Jane Davis. Of Irish-Scottish descent, he was the youngest of five sons and five daughters. It is interesting to note that just eight months later and not more than 100 miles away, another great Kentucky statesman, Abraham Lincoln, was born.

The Davis family came to Nelson County from Georgia in 1793 and to Christian County in 1798. Samuel Davis built a double log cabin. He was a farmer and postmaster of Davisburg. In 1810 the family moved to Louisiana and then to Mississippi. Young Jefferson attended St. Thomas of Aquinas Catholic School in Springfield, Ky., from 1816-1818. Later, while a student at Transylvania University in Lexington from 1823-24, he developed a friendship with Albert Sidney Johnston, who later became a general in the Confederate army.

Young Davis entered the U.S. Military Academy at West Point in 1824 and graduated 23rd in his class, a second lieutenant, in 1828. While as West Point he displayed his stubbornness and his disposition for having fun. In fact, at one point he barely avoided expulsion.

Shortly after graduation he was sent to the Wisconsin Territory, where he met and married Sarah Knox Taylor, daughter of Col. Zachary Taylor. Taylor hated the idea that his daughter would marry a military man, so Davis retired from the army for a time in 1835. Sadly, she died in his arms three months later of malaria at the plantation home of his brother.

For nearly a decade Davis lived alone at his Brierfield plantation in Mississippi, managing his farm and grieving. Never was a widower more crushed.

In the mid-1840s, he abandoned seclusion in favor of a very public life and the heated political arena of the day. The most important factor in his new outlook was his courtship and eventual marriage to Varina Anne Howell in 1845. They eventually had four sons and two daughters together.

Davis was appointed to the U.S. House of Representatives and served from March 4, 1845, until he resigned in June 1846 to enter the Mexican War. He led and commanded the 1st Mississippi Volunteers Regiment, and was wounded in the foot and emerged a hero. Zachary Taylor later said of Davis, "My daughter was a better judge of men than I was."

The monument is the fourth highest in the United States.

Davis was appointed to the U.S. Senate in 1847 by the Mississippi Legislature and was received as a hero. A year later he was elected to a full six-year term. Only one year later, he resigned to become a candidate for governor of Mississippi...and was defeated by a slim 999 votes.

On March 7, 1853, President Franklin Pierce appointed him secretary of war, where he served until 1857 when he returned to the Senate. He resigned the Senate on Jan. 26, 1861, after Mississippi's secession from the Union.

A provisional Confederate Congress, in a meeting in Montgomery, Ala., named Davis president of the Confederate State of America on Feb. 9, 1861. Davis acted with dignity, sincerity and decisiveness, with a strict devotion to constitutional principle. Davis showed strong leadership even with the limited manpower, materials and other resources that placed the Confederacy at a great disadvantage throughout the war. Davis, fellow leader, Robert E. Lee, and the Southern people endured four years of bloody battles, hardships and horror.

Davis and his family tried to flee to Mexico when the Confederate military collapsed and Richmond fell. They were captured by Union forces near Irwinsville, Ga., on May 10, 1865. Davis was imprisoned at Fortress Monroe, Va., for two years, and was released on bail. After spending a year in Canada and a year traveling, Davis settled in Memphis, where he served as president of the Carolina Insurance Co. from 1869-1873.

In 1879 he bought a 600-acre plantation, Beauvoir, on the Gulf Coast at Biloxi, Miss. During this time Davis diligently worked on his two-volume *Rise and Fall of the Confederate Government*. Davis came back to Kentucky twice during his later years, on one occasion speaking to more than 10,000 in Hopkinsville. He also returned in 1886 for the dedicated of Bethel Baptist Church on the site of his birthplace at Fairview.

The Confederate president died in 1889 in New Orleans at 81.

Building the monument: Plans to build a monument at the birthplace of Jefferson Davis were conceived in 1907 by the Orphan's Brigade of the

Confederate Army. A short time later a group called the Jefferson Davis Home Association organized with the purpose of raising money, choosing a design, selecting a site, and beginning the work on the monument. A variety of groups raised $200,000 over eight years for the construction of a concrete obelisk in the park.

First, seven tracts of land totaling nearly 20 acres were secured for the park, costing $7,052. In March 1917 the construction of the world's tallest concrete obelisk began, and over the next five months it had progressed to a height of 30 feet. C.G. Gregg of Louisville, was the primary design engineer, stuck with the project until its completion.

By October 1917 the construction had reached 60 feet before being halted for a time to allow for World War I. The monument stood untouched for several years. When work resumed, costs had soared and the project ran into serious financial difficulties. The United Daughters of the Confederacy raised another $20,000 and the state appropriated $15,000 to pay for the costs of the elevator.

By the summer of 1918, the monument was 100 feet tall and telephone lines and elevator shaft were installed. A huge steam engine provided power up to this point for operation of the construction elevations and other power needs.

Construction was again halted in early fall of 1918, at 176 feet. The top was covered and the structure stood capped off for more than three years. More money was raised, and during the mild winter of 1923-24, progress zoomed the obelisk to about 270 feet tall. By spring 1924 the tower stood at 340 feet in height.

Now the monument was in the final stages, and from this point on concrete was poured from an outside platform; all previous work had been done from within the structure. The final details were completed in late May 1924 and the dedication ceremony was conducted on June 7, 1924, seven years after construction started on the 351-foot tower. The structure is the fourth highest monument in the United States.

Presiding at the festivities were local dignitaries and workers on the tower. A barbecue dinner, lemonade, Boy Scout escorts, Confederate

Veterans, vintage automobiles and fellowship all added to the historic day.

The electric elevator was dedicated in 1929. The monument was rededicated in connection with Kentucky's observance of the 175th anniversary of statehood on Sept. 16, 1967. The monument was listed on the National Register of Historic Places in 1973 and renovation work was conducted in 1977-78 and 1988-90.

Gift shop: The small gray-colored shop is where you purchase tickets for the one minute, 47-second elevator ride to the top of the monolithic monument or where you can buy lots of Civil War related stuff. Hats and caps, T-shirts, books, wooden items, play swords, kiddies toys, fun license plates, jams and jellies, and much more are available.

Day-use areas: Two small picnic shelter buildings, hard-surfaced walkways, plenty of parking, scattered picnic tables, a basketball goal, and plenty of open spaces are located around the towering monument. A public restroom and drinking fountain are behind the gift shop. About half of the perimeter of the park is surrounded by a low stone wall.

For youngsters there are a sandbox, climbing structure, six swings, kid-powered merry-go-round and spring loaded mini-riders in the shape of a porpoise and duck.

20 *Jenny Wiley State Resort Park*
Land: 1,771 acres Water: 1,100-acre lake

The scenic park was named after a young pioneer woman, Virginia
Sellards Wiley, known as Jenny Wiley. The legend of Jenny Wiley is one
of courage, personal tragedy, heroism, pain and suffering that was all too
common during the fiery pioneer days.

The capture of Jenny and killing of the Wiley family by Indians actually
was an error. Neighbors of the Wiley family, the Harmons, shot and killed
two Indians, and Oct. 1, 1789, in Ab's Valley, Va., a group of Cherokee
Indians sought vengeance. Not knowing the exact location of the Harmon
cabin, they fell upon the Wileys instead.

Jenny, her brother, and her four children were alone in the cabin while her
husband, Tom, was at a nearby settlement. Jenny knew there were hostile

Indians—and often settlers—in the area and was prepared to go to a relative's home until her husband returned when a group of Shawnee and Cherokee cruelly raided the cabin.

In a horrible surprise attack, Jenny saw her brother and all of her children, except the infant, brutally tomahawked and scalped. Jenny and her tiny infant were taken hostage, beginning months of incredible hardship and courage.

When her husband Tom Wiley returned, he organized an immediate and exhausting but fruitless search. The march toward the West with the Indians was a hard and continuous strain on Jenny, who desperately tried to take care of her infant son. When it was apparent that she was lagging behind, her son was coldly slain so that she might keep up with the fast moving Indians.

Months passed and Jenny hardened, becoming almost accustomed to the trek. A few months into her captivity she gave birth to a son. At the age of three months, the tiny baby was given an Indian test of courage, whereby he was tied to a flat piece of wood and slipped into a cold stream to see if he would cry. Sadly, he screamed furiously and met the same fate has as his brother only months before. Jenny was also sentenced to die at the stake but was bought, at the last moment, by an old Cherokee chief impressed by her stoic calm in the face of a painful death.

Her life spared, she was forced to do menial chores but also, became valued as she taught the chief's squaws to make cloth and gave them other skills.

More time passed and the band of Indians moved to an area around the Little Mud Lick Creek in Johnson County, Ky., and set up permanent camp. Within a few weeks the Indians relaxed their vigilance toward Jenny. On a dark and rainy night much like the night of her capture, Jenny escaped.

She had no idea where she was, or which way to run, but knowledge of the woods and survival skills learned from the Indians offered her a chance to both elude them, and remain strong. Variations of the legend have Jenny guided by dreams, psychic phenomena, fantasies, and divine providence. She ultimately made her way to a new settlement and with the help of pioneer Henry Skaggs, crossed the Big Sandy River to safety just as the Indians caught up to her.

Finally, in the spring of 1790, she was reunited with her husband, Tom, and amazingly, the Wiley's began to rebuild their shattered life and family by having five more children. Jenny died at the age of 71 and is buried in the Big Sandy area.

Jenny's park, in the heart of coal country on Dewey Lake, includes a wonderful lodge that was dedicated in 1962.

Information and Activities

Jenny Wiley State Resort Park
HC 66, P.O. Box 200
Prestonsburg, KY 41653-9799
(606) 886-2711
(800) 325-0142 - toll-free reservations

Directions: In Prestonsburg, off U.S. 23/460 on South KY 3. About 120 miles east of Lexington in Floyd County.

Lodge: Lampposts that line the roadway up to the lodge are almost candy-cane shaped, helping to outline the rustic-looking, but very modern, lodge that's built on a low ridge line and overlooking Dewey Lake and marina. The lodge has 49 rooms.

Complete with a gift shop filled with Kentucky crafts, small jewelry, books, T-shirts, mugs and other small souvenirs, the lodge has a giant fireplace, comfortable lobby seating, and a nearby 224-seat dining room that serves delicious Kentucky cuisine. Two private dining facilities accommodate up to 70 people. The view from the dining room of the lake, wooded mountaintops and deep-cut valleys is grand.

The lodge swimming pool, with sunning deck and chairs, is for lodge and cottage guests only. There is no lifeguard, but there is a small wading pool for children.

Distance from May Lodge to:

Olympic pool - 2 miles
sky lift - 2 miles
campground - 5 miles
Pines recreation building - 5 miles
Terry Boat ramp - 6 miles
Dewey Dam - 9 miles

The lodge was named for Andrew Jackson "Jack" May, a local politician who served as 7th District congressman from 1930 to 1946.

Meeting facilities: The wooden and fieldstone Wilkinson/Stumbo Conference Center, adjacent to the amphitheater, has three meeting rooms (Iroquois, Shawnee and Cherokee), that have tongue and groove ceilings and quality decor, offering meeting and banquet spaces for up to 800 people.

The lodge contains two meeting rooms that each accommodate 125 people. Audio-visual equipment is available for meeting in the lodge or conference center. Call the group sales office for additional information.

Theatre: The Jenny Wiley Theatre, governed by the Jenny Wiley Drama Association Inc., is a nonprofit arts organization dedicated to enriching the regional community through arts. Each summer the newly renovated 580-seat outdoor facility offers wonderful Broadway-style plays and musicals with performances beginning at 8:15 p.m. The stage is tucked into a hillside, with the natural shape of the terrain setting a mood and enhancing the experience of the professional-quality outdoor performances.

In case of bad weather the production is moved to the spacious Wilkinson-Stumbo Center, where dinner performances and luncheon matinees are often scheduled.

Reservations should be made by calling the box office at (606) 886-9274. Or write: Jenny Wiley Theatre, P.O. Box 22, Prestonsburg, KY 41653. The ticket booth, located in front of the tan-colored amphitheater, is open year-round.

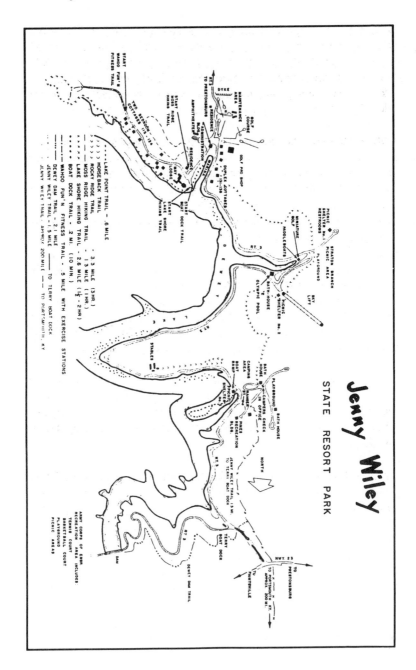

Cottages: The park maintains 17 terrific one- and two-bedroom cottages, each offering a lake or woodland view with cooking utensils and linens. The duplex (two-bedroom) cottages are near the pro shop, while the other small cottages are scattered south of the lodge along the lakeshore near hiking trails and other quiet areas. The cottages have cable television, phones, heat and air-conditioning.

Campground: The cloverleaf-shaped campground has 117 sites on three loops, and is of medium quality. It offers both full-sun and very shady sites in a rolling area of the park on the southwest side of Dewey Lake. It is open April 1 - Oct. 31 featuring two shower buildings that have laundry areas and restrooms. A small camp store has modest grocery supplies. Utility hookups are nearby at sites, and all camping locations have picnic tables and fire rings.

The park's campground staff says that the most popular sites are those in the 30s, 40s and 50s. Sites in the 70s and 80s are sparse of shade and not typically busy. In fact, sites 69-120 are not heavily used, mostly due to their small size. They are not very deep and best used by pop-up units or tents. One exception is site 97, located at the end of a loop, a private, tree-protected spot great for a day or week-long stay.

Area 32-64 is considerably more shady than loop 69-120, with deeper hard-surfaced pads. The single-lane loop offers camping on each side of the roadway so that each camping area has a natural area for a backyard. The best sites in this loop include 37 (near the shower building), 44, 48 and 55.

Loop 1-31 has larger, pull-through sites. Site 28 is probably the finest pull-through site. Families might like sites 11 and 12 located near a basketball goal. If you have a big RV rig, choose this spacious loop. Near site 21 is a stone ring that offers seating for story-telling or quiet relaxing.

Fishing: Fishing on Dewey Lake or along its 52 miles of shoreline is often slow during the summer. Panfish and bass are the primary species and are best taken during the spring and fall.

Fishing can be very good or very bad, depending on the season, rainfall amounts and the clarity of the water. Somewhat plagued by silting

The author "on stage" at the popular Jenny Wiley Theatre.

problems, the lake can be very cloudy after heavy rains in the late winter and spring During the fall weed growth is considerable. Actually, the weedbeds are near deeper water of the old river channel and can yield both bass and tiger muskie.

Dewey Lake has yielded a state record tiger muskie, helping to prove that forage is adequate and maybe the lake is improving. Fish attractors made from brush piles in McQuire Branch, Shade Branch and so on are helping, along with other locations in the main lake. Like the brush piles, deadfalls in the upper end of the impoundment have some good crappie action, and good bass can also be taken there.

Jig fishing with crawlers, flippin' jigs and worm combinations can work in the discolored waters. Many locals like white or silver-bladed spinnerbaits for largemouth. Shad-like lures should also be worked along points and structures. Some anglers slowly troll crankbaits over deep rock points in hopes of picking up a tiger muskie or bass that are feeding. You can also jig fish these spots with rubber worms or light (3/8 ounce) jigs.

Boating: Dewey Lake, an impoundment of John's Creek, was named after a local post office, which was named for Admiral George Dewey (1837-1917), the hero of Manila Bay. It was completed by the Army Corps of Engineers in 1951. The state has a 50-year lease to operate the park and use the lake.

The marina and boat ramp near the lodge offers 199 slips, pontoon rental by the hour or day, and a small store with gasoline and foodstuffs.

The one-lane Dewey Lake boat ramp, located near the campground entrance, is narrow but offers small craft operators a useful access to the popular lake. The hilly tree-lined shore is a terrific background for lake activity that includes pleasure boating, slow motion pontoons putting about, and fishermen casting and reeling in the hazy distance. There are two other launching ramps on the lake operated by the state park.

Hiking: Jenny Wiley has some excellent hiking trails where you'll discover wildflowers, songbirds and maybe a glimpse of a white-tailed deer and other mammals.

There are three fairly short but hilly trails at the park, aside from the access point to the 163-mile Jenny Wiley Trail that connects to the Ohio River.

The path to the boat dock and marina doesn't really qualify as a hiking trail, but it is an easy-walking trail that connects the busy marina to the lofty May Lodge. For a longer hike try the 2.5-mile Lakeshore Hike that is gently rolling until you reach the steep exit at Cottage 123. The trail starts behind the lodge and provides a beautiful view of Dewey Lake and the winding shoreline past ferns, ground cedars, papaws, maples and magnolias. Moss Ridge Trail, a 1.3-mile jaunt to the top of a mountain, is a strenuous hike, ending with a very steep downhill trek along exposed rock of sandstone and interesting flora. The downhill trail can be slippery after rain. The Steve Brackett Memorial Trail offers a 3.5 loop by joining the Lakeshore and Moss Ridge hiking trails.

The Jenny Wiley Trail, which connects to other trails totaling nearly 200

From the pool and beautiful lodge guests have a view of the lake.

miles is a rugged cross-country trail and is thought to be part of the route Jenny was taken by Indians after her capture. The trail is marked with bright blue blazes, and has shelters and cistern water supplies at 15-mile intervals. Hikers will enjoy being in a totally mountainous environment while walking through the Appalachian terrain. Hike with a friend, and enjoy this increasingly well-known trail system.

Day-use areas: The Josie Harkins Schoolhouse, Kentucky's last one-room schoolhouse, is at the entrance of the campground. From Memorial Day Sunday - Labor Day Sunday the house is used for Sunday worship, 8:30-9:30 a.m. (come at 8 a.m. for coffee and donuts). The schoolhouse operated from 1924-1987 and was moved to the park from Daniels Creek in Floyd County.

Community pool: The Olympic-sized pool is open Memorial Day to Aug. 15 each year and has a small fee and lifeguards on duty.

The Pines Grove Recreation building northwest of the campground entrance is offered for wedding receptions and other activities. The narrow fingers of the lake offer many places for scenic overviews. There are a number of pull-offs along the main park roadway equipped with picnic tables and trash receptacles. A variety of game courts is scattered around the park and open for visitor's use.

Skylift: Open Memorial Day to Labor Day and weekends in spring and fall, rates and hours change slightly each season. For information call (606) 886-6303. The lift is about two miles north of May Lodge and takes riders to the top of Sugar Camp Mountain on a mile-long loop.

Airplane rides: Yahoo! Take a airplane ride over the park from the Combs Airport on U.S. 23 between Prestonsburg and Paintsburg. Call (606) 789-5544 on weekends.

Planned recreation: The recreation office in front of the conference center is open by chance, offering schedules of events, handouts and planned recreation activities. Many interpretive programs are offered from Memorial Day to Labor Day including wildflower walks, snake shows, craft making, sports programs, boat rides, kid's story hours, hiking and "wacky" games. Special recreation programs can be created for registered groups.

No bike riding is allowed on foot trails or grassy areas.

Golf: Weather permitting, the nine-hole course is open year-round with a pro shop that rents carts, clubs and sells some small necessities. Call the pro shop for tee times. The course is laid out on rolling hills with narrow fairways lined with mature trees and ankle-deep roughs. From the blue tees, the course measures 2,371 yards.

Hunting: For deer hunting information, call (502) 564-4336.

Special notes: Miami Valley Serpentarium and the Army Corps of Engineers game courts and day-use areas are nearby. A variety of other area attractions include Butcher Hollow, the birthplace and childhood home of Loretta Lynn (made famous in the movie, "Coal Miner's Daughter"); Van Lear Historical Society Coal Camp Museum, call (606) 789-4759; August Dils York Mansion, (606) 432-3092; Breaks Interstate Park near Elkhorn City has the largest canyon east of the Mississippi River; Elkhorn City Railroad Museum, (606) 432-1391; the grave of Jenny Wiley in River, Ky., on U.S. 23 North and much more.

21   John James Audubon State Park

Land: 692 acres   Water: 28-acre lake; 9-acre pond

South of the Ohio River in the western part of the state, the spectacular Audubon State Park skillfully preserves forests where the legendary naturalist once observed wildlife that would become the subjects of his famed paintings.

John James Audubon migrated to Henderson, Ky., in 1810 with his wife and a baby son to pursue a career in business. Audubon was an entrepreneur, setting up a store, running a grist mill and investing in a steamboat. For several years his businesses flourished, until a crippling depression wiped out his ventures and forced him to leave the area in 1819. As this door closed in his life, another one opened that led him to international fame and success as a painter and naturalist.

At this turning point in his life, he and his wife Lucy began the incredible lifelong quest to paint every avian species in North America and sell the life-sized paintings to publishers. The unique stature of John James Audubon among American artists stems from his genius for artistic design and painter's stroke, combined with his genius for meticulous observation and records of birds and animals in the field. Audubon brought scientific observation into his art, and to the world. The worldwide Audubon Society takes its name from him.

His love of nature ultimately changed the way a nation viewed the world. Audubon was a romantic figure of sorts. He was at once a gifted artist and naturalist, sometimes dressed well and wealthy, other times rough and penniless. He was totally absorbed in his study of birds and art.

Lucy Audubon was a great supporter of his wanderings and artistic nature. She taught as a governess to support their sons and sacrificed to enable Audubon to enlarge his portfolio and eventually gain acceptance and success after publication of his work in England in 1838. As his success began, he became even more critical of his own work, driven to total accuracy and methodical field observations.

Information and Activities

John James Audubon State Park
P.O. Box 576
Henderson, KY 42420-0576
(502) 826-2247
(502) 827-1893 - museum/nature center

Directions: On U.S. 41 at the 18-mile marker, at the northern boundary of the city of Henderson, one-half-mile south of the U.S. 41 bridge over the Ohio River. You can't miss the beautiful park entrance sign. The park office is in a wonderful stone building with a slate roof that was built by the WPA in 1938.

The Struggle to Publish: After years of struggling in business including an 1819 bankruptcy, Audubon, with the incredible support of his family made art his life's work. For four years Audubon traveled down the Mississippi River, taught drawing and began to perfect his method of combining pencil and water color with pastel, and later with crayon, ink, and oil to simulate texture, sheen and subtle coloration.

He was fanatical. Audubon studied birds in every conceivable manner. He made notes, hundreds of sketches and paintings. Surprisingly, he loved to hunt birds, using the downed birds as study models, analyzing colors, feather texture, size and more.

In 1824 Audubon left for Philadelphia—the publishing center of America at the time—and received a mixed reception. He could not find an American publisher on this trip.

So, John James set sail for England in June 1826, the first of four trips there, with $1,600 in his pocket and more than 400 life-sized bird drawings in tow. His first stop was Edinburgh, Scotland, where his beautiful works found instant acclaim that led to a business trip to London. There, Robert Havell and his son engraved the entire 435 painting collection into one great book, *The Birds of America.*

Each of the copper plates was delicately engraved by hand, lightly inked, and individually hand-colored by a staff that at one time numbered 50 artists. Accounts vary, but many experts suggest the book took much longer to produce because Audubon stood over each engraving and every process, demanding excellence. The works were produced on 29 1/2 inch by 39 1/2 inch paper. The book sold well and went to a second edition, a smaller size which was more affordable.

Audubon never stopped wandering. He returned to America and traveled from Florida to Texas to Brunswick to Labrador collecting new material. These and other works were recorded in *The Ornithological Biography* and *Biography of American Quadrupeds,* volumes describing many species of birds and animals in America. These two works were created jointly with his very talented sons, Victor and John Woodhouse.

Audubon's last years were spent at his New York estate, enjoying his success and fame. The great nature artist died at age 65 on Jan. 27, 1851.

Museum: Open 10 a.m. - 5 p.m. daily for a fee. Closed during Christmas Holidays. With the wrought of native stone, the museum is a reproduction of a French Norman inn with cobble courtyard, walkways and French garden (chosen for Audubon's French heritage). It houses a huge collection of priceless water colors, oils, engravings and personal memorabilia of the master nature painter.

The 9,500-square-foot museum opened in 1938 (constructed by the WPA) to receive the collection of the L.S. Tyler family, descendants of Audubon. They chose Henderson for the display that included letters, journals, jewelry, silver and clothing. This is the largest collection of Audubon art and artifacts in the world.

The entertaining and educational displays inside the museum are fresh, interesting and professionally prepared presenting Audubon's life and works in four outstanding galleries: Foundation for Success (Audubon's 1785 birth in Haiti through his years in Henderson, Ky.); A Bold Choice (the determination of John James and Lucy Audubon to get his painting published); Fruits of Labor (the folio editions of Birds of America along with silver and jewelry acquired during the prosperous years); and Into the Twilight (from the completion of his master works through his 1843 Missouri River trip to his death in 1851, and Audubon's legacy).

Visitors will see dioramas, sketches from Audubon, natural history lessons, hands-on exhibits and a legacy that is world-renowned. Group tours are available.

The museum shop will give you an opportunity to bring some of Audubon's art home. Here they sell an outstanding selection of Audubon reprints and objects displaying his artwork, many from other museums. There's also a great collection of nature items, books, science experiments, artworks, T-shirts, sculptures, educational toys and much more.

Nature Center: Interpreting the natural world and teaching eager youngsters and adults about man's role in nature are the missions of the modern environmental education center. The nature center, which occupies one wing of the building, opened in 1993 with three educational areas that will dramatically expand your knowledge and experience of the outdoor world. Audubon would have liked the nature center!

The Observation Room has terrific windows and an observation deck—that look out over woodland planting, wildlife feeding stations, a small, stone-lined woodland pond, and forest. Binoculars are placed near the windows to help you see native wildlife, especially birds. The variety of wildlife feeders and expert use of native planting materials almost guarantee novice birders a chance to see songbirds up close and feeding. Both hummingbirds and butterflies are regular visitors to the garden in the summer.

Because we learn best by doing, the Discovery Center is a terrific learning area equipped with lots of hands-on activities. A huge, hop-into-it birds nest, complete with a jumbo fledgling bird sitting in it, sparks the imagination of all ages. Many of the other exhibits are just as unique, featuring explanations of bird locomotion and flight, feeding and avian behavior habits.

The Learning Center features live animal teachers, trained naturalists and a starting point for many outdoor interpretive hikes.

Cottages: The driveway back to the cottages is thickly wooded and hilly. Five, one-bedroom cottages sit like ducks in a row on a single loop. Cottage 101 is near the water, and 102 is closely positioned to the shoreline under a canopy of trees. Cottages have picnic tables, grills and outdoor seating. In the distance is a view of the beach and flat shoreline day-use areas.

The cottage loop has a creative little swing set for small children. The tops of the swings have a cow's face, with the horns of the cow actually holding the chain swings to the bar. This tiny play area is directly across the road from cottage 105.

The cottages are furnished with dishware, basic cooking utensils, cable television, central air-conditioning and heating, a living room with fireplace, telephone, and linens are available daily.

Campground: The tiny campground office, outdoor ice vending machine, has a public information board that lists churches, park information and local attractions. There are 69 camping sites with utility hook-ups.

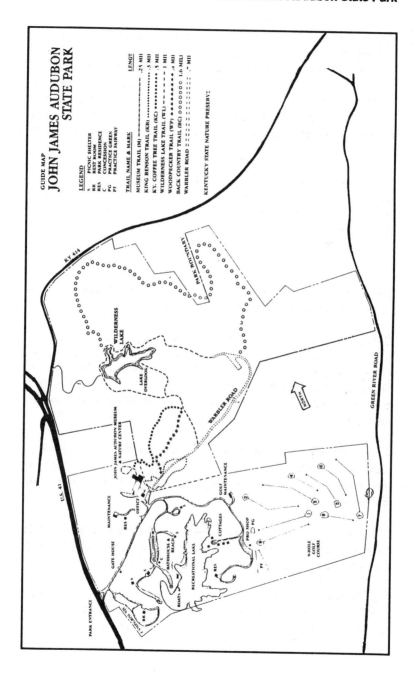

GUIDE MAP
JOHN JAMES AUDUBON STATE PARK

LEGEND

S   PICNIC SHELTER
RR   REST ROOM
RES   PARK RESIDENCE
C   CONCESSION
PG   PRACTICE GREEN
PF   PRACTICE FAIRWAY

TRAIL NAME & MARK   **LENGT**

MUSEUM TRAIL (M) ——————— .25 MIl
KING BENSON TRAIL (KB) •••••••••••• .5 MIl
KY. COFFEE TREE TRAIL (KC) ********* .5 MIl
WILDERNESS LAKE TRAIL (WL) – – – – – 1 MIl
WOODPECKER TRAIL (WP) ★★★★★★★★ .4 MIl
BACK COUNTRY TRAIL (BC) OOOOOOO 1.6 MIl
WARBLER ROAD ═ ═ ═ ═ ═ ═ ═ ═ ═ ═ .9 MIl

KENTUCKY STATE NATURE PRESERVE

The campground is very shady, resting under a canopy of mature trees. Each camping site has hard-surfaced pads, fire boxes and picnic tables. Firewood is available from the camp store. Interestingly, many of the camping sites are "Y"-shaped, meaning you will have one branch of the "Y" to park your RV rig and the other branch to park your tow vehicle, boat trailers, etc.

Sites 10 (especially good for large RV units) and 11 are shady and long, but they are closest to the sometimes noisy commercially developed road (U.S. 41). On the opposite side of the campground, travelers will find quieter sites. Flat and shady sites here are those in the 20s which are large enough to accommodate just about any size RV rig. The shower house and small playground area are centrally located in the tree-covered campground loop.

One of the best sites in the campground is site 34. If you want to be near the small brown shower building, consider sites 37-48. If you can level your rig, sites 51 and 53 would be interesting from which to explore the state park and surrounding community. Site 49 is a good big site in this older campground.

Fishing: The 28-acre lake is occasionally stocked with sportfish, and there are many shoreline access areas where families can try their angling luck. Largemouth bass, bluegill and catfish can be taken from the smooth waters of the recreational lake. Only trolling motors are allowed.

Day-use areas: The primary day-use area is near the lake. Near the Cardinal Picnic Shelter is a lone tennis court. There are four picnic shelters (Sycamore Shelter has restrooms), tables, grills and a playground. Volleyball nets are set up randomly in the park.

Planned recreation programs are offered year-round and are usually natural history based. Naturalist hikes, nature walks, birding hikes, nature arts and crafts, beaver observation hikes, bird behavior bingo and many fun adventures for youngsters are offered.

Golf the 3,018-yard-nine-hole course it is hilly and challenging. Get ready to climb a tall set of stairs up to the pro shop that rents clubs and carts. Many of the fairways are carved out of mature trees and present a long-ball hitting opportunities. There is no water on the course, but bean-shaped sand traps guard many of the medium-sized, slightly elevated greens.

Plan to register in advance for weekend tee times. The hilly fairways, sloping from side to side, are slippery slopes for mortal golfers. This is a terrific little golf course! No hiking is allowed on the course.

Beach: A narrow, brown wood and stone bath house is open Memorial Day-late August. The horseshoe-shaped beach outlined by a low cement retaining wall is a popular cooling off spot during the summer. The beach is narrow, and the sand is clean and a sunning deck is situated in front of the bath house. Free to the public, swim at your own risk. Pedal boats are rented seasonally near the beach.

Hiking: More than 5.7 miles of maintained hiking trails wander the through the nature preserve with variations in difficulty and length. Access to the trails are from the nature center. The one-mile Wilderness Lake trail takes hikers along the water's shoreline. Other trails include the Museum Trail (.25 mile), King Benson Trail (.3 mile), Kentucky Coffee Tree Trail (.5 mile), Woodpecker Trail (.4 mile), Back County Trail (1.6 miles), and Warbler Road (.7 mile).

More than 20 species of spring warblers can be seen.

Nature: The appreciation and understanding of nature is a strong theme at the park. From observing the beautiful paintings of Audubon to hiking the trails, visitors can learn about birds, trees, shrubs, ferns, wild flowers, insects, ecology and much more.

Originally dedicated as a bird sanctuary, the park has seen a variety of changes in both numbers and types of birds inhabiting the area. Audubon loved the Henderson area, in part because it is on the Mississippi Flyway over which countless birds migrate annually. About 170 species are seen over a five-year period that is listed in the handy "Birds of Audubon State Park and Wolf Hills."

One of the most important—for ecological reasons—and beautiful features of Audubon State Park is the graceful trees that comprise a variety of associations and woodland communities. There are basically two tree communities at the park the beech-sugar maple-basswood association, which occupies mainly the moist, rich northern portions of the park; and an oak-sugar maple-tulip tree association found in the drier southern part of the park.

The beech-sugar maple area is charming. The beautiful area is heavily used by birds, and wildflowers are found in abundance in the "climax forest," due to the large older trees found there. Some of the biggest tree species found include sugar maple, basswood, oak, white ash, elm, hackberry, coffee tree, sycamore and honey locust. Smaller trees are the dogwoods, redbud, hornbeam and sassafras.

The tallest tree in the park is a tulip tree that towers 120 feet and has a girth of 15 feet. The tree with the biggest girth is a rotund white oak that measures 18 feet around. Also in the park is a burr oak with a crown more than 100 feet wide. Audubon has 61 species of trees, covering 692 acres.

Because of the tight tree canopy that allows little sunlight to reach the ground, shrubs are somewhat scattered. There are 42 species of common shrubs found in the woods that include spicebush, pawpaw, wild hydrangea, arrowwood, honeysuckle, poison ivy, Virginia creeper, wild grape, sumac, wild rose and many other fairly common varieties. Two unique shrubs are the buttonbush, which is found only in or near the water, and mistletoe, a parasitic shrub found high on the branches of trees can easily be seen in the winter.

Moist rich soils favor many types of beautiful ferns. Common ones include Christmas fern, gladefern, grape fern, fragile fern, rattlesnake fern and 13 other types. The park is also home to 40 species of mammals and thousands of species of lower animals such as snails, worms, crayfish, spiders and insects.

The bird life and wonderful mature forests may be Audubon State Park's best known features, but during the spring the blooms of wildflowers rival all other natural gifts. The spectacular flora display includes larkspur, phlox, blue-eyed Mary, trilliums, trout lilies, bluebells, Dutchman's breeches and bloodroot. About 280 species of herbs and various shrubs and wildflowers have been identified at the park by staff naturalists.

22 Kentucky Dam Village State Resort Park

Land: 1,351 acres   Water: Kentucky Lake

The Tennessee Valley Authority was established in 1933 to manage the expansive Tennessee River flood plain. As part of this work to control flood waters, improve water quality and generate power, the TVA built the massive Kentucky Dam over a six-year period. The 1.5-mile dam opened in 1944 —after being dedicated by Harry Truman— creating the biggest man-made lake in the eastern United States. With a canal connecting neighboring Lake Barkley, the two lakes make up the biggest man-made body of water in the world.

The 206-foot-tall dam was a massive undertaking and ultimately fostered the state park's intensive development. While the project was under construction, the TVA built a small village to house the workers, and when the work was completed, the village and surrounding areas were sold to the state. Kentucky public employees quickly upgraded the existing buildings, landscaped the area, and built roadways. The sprawling and highly developed park opened in May 1948.

Kentucky Dam is the only state park to have begun from a group of existing buildings and as the result of a major public works project. This resulted in the largest marina and most lodging space of any unit in the Kentucky state parks system. The park is also a perfect place for water sports enthusiasts and is one of the busiest in the state.

The park is in the heart of Western Waterland, next to the 40-mile peninsula bounded by Kentucky Lake and Lake Barkley. The Land Between the Lake recreation area and considerable amenities make this region one of the top vacations spots in the country. The area has more than 200 miles of hiking trails, 300 miles of back roads, more than 100 paved roads ideal for cycling, picnicking sites, windsurfing, hunting, sightseeing, camping, 300 miles of shoreline and lots more. For more information on the recreation area call (502) 924-5602.

Information and Activities

Kentucky Dam Village State Resort Park
P.O. Box 69
Gilbertsville, KY 42044-0069
(502) 362-4271 - lodge
(502) 362-8386 - marina
(502) 362-8658 - pro shop
(800) 325-0146 - reservations

Directions: 21 miles southeast of Paducah, off I-24 to U.S. 62 to U.S. 641.

Village Green: The cluster of gray-colored shops near the golf course and across the road from the inn include a game room (bumper pool, billiard tables, video games, table tennis, etc.), post office, gift shops (wood crafts, some cloth and dishware, hard candy by the pound, hats, souvenirs, and one of the few beach shops in Kentucky, the Wooden Wave, a shop that sells mountain bikes, beachwear and outdoor accessories). The ice cream shop is next to the park's office at the end of the mini-shopping complex.

Lodge: The Village Inn Lodge opened in July 1962 featuring 72 rooms overlooking the glistening lake. A brass, free-standing fireplace greets visitors to the lodge lobby, with nearby comfortable rose-colored furniture and polished wooden floors under foot. Video games and snack machines are also located in the large lounge area.

A carpeted alcove has a large-screen television that is said to be a busy place when big games are broadcast.

The gift shop sell quilts, Kentucky handcrafts, and a mixture of other items.

The jumbo-sized dining room can seat up to 346, serving breakfast at 7 a.m. and lunch and dinner daily. The restaurant has a buffet, lake view, and a comfortable atmosphere.

Swimming pool: The diamond-shaped pool shimmers and refreshes lodge and cottage guests during the hot summer season. The maximum depth of the pool is eight feet, and blue deck chairs and umbrella tables are popular places during the daytime and evening hours. From the tiled pool deck you can see the large marina and small craft on the lake. Hours are 8 a.m. - 8 p.m. seasonally.

A small, 12-inch-deep kiddies pool is next to the swimming pool. Rooms for the disabled guests are available at the lodge.

Village Green Lodge: Once a hospital for the TVA, the small lodge now has 14 rooms with shower and tub, air-conditioning, cable TV and telephones. Six rooms have two double beds; two have one double bed; four rooms have one double bed and one twin bed; and two rooms have queen-sized beds. Two of the smaller lodge rooms include a convenient wet bar.

Meeting facilities: The park staff markets to meeting planners regionally, offering catering for outdoor picnics and at executive cottages and fine, modern meeting spaces. A meeting room off the Village Inn lobby accommodates 65 people, and the Village Green Inn has a room that seats 70 people.

Near the main lodge, a convention center bills itself as the "Super Natural Meeting" site. Surrounded by tasteful landscaping and soaring trees, the facility has one large multi-purpose room of 132-by-60 feet that can seat 463 (if storage areas are used for seating, the room can seat up to 525 people—6,940 square feet), and can also be divided into three smaller rooms. Meeting room A is 60-by-48 feet; meeting room B is 48-by-36 feet; and meeting room C is 60-by-48 feet in size.

The conference center has its own kitchen, storage, floor outlets, lobby and modern sound system.

Cottages: Many of the cottages at the park are renovated from the original TVA workers' village. Twenty executive cottages were built for the Southern Governor's Conference in 1966. There are 72 cottages with one, two, or three bedroom models, with one or two baths. Tableware, cooking utensils, and fresh linens available daily.

The bulk of the cottages are positioned around a large loop with one spur, with an entrance off Route 641 and from behind the village shops. The area is almost like a suburban neighborhood in feel and quality. The fancier Executive Cottages (301-320) are east of Route 641 on a single loop not far from the huge marina, where large houseboats and other pleasure boats can be seen cruising the sparkling surface.

In the main cottage loop, 101-155, is a mixture of light-brown cottages sitting on the rolling terrain. Some are more modern and larger than others. Modest cottages include 122, 123 and 125. Cottage 126 has a golf course view.

Farther back in the loop, the cottages change colors to a pleasing gray and tan. This group is shaded with small side yards. Cottage 140 is perched on a low ridge line. Cabin 142 is shaded by the broad-reaching branches of a tall sycamore tree.

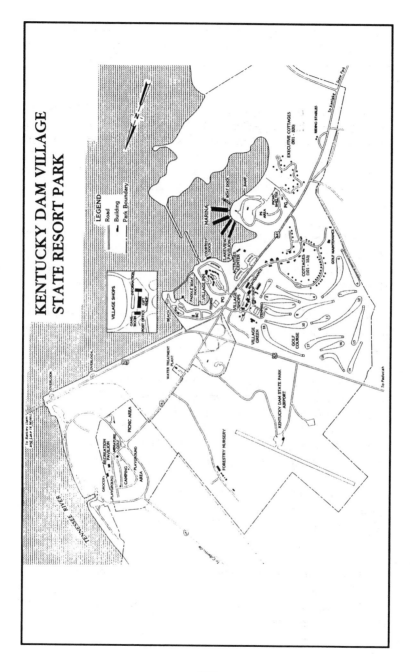

For families with small children, consider cottages 146, 148 and 155 adjacent to a small timber-structure play area.

The roadway that wanders among the cottages is large enough for pleasure boat trailer traffic. Some of the cottages have ample-sized driveways or sideyards where a boat and trailer could be readily parked.

Loop 121 (Efficiency Drive), the gray and tan cottages, are stucco with mixed light shade. Cottage 115 is handicapped accessible and near a small grove of airy white pines. If you like cute, try cottage 119, with a short walkway and fresh paint. For privacy in this loop, consider cottages 120 or 121.

Executive cottages are contemporary, bi-level units with living rooms, dining room and kitchen. One floor will have two bedrooms and one full bath; the other will have the third bedroom, another bath and the other rooms.

Regular cottages have one double and one twin bed in each bedroom; upgraded executive cottages can have two bedrooms with two double beds each, with one double bed and one twin in the third bedroom. Upgraded units can also have a second television, dishwasher, microwave oven and outdoor deck. Executive cottage 313 is one of the finest in the well-spaced loop. Unit 320 has a partial view of the lake and has lots of room around it for a large family to play.

Campground: Open year-round, the 221-site campground is a popular destination offering water and electricity with each site, three dump stations, four bathhouses, grocery store (open 7 a.m. - 10 p.m.), laundry facilities, and an older miniature golf layout near the entrance that is lighted and open seasonally. The facility is usually full on holiday weekends. Larger RV rig pilots will like the layout and space to maneuver.

Pads are hard-surfaced and outfitted with picnic tables and elevated grills or fire boxes.

About 65 percent of the sites are shaded. The grocery store is at the back of the facility. The general layout of the campground is one large loop

Fishing near the huge dam is popular.

with six lanes bisecting the circular area. A small amphitheater has six sets of seats on aluminum bleachers and a movie screen.

Sites 208 and 210, at the end of a loop east of the grocery store, are two of the better locations in the facility, offering shade and privacy. These two sites are very large for big RV rigs, and they have gravel pads.

Site 55 has two huge trees and is located near the store. Sites in the 40s are paved, shaded and often requested, according to the campground staff. Site 44, an extra wide camping site ideal for a large RV rig, is on a curve backed up against woods. A huge oak tree with a diameter of 3 1/2 feet shades this site. Many of the sites in the 30s are open, except 32 and 34 that are great for medium-sized trailers.

Sites 23, 25 and 27 are under the refreshingly shady canopy of a grove of mature oak trees. Site 6 is also protected by a towering oak, which is often visited by fast-moving squirrels collecting acorns or chasing each other constantly.

If you like open, sunny lots, try sites 78, 79, 80-82, 101 and others.

Smaller, more closely situated sites are in the 60s, 70s, 80s and 90s. Near site 156 is a huge vine of poison ivy growing up the side of a large hardwood. Be careful! The campground has two play areas, both equipped with swings, slides and routine play apparatus.

Fishing: (See the Kentucky Lake State Resort Park chapter for general information on fishing Kentucky Lake.) The huge Kentucky Dam is a popular congregating site for rock fish anglers. There is a 15-inch minimum, three per day maximum on rock fish. Detailed fishing maps of the lake are available at most area bait and tackle shops.

Local experts recommend rubber worms in the weedbeds, fishing near the dam, and hiring a guide for your first few times on the lake.

Boating: From the protected waters reserved for paddle boats to the largest marina in the region, water sport lovers will relish a visit to Kentucky Dam Village. Two-and four-passenger paddle boats are rented seasonally from the floating contact office.

Kentucky Dam Marina (call (502) 362-8386 or outside Kentucky, (800) 648-2628) offers a wide variety of marine service and repairs, boat rentals, tie-ups, slip rentals, fuel, ice, snack foods and a three-lane launching ramp. The newer, 25 hp fishing boats are great for fishing.

Hiking: There are no hiking trails at the park, but there are many great informal places for a relaxing walk, including quiet park roadways, along the shoreline, and on the breakwall-walkway that connects the beach to the Village Inn.

Riding stables: A circular paddock outlines the small riding stable on Route 641 south of the entrance to the park. Rides are guided and offered daily during the summer. The gray-colored stable is flanked by port-a-potties and a parking lot for guests.

Day-use areas: Day-use areas include picnic shelters (one with restrooms that is rentable), grills and tables; two tennis courts near the lodge and two near the golf course; a shuffleboard court near the pro shop; playgrounds along the park roadways and in open day-use areas; limited shoreline fishing; pavilions; and overlooks along Highway 62/641 north.

Planned recreation programs are offered to overnight guests that include activities like ice cream social, wildlife show, gospel singing, folk music, kiddies Olympics, free-throw contest, finger painting, beach blasts, bingo, scavenger hunts, kickball and much more. A schedule of activities is available at the lodge and other park offices.

Golf with one of the most modern pro shops, Kentucky Dam's 18-hole golf course is heavily used and challenging. The course is open year-round, weather permitting. The layout is fair, but a challenge to those golfers who tee it up from the back tees—it's a long-ball hitter's course. Eight of the holes are more than 400 yards, with the finishing hole a lengthy 546-yard dogleg to an oval green that is protected on the left by sand. The par 3 seventh hole has a small water hazard, and most of the greens have small sand traps strategically placed to protect the hole. The rolling and wooded course is a total of 6,704 yards from the blue tees. Securing a tee time is always a good idea.

The newer pro shop is well-stocked compared to many state courses. Green in color, the shop has vaulted ceiling and houses clothing, hats, balls, limited equipment and cart rentals. Two black, wrought iron tables and several chairs are under the cover porch where golfers can relax and tell stories—some call them "golf lies"—about the day's round.

Beach: The beach is across the cove from the Village Inn and next to the controlled water impoundment that is used for paddleboat rentals. Picnic shelters, tennis courts and open spaces are in the area. The beach is about 100 yards long with three lifeguard stands. The beach is closed when no lifeguard is on duty.

Airport: A sign in the window of the small tan building says to *"Watch out for geese and deer."* The 4,000-foot paved (100-foot-wide) strip is lighted. Tie downs, Jet A and 11 L.L. AV gasoline is sold. The small building is well designed for visiting pilots featuring restrooms, showers, lounge area, air camping (grill and picnic table are nearby), courtesy transportation to the Village Inn, and a computer where weather data can be obtained. You can also purchase a Kentucky Dam Airport cap at the friendly airport. Pilots can also get NOTAMs, use the phone, or buy a soft drink while watching the television that is surrounded by nine chairs in the lounge/lobby area. Elevation is 379 feet.

23 Kenlake State Resort Park

Land: 1,795 acres Water: 160,300 acres

Kenlake, Lake Barkley State Resort Park and Kentucky Dam Village State Resort Park all surround the wonderful 170,000-acre Land Between the Lakes (LBL) National Recreation area. The area is a nature lover's paradise offering environmental education, camping, hiking trails, natural areas and many other amenities that complement your visit to the state park.

This region of the state is in the heart of the nation's finest outdoor recreation areas. The Land Between the Lakes visitors center helps to interpret the Tennessee Valley Authority national recreation area by offering significant educational programming. The center has a planetarium, gift shop, informational displays, Golden Pond, and an entire complex of amenities and nearby attractions that include a buffalo herd

(12 miles south), 18 campgrounds, and dozens of lake access points and boat launches.

The interesting little Golden Pond is an actual small pond, near the visitor center. The once thriving community of Golden, Ky., took its name from the pond's bright yellow clay sediment. A popular story tells of how a farmer noticed the shimmering gold waters while passing the pond on a bright sunny day. The story soon spread about the phenomena, and the name Golden Pond was thereafter applied to the small area. A small wooden boardwalk overlooks the tiny pond near the parking lot of the visitor center. The golden-colored clay is readily seen under the brownish, stained pond waters.

With the longest shoreline of any manmade lake in the world, Kenlake is the perfect destination for eager water sports enthusiasts. Sailing is especially popular in and around the waters of the resort complex, and more and more fast-moving water craft—Jet Skis and powerful jet boats—are skimming the surface of the flat lake.

Kentucky Lake was formed by the impoundment of the Tennessee River. It extends 184 miles from the dam at Gilbertsville to the Pickwick Landing Dam just north of the Tennessee and Alabama state line. The need for power, transportation and flood control were the initial reasons for the development of the lakes.

In 1933, President Franklin Roosevelt created the Tennessee Valley Authority to develop the valley's resources. In 1944, the TVA completed the Kentucky Dam, impounding the huge area that equaled 2,300 miles of shoreline. During construction of the dam, the TVA bought a tract of land near Egners Ferry Bridge and called it Aurora Landing. This section of land was transferred to the state in 1948, and the name was changed to Kentucky Lake State Park.

The land north of Highway 68 was developed as a separate state park for "Negro's" and named Cherokee Park. Happily, in the 1960s, Cherokee Park was closed and the land annexed to the state park for all to use.

The Kenlake Hotel is the only hotel with interior room doors in the parks system. It was built in 1952.

Information and Activities

Kenlake State Resort Park
Route 1, P.O. Box 522
Hardin, KY 42048-9737
(502) 474-2211 - lodge
(502) 474-2245 - marina
(800) 325-0143 - reservations

Directions: Forty miles southeast of Puducah. Take I-24 to the Purchase Parkway then U.S. 68E. Located on the midwestern shore of Kentucky Lake.

Hotel: The entrance and front courtyard-like area have an enchanting 1950s-like feeling. The 48-room hotel was also the anchor of the first resort park in the state. Annual flower beds, terrific lake views, and pure Kentucky hospitality make this resort one of the best in the system.

The stucco hotel features classic outdoor sitting areas. Inside the front door is a tiny waterfall. Nearby is a gift shop that is open 8 a.m. - 9 p.m. and stocked with jams and jellies, beautiful quilts, T-shirts, Kentucky handcrafts, children's toys and other small items.

The outside deck looks down on the popular swimming pool and immediate environs, with the shimmering lake in the distance. Behind the front desk are a huge television, three large couches and other seating for reading, relaxing or watching a game.

An outdoor patio greets guests where three umbrella tables and additional seating provides a casual place for a cool drink on a hot afternoon.

Three walls of the dining room have windows for wonderful views of the placid lake. The room can seat 182 guests and offers excellent Kentucky cuisine and gracious service. Small water gardens and bird feeders placed outside the vast walls of glass also entertain breakfast, lunch or dinner guests.

Meeting facilities: The lower level of the hotel is the site for meeting rooms that are adaptable for many uses and group sizes. The Garden Room, a glass-enclosed room overlooking the lake, can accommodate groups up to 100 banquet-style. The three other meeting rooms can seat from 30 to 210 people, depending on the configuration of the room(s).

Cottages: Private and secluded, some very close to the water and others near the hotel, guests may choose from 34 one, two, or three-bedroom cottages. All of the cottages have views of the beautiful lake, woods, golf or peaceful natural areas. Tableware, cooking utensils and linens are provided.

Cottages near the hotel are units in loops 260-275 and 276-281. A medium-sized play area, equipped with traditional play apparatus, is at the entrance of these neighboring loops. These somewhat more modern units are a good choice for families; they are close to the hotel and other recreational amenities.

Cabin 280 is near the tee-off area for hole No. 4 on the golf course, where you can hear the snap of the clubhead against the leathery golf ball, and sometimes the comments about the shot. Cottage 281 has both a lake view and a partial view of the fairway.

Loop 260-275 has exterior lampposts. The cottages made of cement block, are smaller than cottages in other loops. Cottages 265-270 have a partial lake view and are perched on the high bank above the water. Some have wooden ramps up to the doors, and parking is easy. In front of 267 is a mini-play area for toddlers and young children. All of the units in this loop have shade, cooking grills and picnic tables.

If a water view is not very important to you, unit 275 would be perfect.

Along a long loop in the central part of the park are cottages 283-293. Neat and tidy with fresh tan paint and gray slate-colored roofs, the teal doorways make the air-conditioned units inviting for a long weekend or an entire vacation. Each of the cottages has a screened porch, and is backed up against the woods with views of forested ravines.

Cottages 288-290 at the end of the loop have a view of the lake, and are the most private of the orderly group of cabins. All of the cabins in this

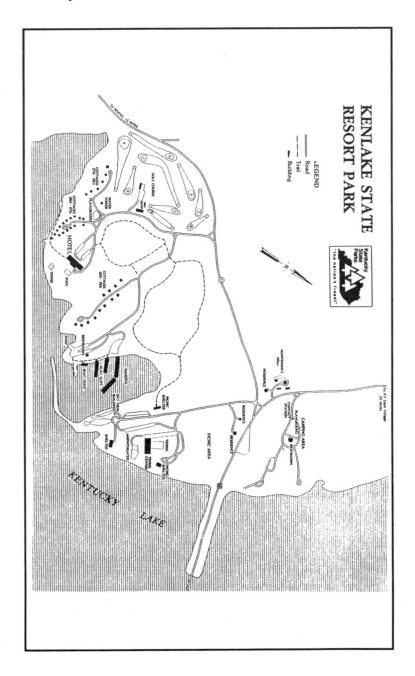

area have plenty of parking and shade.

Campground: Firewood and ice are sold at the small campground check-in office north on Route 68. The campground is open seasonally, April 1 - Oct. 31. The rolling facility has 92 sites with utility hook-ups and a service building with showers and restrooms. The campground is filled only on holiday weekends.

Sites 1-7 are very small; many of the sites in the campground are small. Sites 21-32 have an excellent view of the bridge that connects the park with the Land Between the Lakes recreation area. This loop has some great views and wonderful camping sites and is the premiere area for camping.

Sites 62-72 are small to medium-sized, shaded camping sites with a big view of the sparkling lake and tree-lined shorelines in the distance. Sites have access to the water and include grills, picnic tables and hard-surfaced pads.

Sites near the service building are in the 80s (but are very small). Near the shower building is a small kids' area with some playground apparatus. The service building has laundry facilities, vending machines and pay phones.

Emergency phone: state police, 856-3721.

Fishing: (Also see Barkley Lake State Resort Park for regional fishing information.) Kentucky Lake is on the western boundary of the 270-square-mile Land Between the Lakes national recreation area. The lake has a maximum channel depth of 72 feet and at summer pool, exceeds 160,000 acres in size. About 48,000 of these acres are in Kentucky.

The lake is the result of impoundment of the Tennessee River by the Kentucky Dam. The dam is about 22 miles above the confluence with the Ohio River near Paducah. Kentucky Lake is the sister lake to Barkley Lake; both surround the Lake Between the Lakes recreation area. There are about a dozen marinas on the lake, dozens of tackle and bait shops, and unlimited boating on the waters.

Kentucky Lake is one of the state's finest fishing lakes. There's plenty of access points and support services, including about 40 fishing guides who work on the lake.

Crappies are probably the most popular fish taken, with the most caught in April of each year. Either use a bobber and live bait near shoreline cover, or jigging in deeper water—crappies stay near cover during the spring season. Look for stumps, brush piles and channel edges during the summer. Two-pounders are common.

Knowing where to fish for crappies is important. Seek out local knowledge or try locating hump-backs along the old river channel, fence rows, rock piles, old building foundations, stumps, brush or dropoffs. These deep water locations are especially important during the early season. "Kentucky crappie rigs," or tandem rigs with two drop lines, work well in these waters.

Ultra-light spinning gear (light line) can help make the action faster by offering a more sensitive touch in the early season. You'll get better jigging action and more "feel" with the light equipment. Try pinky's, maribou jigs, fuzzy grubs, sassy shads, or other 1/16-1/8 ounce jigs. Remember the old saying, "crappies will be at the shoreline when the oak leafs are the size of squirrel's ears." Don't forget any weedbeds or stickups in the springtime. This offers some of the best fishing, when the fish are moving from shallow beds to deeper water.

Right at spawning run time, many locals use long poles and larger minnows. For super crappie fishing, time your visit during the spring spawning run.

Sauger anglers who visit during cool weather should try creek channel flats in front of the state park.

Largemouth are found in back coves or areas containing buck brush in the spring, and are best brought out by flipping jig n' pigs. Post-spawn largemouths hold to secondary points within the coves or in developing weedbeds. During this time of the year, spinnerbaits pulled across the weedbeds can be productive.

The 48-room Kenlake Hotel is a classic.

When summer comes, Kentucky Lake bass anglers can find the fish with plastic worms worked along deep weedbeds. Don't forget to work the points or any dropoffs you can find. Pull out the crankbaits and head for deeper water when autumn weather comes in late September and October.

Smallmouth can be taken on the east side of the lake along gravel or cobble areas, outside weedbeds. Night fishing for smallmouth is popular in the summer on Kentucky Lake.

Kentucky Bass (spotted bass) tend to hold to rocky shorelines and suspend near the bottom. Crankbaits should be tossed near rocks, and jigs can also be thrown toward rocks, letting the lures flutter to the bottom.

Catfish anglers typically use cut shad and big minnows, or big gobs of nightcrawlers during the summer season worked along irregular bottoms.

Boating: The Kenlake Marina, (502) 474-2245 or out of state, (800) 624-4124, is a privately operated facility one-quarter mile from the hotel. Open year-round, the marina has three large covered slip docks that can accommodate 140 boats, and 75 open slips. A small coffee shop, nearby launching ramp, and rentals of fishing boats and motors, pontoons, ski boats and wave runners are offered. All rentals include life jackets and safety equipment, but not gasoline and oil.

The state park's boat launching ramp is a two-lane ramp just past the main marina area across from the barge restaurant (open daily to about 3 p.m.). A fish cleaning station and restrooms are in the immediate vicinity. The screened fish cleaning station that looks down on the barge has sinks, running water, and table-top surfaces for cleaning and field dressing your catch of the day.

Hiking: Hikers can enjoy the .7 miles of trails at the park that connect the hotel with the marina and beyond. If you are an avid hiker or would just like to enjoy some great trails, you are only minutes away from miles and miles of quality trails at the Land Between the Lakes recreation area, east of the park across the bridge.

The marina has full-services for boaters and anglers.

Day-use areas: On the point near the tennis center and Bay View building are two picnic shelters, scattered picnic tables, volleyball courts, amphitheater, walking trailhead, shoreline access and parking. A shuffleboard court is near the swimming pool at the hotel (equipment can be checked out).

Swimming pool: Refreshing on hot days, the clean pool has a maximum depth of nine feet. Salmon-colored deck chairs line the sunning area and surround a number of comfortable umbrella tables. Hotel and cottages guests may use the pool and all visitors may use the public beach for a dip in the waters of Kentucky Lake.

Golf: Northwest of the hotel, the compact, nine-hole golf course is hilly with a couple of narrow fairways, and water on No. 4. From the men's blue tees the course is 1,919 yards long and a par 30. Weekends can be busy, but advance tee times are not necessary. Kenlake Golf Course is one of the shorter, better courses for the average player. While no golf course is easy, this handsome course is fun to play.

Bay View Building: On the west bank of the peninsula near the tennis center, and directly across the cove from the large marina, is the white, two-story, octagonal Bay View Building. The 40-foot-long meeting room is used by a variety of groups.

Planned recreation programs are offered during the summer, and special events like the Blue and Barbecue Festival, are offered annually. Many summer activities are held outdoor for hotel, cottage and campground guests featuring games, fishing, arts and crafts, family feuds, storytelling and much more.

Tennis center: Four indoor courts are open seven days, from Oct. 1 - April 15. Outdoors, four lighted and screened courts are open year-round. During the indoor season, pro shop, showers and locker facilities are open. There is also one outdoor court near the hotel. Two large picnic shelters (one with a fireplace and a great view of the lake) are situated near the tennis center and available for rent by groups.

Special notes: A Kentucky Lake visitor's guide can be requested from the Marshall County Tourist Commission at (800) 467-7145.

24   Kincaid Lake State Park

Land: 850 acres   Water: 183-acres lake

The placid setting of wooded hillsides flanking its shining lake, Kincaid Lake, is a family-oriented state park offering many opportunities for outdoor fun with your clan. Adults, as well as youth, will love splashing in the swimming pool, a boat ride on quiet waters, catching a stringer-full of panfish or catfish, and camping in the well-tended campground that is just a short walk from the recreational complex.

The park was named after tiny Kincaid Creek from which the lake was created in 1960. The tree-lined and hilly shoreline of the lake equals more than five miles and is the perfect setting for a quiet state park facility.

The park also features a 300-seat amphitheater where movies are shown weekly during the summer season, a heated and air-conditioned multi-purpose building, nine holes of miniature golf and game and sporting equipment loaned to park guests.

The unit also helps, in cooperation with the Kincaid Lake State Park Development Association, to maintain a simple log house that was built in 1878 by Boston Steele, the plain and functional structure is now the second oldest house in Pendleton County. Visitors to the humble log home should notice that no nails were used in the house because at the time they were far too expensive and almost unobtainable in the region. Carefully made wooden pegs and skillful dovetail joints were the high-skill and low cost ways this and many other similar structures of the era were crafted.

Information and Activities

Kincaid Lake State Park
Route 1 Hwy 159, P.O. Box 33
Falmouth, KY 41040-9203
(606) 654-3531

Directions: 48 miles southeast of Covington, take I-275 east to U.S. 27 south to Falmouth in Pendleton County. About 4 miles off U.S. 27, six miles from the city of Falmouth, Ky.

Campground: The 84-site campground is open April 1 to Oct. 31, with quiet hours 11 p.m. to 7 a.m. the sites are spread-out along a series of small ridges following the contours of the land and the wooded lake shoreline. Reservations are not accepted.

Kincaid Lake campers will find medium amounts of shade at gravel and camping pads that all have a picnic table and fire rings. Sites 1-17 are small and best used by pop-up or other small camping units and have adequate shade. Site 18 is larger and can accommodate medium to larger rigs. Many campers like to cluster near the bathhouse that has a laundry area, soft drink machine, phone and nearby children's play apparatus. Sites 26-35 in this area are larger and adequate for medium-sized trailers and motor homes.

Across from sites 42 and 43 is a small picnic and tent area with tables and a water hydrant and a new bathhouse. Large RV drivers will want to tour the campground to identify a sufficiently sized site along the linear layout. Sites 1-52 back up against a shady nature area and provide some rearward privacy.

One of the most popular campground areas is a spur from the main campground with sites nearer the lake situated in a quiet area. This spur is great for large RV rigs. These sites are numbered 77-84, watch for level sites when you inspect this area. At the end of this loop is a narrow foot trail that takes campers down to the lake. Sites 81-83 are the best site in the park for large RV rigs.

Along the lake and on this spur is a terrific tent camping area that offer lake access and great scenic views up and down the lake. Bring your small boat and fishing rod and reel for nearby waterside enjoyment. Camping is not allowed within 50 feet of the lake shore.

Campers can find 125 primitive sites throughout the season along the last camping loop. All sites do not have picnic tables and/or fire rings. The sites are not designated. That allows tent campers to select the best level spot in the shady area. Tents should be placed behind gravel pads when appropriate.

Emergency numbers: state police, rescue and ambulance, 654-3300. Firewood and ice are sold at the campground office.

Meeting room: Overlooking Lake Kincaid with a satellite dish pointed skyward, a rough-sawn, wood-sided multi-purpose building can seat 240 people and awaits use by groups, families and special events. The carpeted building has an old piano for singalongs, or can be quickly set up with banquet tables and kitchen equipped only with a deep freeze and refrigerator. There are no amenities such as table cloths and place settings. Advance reservation are required and there is a rental fee.

Boating: The concrete launching ramp past the multi-purpose building along a small cove offers parking for about 60 trailers and vehicles and 38 rental slips by the month. Basic marine supplies and bait are available at the dock that is open 8 a.m. - 9 p.m. seasonally. Call (606) 654-9916.

Boat motor size is restricted to 10 hp or less. Pontoon boats, fishing boats and motors and row and pedal boats are rented at the dock by the hour or day.

There is no swimming in the lake. The marina/dock is open April 1 - Sept. 30.

At the lake Dam there is a launching ramp, which is best used for bass tournaments. A large shelter house above the ramp offers an excellent view of the lake, anglers and boaters. The half-gravel, half-asphalt parking area is shared by the shelter house and boaters.

A handicapped fishing pier is provided at the dam There is also a docking pier for boats 18 feet or less.

The nearby North Fork of the Licking River drains portions of Lewis, Fleming, Mason, Bracken and Roberts counties before joining the Middle Fork southeast of Falmouth. Canoeing is popular during high-water times. This part of the watershed is a Class I stream with deadfalls and logjams.

The Middle Fork of the Licking River starts in southern Magoffin County and runs north to just south of the state park past the Blue Licks Battlefield State Park at its boundary. The South Fork of the Licking River has its confluence at Hinkston and Stoner creeks near Ruddels Mills, south of Cynthiana. It flows northward over mud and sand bottoms and joins the Middle Fork and the North Fork near Falmouth, about 10 miles from the state park entrance. The river is about 40 feet wide in most places, with many dams along its length. The river is a good canoe run year-round.

The Licking River, which is runnable year-round below the confluence, offers pleasant scenery, and lengthy curves through broad valleys bordered by tall ridge lines and hillside. This is an easy, generally quiet (including the lack of motorboats) stretch of river that families camping at Kincaid Lake can reach in minutes. There is access off 159 and 177, both north of Falmouth.

Fishing: Shoreline angling near the boat ramp, at the small pier, or along the grassy shoreline access points is popular. Worm and bobber fisher-

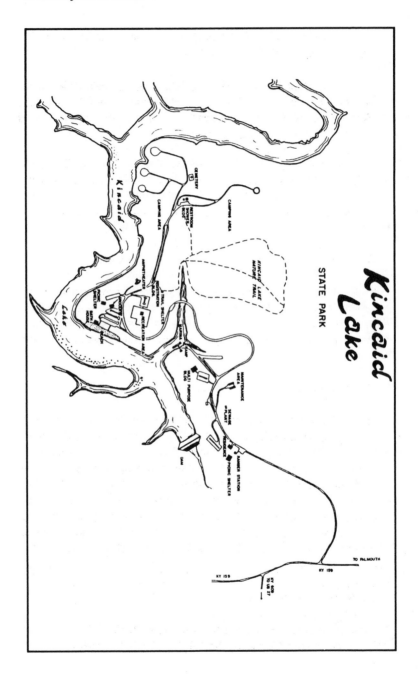

men hope to hook panfish, bass (large- and smallmouth and spotted), crappies or a big catfish.

Bass anglers should try pig n' jigs and rubber worms with scent around fishing holding structures. The lake is known for lots of bass. Bluegill anglers should try the weed lines and use live bait, according to local experts. Catfish are stocked annually.

One recommended productive area to fish is a narrow spur-like cove directly across from the bath house south of the swimming area. On the other side of the swimming area, along the east shoreline, is another preferred fishing area that contains some fish-holding structures and weedbeds.

Fishing regulations: There is a 12 inch size limit on bass.

Hiking: The Ironwood Trail is a 1.5-mile loop, and Spicebush Trail is a one-mile loop with trail heads at the campground check-in station. The hiking is moderately difficult and offers some good views of wooded ravines. It lies near the lake, taking hikers up and down some hilly regions.

No horseback riding is allowed in the park.

Day-use amenities: Swimming is restricted to the swimming area only, and only when lifeguards are on duty during the summer season. You can whoop it up in the outdoor junior-size Olympic swimming pool. The pool facility, which has a small, shallow kiddies pool, and charges a small admission, is typically (depending on the weather) open Monday - Friday, noon to 8 p.m., and weekends 11 a.m. - 9 p.m. The eight-foot-deep pool has plenty of deckside lounge chairs for sunning and watching the children swim in the filtered waters, a changing room, and soft drink machines. The pool is open Memorial Day to Labor Day and is available for after hour rental.

Near the pool are also some pedal boat rentals for out on the lake.

There are two picnic shelters, with restrooms and tables. Shelter One has a fire pit and Shelter Two has grills and play apparatus. Both shelters can be reserved and rented in advance.

Above the pool on a shady ridge is a shelter. Further above on yet another ridge is the small, but well-stocked park store that is also near the campground entrance. The store is open Monday-Thursday, 10 a.m. - 6 p.m. and Friday - Sunday, 8 a.m. - 9 p.m.

The park gift shop is open April 1 to Sept. 30. The mini-golf course is open daily between Memorial Day and Labor Day and square dancing on the weekends is often held during this time frame also.

Planned recreation: Pick up your schedule of Kincaid Lake activities at the park office or campground office. Planned recreation is offered Memorial Day - Labor Day, and recreation center hours are Monday - Thursday, noon - 8 p.m. and Friday - Sunday, 9 a.m. - 9 p.m. The little recreation center is north of the grocery store at the Kincaid Lake Nature Trailhead. The mini-golf, many game courts and play apparatus are centrally located in this area of the park.

Activities might include coloring contests, kiddies crafts, badminton reptile shows, nature walks, Frisbee, shuffleboard and many other games for the entire family.

Church services are offered at the small recreation center at 9 a.m. each Sunday.

Game courts: Tennis, paddleball, basketball and handball courts are available.

Nature: The non-poisonous black snake is often seen at the park.

Special notes: The Kentucky Wool Fest is held each October in Falmouth. Kincaid Lake State Development Association annual picnic is held the last Saturday in June. Boston Steele Day held the first Saturday in September. Christmas at Kincaid Lake is held the first Saturday in December with camping available for this event.

25 Kingdom Come State Park

Land: 1,027 acres Lake: 3 acres

It's a tree-lined, nearly vertical climb up the park roadway to the official park entrance of Kingdom Come State Park from the steep and winding U.S. 119. The two-lane road curves through abrupt valleys and mountaintops in southeastern Kentucky. The rock outcroppings, steep roadside valleys and switch back roads are half the fun of visiting Kentucky's highest park, located at the top of Pine Mountain. The park has an elevation of 2,700 feet above sea level.

The park is named after the popular Civil War novel, *The Little Shepherd of Kingdom Come* (the first book in the U.S. to sell one million copies!) by Kentucky author, John Fox Jr. The park offers mountain views that are spectacular, gorgeous scenery (especially in the fall), and some of the most unusual and striking rock formations in the Kentucky parks system.

parks system. The park has eight overlooks and turnouts, Bullock , Creech, Holcomb and a "12 o'clock" overlook that faces north: When the sun is at high noon, the shadow on the rock face is vertical.

Log Rock, Raven Rock and the Gazebo overlooks where Big Black Mountain, the highest mountain in the state at more than 4,000 feet, can be seen. The mountain is often covered by light haze; many call it "smoky."

The natural features of the park are curious. Log Rock, a long and narrow natural sandstone arch, resembles a log and can be easily viewed from the parking lot at its base. Or you can take a short hike to touch and see the exposed slab of sandstone rock. Raven Rock, a giant sandstone rock exposure, is in the center of the park and requires a one-quarter-mile walk to see. The bald rock is huge and walking on the top of it is great fun, but do not try to walk down the steep-angled face of Raven Rock.

The park was dedicated in 1962.

Information and Activities

Kingdom Come State Park
P.O. Box M
Cumberland, KY 40823-0420
(606) 589-2479

Directions: Situated 50 miles northeast of Middlesboro, take U.S. 25 East to U.S. 119 to Cumberland.

Camping: Kingdom Come keeps four small gravel tent camping sites near the cement block picnic shelter in a grove of mixed deciduous trees. These are shady walk-in sites that receive light use during most of the year and are outlined by pressure-treated timbers. Restrooms are at the two main day-use shelters. There is no other developed camping at the park.

Gift shop: Overlooking the tiny dark lake, the tan and burgundy-colored

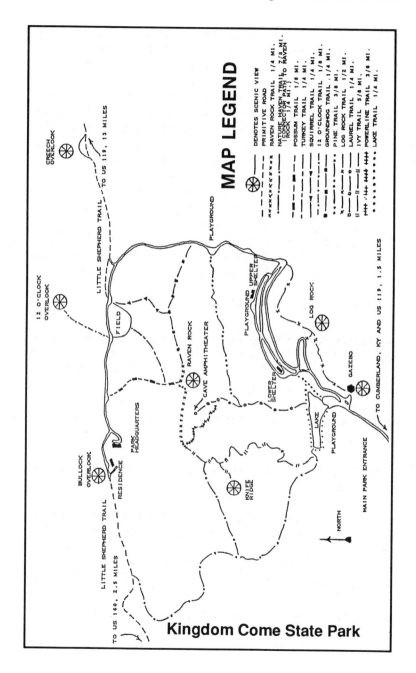

MAP LEGEND

⊕	DENOTES SCENIC VIEW
	PRIMITIVE ROAD
xxxxxxxx	RAVEN ROCK TRAIL 1/4 MI.
	NATURE/CREECH PATH TO RAVEN ROCK 1/4 MI. (CONNECTION PATH TO RAVEN 3/8 MI.)
	POSSUM TRAIL 1/8 MI.
	TURKEY TRAIL 1/4 MI.
	SQUIRREL TRAIL 1/4 MI.
	12 O'CLOCK TRAIL 1/8 MI.
	GROUNDHOG TRAIL 1/4 MI.
	PINE TRAIL 1/2 MI.
	LOG ROCK TRAIL 1/4 MI.
	LAUREL TRAIL 1/4 MI.
	IVY TRAIL 5/8 MI.
	POWERLINE TRAIL 3/8 MI.
	LAKE TRAIL 1/4 MI.

Kingdom Come State Park

Mountaintop lake at Kingdom Come.

gift shop is open 11:15 a.m. - 6:45 p.m. Items sold include T-shirts, small Kentucky crafts, postcards, and brochures. A couple of picnic tables in front of the gift shop face the lake, where visitors can often see large carp feeding in the weedy shallows and waterfowl cruising the mirror-like water surface during the summertime.

Fishing: The tiny three-acre mountain lake is a fun place for children to shoreline fish for carp and panfish. A gravel foot path circles the pond where anglers may try their luck, or rest on a picnic table under a canopy of mature trees. Some bluegill, bass and trout are taken from the tiny lake.

Boating: Pedal boats are rented on weekends only, April - October. There is no boat launching ramp.

Hiking: The Little Shepherd Trail is a narrow dirt and gravel road that runs 38 miles near the crest of Pine Mountain in Harlan and Letcher counties. This road traverses the park near the top of the mountain. Four-wheel drive vehicles are recommended, and sometimes required for certain sections of this road.

The walking trail system is like a giant spider web, with Raven Rock in the center. The steep Raven Rock Trail is a one-quarter-mile path that skirts the top of the rock. Although there are trails leading from nine points around the perimeter of the park that you can take to access the Raven Rock, the Possum Trail, located at the top of the mountain near the park office, is the easiest and shortest route.

The trails at the park are usually short, and moderate to difficult. A trail guide will help hikers piece together routes they can travel to all points of interest in the park. There are a total of five miles of interconnecting trails.

Day-use areas: There are many picnic areas with grills that are open April -October, overlooks, hiking trails, and a nine-hole miniature golf course on three levels along the natural hillside contours overlooking the lake and gift shop. It is lighted for evening play. The playground on the east side of the park includes brightly colored play apparatus and an old black play cannon. There's parking for about 15 cars at this day-use area.

Special notes: Pack a lunch and enjoy the terrific views and quiet park lands. Route 119 between Kingdom Come and Pine Mountain State Resort Park is one of the most scenic drives in Kentucky.

KY 0072 BK

26 Lake Barkley State Resort Park
Land: 3,600 acres Water: 57,920 acres

Connected by a canal, the waters of Lake Barkley and Kentucky Lake form the largest man-made body of water in the world.

The park's original land area on the east shore of sprawling Lake Barkley officially became part of the parks system in 1964, when the state leased thousands of acres from the U.S. Army Corps of Engineers. In the spring of 1966, construction of the luxurious lodge began. It was completed in 1970 and is celebrated as the largest single-story wood structure in the United States built since 1950. The incredible 120-room lodge was crafted from large timbers of western cedar, Douglas fir, and 3 1/2 acres of glass. It opened for business in 1970.

Lake Barkley park is located in Trigg County, Ky., the county is named after Stephen Trigg, who came to the area in 1779. Today, the resort is well established and considered a premier conference center and a complete family vacation destination. The park was recently named one of the best 12 state parks in the nation by *Money* magazine.

The Barkley Reservoir and the lodge was named in honor of the late U.S. senator and vice president from Kentucky, Alben W. Barkley. This huge project called for the construction of a multi-purpose earth and concrete dam, navigation lock, and a hydropower generating plant. The project was designed to develop the water resources of the Cumberland River and its tributaries in Kentucky and Tennessee. The effort also provided flood control to the Ohio basin.

Today, the lake and state park lands offer excellent recreation opportunities, including boating, fishing, a fitness center, cottages, camping, hiking, court games, golf, an airport, fine dining and much more. Barkley Lake has 1,004 miles of shoreline, an average navigating channel depth of 25 feet, and an average non-channel depth of 10 feet.

Information and Activities

Lake Barkley State Resort Park
P.O. Box 790
Cadiz, KY 42211-0790
(502) 924-1131
(800) 325-1708 - reservations

Directions: 29 miles west of Hopkinsville. From Hopkinsville, take U.S. 68 west to KY 1489. 200 miles from Louisville.

Lodge: The impressive, rich-looking lodge, accessed by driving over a land bridge, was designed by Edward Durrell Stone and has a circular footprint (shape) offering outstanding views of the lake in almost every direction. All of the 120 rustic rooms have private balconies. The lodge also has four suites.

Immediately upon entering the angular lobby are a large fireplace, lounge seating, television and a vaulted ceiling of large timber framing. The massive main lodge is actually two buildings connected by a roof that covers a driveway and dropoff area. The rear building houses the 331-seat dining room that occupies the second level. The gift shop and a variety of multi-use meeting and conference rooms are also in this annex. The gift shop has a full supply of Kentucky handcrafts, figurines, gift boxes, mugs, hats, T-shirts, wall hangings, and country-style decorations.

The huge dining room opens daily at 7 a.m. for breakfast, and closes after dinner. The popular Sunday buffet is offered to the public. A large square fireplace and walls of glass create a traditional elegance in the dining room, while expert chefs prepare high quality dishes to suit every member of the family.

Down the stairs from the dining room is a a small exhibit of mounted hawks, owls, eagle and American bald eagle. This lower level accesses the pool area and game room, which has a pool table, video games, table hockey, classic coffee shop and the recreation office.

The swimming pool is for the exclusive use of lodge and cottage guests and has a maximum depth of nine feet. The entire poolside sun deck is filled with lounge chairs and tables offering an excellent view of the busy lake. There is also a covered patio area above the swimming pool that offers a mile-long view of the tree-lined lake and two wooded islands in the distance. The pool is open seasonally.

A two-foot-deep kiddies pool is near the large swimming pool in a separate fenced-in area.

Below the swimming pool behind the lodge, are a temporary boat mooring dock and a cement walkway that guests may use to walk along the improved shoreline. Some segments of the lake's shoreline are treated with stone and rip-rap erosion and shoreline protection aids.

The wooded two-story Little River Lodge, once a dormitory for seasonal park workers, was renovated into 10 guest rooms. The entire building can be rented for special meetings or family gatherings. The Little River Lodge is south of the main lodge; it has no lake view.

Meeting facilities: Two elevated walkways access the wood and glass

Lake Barkley Conference Center that can accommodate 500 people banquet seating and 1,000 people theatre style. Set along a medium-height ridge line and shaded by towering hardwoods, the center is adaptable and large enough to serve many types of functions.

Two other larger meeting rooms are in the main lodge that can accommodate groups up to 150.

Cottages: A large loop is home to nine two-bedroom, two-bath cottages with lake or wooded views (cottages 501-509). For more rustic charm, cottages 510-513 on the south side of the loop are two-bedroom log cabins with long porches nestled in the shade of a deep forest. This group of cottages not as heavily used as the 501-509 group. All of the cottages have tableware, cooking utensils, linens and picnic tables. Grills are provided.

Cottage guests can wander an almost beach-like area along the lapping waters.

The rolling, hilly, densely wooded area south of the main lodge is the perfect site for a family getaway in one of the park's clean cabins.

Fitness center: With an inspiring view of the lake, the first floor of the center has exercise bikes, two Wolff tanning beds and a 12-piece nautilus equipment, along with open floor space for aerobic programs and classes. In the lower level is the fully-equipped Olympic free-weight room and racquetball (wally ball) court. There is a small daily fee for walk-ins and overnight guests.

Open year-round, Monday-Friday, 8 a.m. - 9 p.m., and weekends, 8 a.m. - 4:30 p.m., other amenities include sauna, wet-steam room, leverage equipment, eight Schwinn Airdines, Star treadmill track, Jacuzzi spa and shower/locker room. The staff of trainers offers instruction and information to regular members and lodge and cottage guests. A certified massage therapist is available by appointment.

Immediately next to the fitness center—and across the street from the Little River Lodge—are basketball and tennis courts. The fitness center checks out tennis rackets and balls, basketballs and shuffleboard equip-

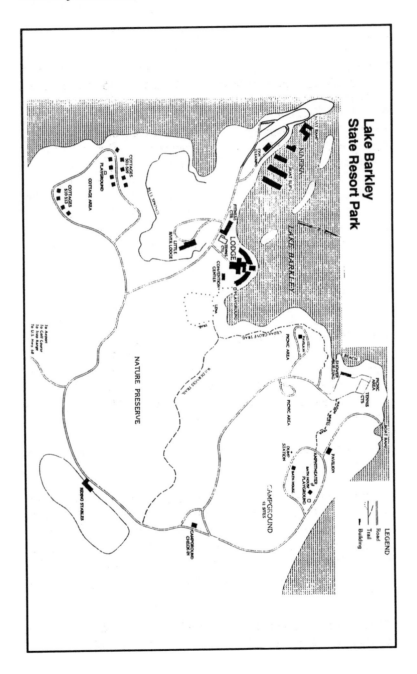

ment at no charge.

Campground: Upon passing through the yellow gates, campers are in a very shady area with a narrow one-way road. Sites 1-53 are considered by the staff to be the most heavily used. The first service building inside the entrance has toilets, showers and laundry, while the second service building is a shower house and restroom. The campground is a two-tiered facility, with sites 1-53 on the upper level and other sites stepped down in elevation, where a lot of tent camping takes place.

The 78-site campground is open year-round with utility hook-ups. There is no advance registration. The campground is above the lake and some of the sites (20-31) have a partial view of the lake. All of the sites have hard-surfaced pads, picnic tables, and plenty of nearby trash barrels.

A fine set of large timber play apparatus are near the first bathhouse. The bumblebee spring rides are the cutest of the pieces of play equipment. There is also a red, spaceship-looking merry-go-round that kids will love.

Some of the even-numbered sites have a gentle slope in front, while odd-side camping sites in this area are typically flat. A small boat ramp access road is between sites 46 and 47. The ramp is for small fishing boats only. Many campers enjoy walking down the lane to the water's edge. Many campers also scurry down the bank behind sites 1-50 for some shoreline fishing.

Sites 65-80 are densely wooded. The campground is full on holidays and many summer weekends.

Fishing: Fishing on the 57,900-acre lake is considered good to very good. Local knowledge from area bait and tackle dealers should be sought, and some fishing guides operate on the lake. The average depth of the water is 12 feet, with a maximum of 68 feet found in the deepest channel. First-time anglers may also want to purchase a *Fishing HotSpots* or similar quality map that details depth, underwater structures, and access points.

The lake's major tributaries are the Little River and Eddy Creek. The irregular shoreline of Lake Barkley is more than 1,000 miles long. Most of the high banks are clay, with scattered sandstone cliffs. All of development is along the eastern shoreline.

The lake's bottom is made up of 70 percent clay, 10 percent muck and 15 percent broken or layered bedrock. The remaining 5 percent is composed of flooded manmade features like old roadbeds, bridges, or stumps and timber. The water is light brownish. Oxygen levels in the lake are good, except late in the summer in back bays and channels. Large weedbed of milfoil, coontail, and pond weeds can be found and often hold good populations of largemouth bass.

The primary sportfish on the lake is largemouth bass—some say this is Kentucky's best bucketmouth waters—with panfish (especially crappies) a close second. Largemouths are actually on the rebound, with an increasing percent of the population over the 14-inch minimum.

A strong effort by the Kentucky Fish and Wildlife Resources, Corps of Engineers and volunteers to place fish attractors has helped bass fishing dramatically. This is why fishing in the open water rather than along the shorelines is a good idea.

During the spawning season from late April to early June, bass anglers can find lots of fish in four feet of water using jig and pigs on deeper points, or plastic worms (black or purple) fished across stump rows along dropoffs. Buttonbush (buck bush) holds lots of fish at this time of year. Try flipping close to the submerged portion of the vegetation. Crankbaits in natural colors, black and white, or yellow-skirted can be fished over the flats and near stick-ups. Night fishing the flats with plastic worms and dark buzzbaits is a popular summertime activity that can produce good catches of bass.

From June to the first of October, fish move out to the brush piles, stumps, deadfalls, weedbeds and other submerged structures. Good places to try during this time of the year are points within coves, along brush and weeds in the morning or evening. Light-colored spinnerbaits run along deadfalls or floating diving lures during the day can trigger active fish. Summer fishing also calls for lots of worms in the thickest cover you can find.

As the water cools in the fall, concentrate on rocky points with deep diving crankbaits of natural color. Creek channels and heavy cover can produce lunkers for worm anglers with spinnerbaits tossed along stumps, edges, and other natural cover.

Local crappie angling experts use lively minnows and small tube jigs in the spring—they also argue about the best color. In the summer crappies often suspend in 8-15 feet of water and can be taken with a 3-inch white, yellow or chartreuse twister tail. In the fall the tasty panfish head for deeper water.

White bass are often taken when panfishing (or bass angling). If you see the schools surface feeding, get out the small spinner (beetle spins, rooster tails, etc.) and cast to them. If they go deep, try small spoons or Little George-type lures jigged gently in the deeper, open water.

Striper and hybrid striped bass, rock bass, sauger, and channel cats on live bait are also taken. A number of bass tournaments are held on the lake each year, including the Coca Cola Classic and Red Man events. Some of these events attract more than 400 boats.

Boating: Lake Barkley State Resort Park Marina, (502) 924-9954, is on Little River Cove, just off Barkley Lake and right in the middle of all the fun you could imagine. The marina is the busiest and most completely stocked, full-service marina on the lake.

You can pamper your boat with the facility's 112 covered slips that have freshwater supplies, electricity and docking for up to 55-footers. Your family can relax by renting a pontoon boat, fishing boat to probe the coves and bays of the lake, or a heart-pounding "wave runner" Jet Ski that will let you skim the surface of the huge lake. Guests can also rent jet boats for those that would like to spend the day skiing.

A service building with laundry machines is at the marina near the large parking area.

The fairly steep, three-lane launching ramp is open year-round for pleasure boaters. A well-designed fish cleaning station is at the end of the parking lot.

Lake Barkley has a 4,800-foot-long landing strip.

Whether you rent or bring your own boat, the marina sells fuel, both gasoline and diesel. Supplies at the store include ice, groceries, ski supplies, microwave snacks, charcoal, hats, rope, fishing tackle, bait and other items.

Biking: The staff at the fitness center has prepared a number of fun fitness bike ride maps and walking/jogging routes, from a long 55-mile ride to a fun one-mile walking course. The bike course is winding loops that are scenic, passing through some excellent areas and stopover points. The 15-mile course features a grand tour of the park, using all park roads traveling over hilly areas, and along the lakefront. The course is marked on the road with white paint.

Hiking: Lake Barkley has five hiking and nature study trails, varying in length from .3 mile to two miles. All are easy hiking.

Lena Madesin Phillips Memorial Trail (.75 mile) starts below the lodge's east playground. It meanders through the lakeshore woodlands, featuring scenic views and a swinging bridge.

Cedar Grove (2 miles), the longest trail in the park, begins at the lodge. It travels to the beach and picnic areas to the north.

Wilderness Trail (1.25 miles) starts part way along the Lena trail and comes out north of the stables.

The Blue Springs Trail (1.75 miles) access is between the main park road and the Little River Lodge. It takes walkers along a hard-surfaced pathway and outlets at the Fitness Center.

The Short Wagon Wheel Trail (.3 mile) offers access to the beach for campground guests.

Riding stable: On the park road south of the campground entrance, a small brown riding stable with walk-in stalls is open seasonally. The horses take visitors on a gently rolling, wooded riding course. The walk-only ride takes 40 minutes. The stable is open Monday-Saturday, 9 a.m. - 5 p.m., and Sunday, 1-6 p.m. There is a 240-pound maximum weight limit per horse.

Day-use areas: The park has many open spaces, two lighted tennis and two other courts near the beach, plus other court games. Many of the picnic areas are actually large open sites, notched out of the woods, with tables, shelters, grills, drinking fountains, parking and other useful amenities. These areas (one has a pavilion) are south of the beach on low ridges.

Many of the park's roadways have mowed, wide and grassy shoulders where visitors may walk during the evening—or anytime.

Swimming beach: The large public beach (125 yards long) is open seasonally, 10 a.m. - 6 p.m., weather permitting. Four large parking lanes, a blue and yellow bath house, volleyball courts, and taffy-colored sandy beach make this a popular cooling-off spot for day-use visitors and overnight guests. Two tennis courts are also near the bath house and

Boots Randolph Golf Course.

beach. Lots of picnic tables are also in the area. There are two outside shower heads at the bath house for swimmers' use.

Golf: Known as the Boots Randolph (a world renowned Kentucky sax player and entertainer) Golf Course, the lush layout with slightly terraced greens winds through two wide valleys along a narrow creek bed. Big Blue Spring, stocked with rainbow trout, feeds the creek that adds interests and steels a few poorly struck golf balls. The stream bisects holes 12 and 18. From the back tees the 18-hole, 72 par course is 6,751 yards long. There is water on holes 8 and 17. Sand traps of various sizes guard every green but two. There are designated cart paths, driving range, large practice green, and gently rolling fairways.

The course was dedicated in 1972. Tee times are required on holidays and weekends.

The dark-brown, modern pro shop is one of the largest in the parks system offering a lounge, dressing rooms, snacks, club repair, cart rental, outdoor seating, showers, vending machines and equipment for sale. Look for the prehistoric golf ball display.

The small Blue Spring that is fed by a rock outcropping, complete with large, 16-inch rainbow trout that are easily seen, is behind the pro shop. The water is actually blue!

Trap range: Five trap shooting stations and some small bleachers are on the lighted range. Open seasonally, all shooting is supervised. There is a charge for shells and clays. You must be at least 13 years old to shoot and no one under 16 years old may shoot without a parent or guardian. The range is open Wednesdays and Saturdays.

Airport: Laid out on the flat top of a ridge, the 4,800-foot field has an elevation of 570 feet and is lighted. It can be keyed by mike clicks. Overnight tie downs and AV gasoline and jet fuel are available. Courtesy transportation is offered to the lodge. For airport information, call (502) 924-1171.

Special notes: One mile east of the park is the Woods and Wetland Wildlife Center, a roadside animal attraction, adjacent to the Land Between the Lakes national recreational area.

27 Lake Cumberland
State Resort Park

Land: 3,117 acres Water: 50,000 acres

Lake Cumberland is one of the most scenic, best fishing and pristine pleasure boating lakes east of the Mississippi River. The rugged 1,225 miles of shoreline are framed by wooded mountains and steep, shady ravines that are home to many types of wildlife and wildflowers. Lake Cumberland, in Wayne, Russell, Pulaski, Clinton, McCreary, Laurel and Whitley counties, was created by the Corps of Engineer's, who built a dam that went into operation in August 1952.

The dam was completed for flood control, hydroelectric generation, and recreation at a cost of $80.4 million. Today, the entire region is busy with vacationers, but it wasn't always a mecca for tourists, houseboaters, campers and bass anglers.

In 1750, Dr. Thomas Walker and his party explored the mountainous region that is criss-crossed by wild rivers and high bluffs. He was so impressed by the raw power and beauty of southeastern Kentucky, he honored Duke Cumberland (son of George II of England) by calling the mighty river, Cumberland. And the rest is history.

More than one million visitors annually explore the area with much the same excitement as Dr. Walker. The steep, rocky shorelines are of great interest, made from layers of sedimentary rock that underlies this entire region of the state. These craggy layers were formed as sediments in the bottom of ancient seas. Much of this structure provides excellent fish habitats, and the perfect shorelines to explore in a pleasure boat on a warm summer afternoon.

Information and Activities

Lake Cumberland State Resort Park
5465 State Park Road
Jamestown, KY 42629-7801
(502) 343-3111 - lodge
(800) 325-1709 - reservations
(800) 234-3625 - marina

Directions: From I-65, exit onto the Cumberland Parkway, then take U.S. 127. From I-75, exit onto KY 80 west.

Lodge: Five miles from the main park entrance, on a winding, shoulderless road along ridge tops and through ravines, the 63-room Lure Lodge overlooks beautiful Lake Cumberland from a high knoll.

The Lure Lodge opened Sept. 8, 1962. Originally built with just 24 rooms, in 1965, the golf course and 24 more rooms were added in 1965. During the winter of 1980, the Pumpkin Creek Lodge underwent major renovations to include 10 guest rooms, three suites and a meeting room.

The Lure Lodge has a large stone fireplace, lobby seating, gift shop and a 200-seat dining room that is open for breakfast, lunch and dinner. The Lure Lodge dining room has one of the finest lake views in the entire Kentucky park system. Diners will relish the fine service and Kentucky cuisine while watching houseboats slowly motoring across the lake's sparkling surface. The rugged shoreline and mountain view are celebrated by diners. Fresh cut flowers are placed for the dinner hour each evening in the lofty dining room with the million dollar view.

A game room in the lodge is particularly popular with older children and young adults. It has one pool table, seven video machines, foosball, and a ping pong table. Even the game room has a great view of the rocky shoreline and recreational lake in the distance.

Cottages: East of the lodge in a rolling, heavily wooded area are cottages 511-520 and loop 521-530. The impressive Chalet-style cottages in the 521-530 loop are private and about 1.5 miles from the high-energy lodge complex. Angular and modern, these brown cottages have fireplaces, outdoor grills, porches, picnic tables, air-conditioning and walkway-like entrances. The most private cabin in the group is 521. Cottages 529 and 530 blend into the shady forest, offering guests extra quiet accommodations. These cottages are about 150 feet above the lake, and some of them have a partial view of the water.

The road to cottages 511-520 ascends a bluff and penetrates the forest where these traditional square cottages are nestled parallel to the shoreline. Each unit has a mowed yard, and in many ways they resemble a small rustic neighborhood. Cottages 516-520 have a partial lake view through the leafed-out trees. At the end of the loop, cottage 520 has a lake-facing porch and is the most private and most often requested. Cottage 519 is handicapped accessible. Cabin 512 has an extra parking space for a boat trailer or extra vehicle.

Cottages 501-510 are near the lodge complex. Cottages 501-504 is a mini-loop with parking on an elevated area. These older-style wood-structure cottages are shady with open porches, and close to amenities, and are popular with families.

All of Lake Cumberland's 30 (one- and two-bedroom) cottages have tableware, cooking utensils and linens provided fresh daily.

Meeting facilities: The primary meeting space is in the modern Activity Center that seats 300 and has a great lake view. Other meeting spaces include a room adjacent to the Lure Lodge dining room that can accommodate 50, a 40-person room at the Pumpkin Creek Lodge, and a hospitality patio that can be arranged to accommodate 70 people.

Campground: At the grocery store and outdoor pool area, the roads to the cottages, campground, boat ramp and lodge converge. Take the only westbound road (it's marked) to the linear 147-site campground that has utility hookps, two central service buildings with laundry and showers, and day-use areas. The campground is open April through November and no advance registration is taken. Church services are set for 8 a.m. each Sunday.

Staff says some of the most popular sites are 12-21, and sites in the 50s and 90s. Many of the camping sites at Lake Cumberland are small—the campground roads are also quite narrow, often with a tight turning radius. Sites 19, 64 and 67 are fine for tent camping. At the second service building is a play area for children complete with climbers, red-colored teeter-totter, and a play apparatus with daisy-petal designs on them.

Sites 41-53 are on a narrow road along a ridge about 100 feet above the water. Sites 71-76 are the largest and are adequate for larger RV rigs, as are sites in the 80s and low 90s. Although site 100 is very tiny and on a narrow road, it is one of the most private and shady sites in the campground. Sites 112-122 and 129-133 are for small RV units only or tents.

Almost all of the sites have shade by mature trees. Each pad is hard-surfaced with picnic tables, grills or fire boxes nearby.

Grocery store: Lake Cumberland's country store has a wide selection of grocery items, sundries and souvenirs. The store is open seasonally and near the entrance to the campground and public pool. A restroom is at the country store.

Fishing: The average depth of the lake is 90 feet, but there are many shallows and weedbeds to explore. A dozen species of sportfish are in the lake including crappies, bream, walleye, bluegill, three species of black

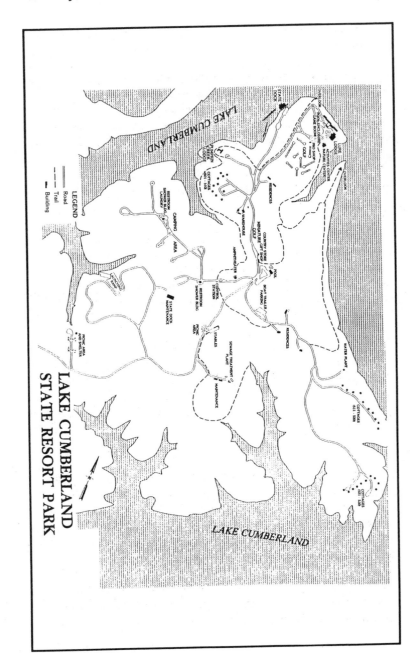

LAKE CUMBERLAND
STATE RESORT PARK

bass, white bass and striped bass. A 58-pound rockfish has been taken from the lake.

When the water temperature in the spring reaches 60 degrees, the white bass begin their annual run. About this same time walleye fishing can be excellent. Trout fishing is fair to good above Wolf Creek Dam, and probably is best in the Cumberland River, below the dam. The national record brown trout and state record rainbow trout came from these cooler waters.

For crappies, fish the fallen trees, driftwood, flooded willows and other structures.

Lake Cumberland walleye like rocky points, gravel flats and other similar structures along the main river channel. Nightcrawlers on a Lindy Rig and backtrolling can be productive. Fish across points with shad-like lures or threadfins. Jigs tipped with a minnow worked quietly can also attract some attention from this member of the perch family—one of the best-tasting fish around.

Early-season bass anglers should concentrate on embayments where runoff waters move into the lake. The lake warms slowly in the spring, so finding the right temperature zones will prove to be the most productive waters. Correct water temperature, combined with flooded timber, stump beds, weedbeds and stick-ups in the back end of embayments are popular locations during the spring. Largemouths are hard to find after this time of year.

Near warmwater discharges or any of the many fish attractors that have been placed in the lake are your best fishing opportunities during much of the year. Many bass anglers say the lower five miles of the lake offer the best largemouth bass fishing in the country during the early to middle spring. The high water submerges extra cover. These areas can be fished with crankbaits, working toward the shallows.

Vertical jigging spoons, bucktails and/or jigs with pork trailers are the standard methods for rockfish in deeper open water. They often suspend over breaklines, old roadbeds, and off-shore of islands in 30 feet or more of water.

Houseboating on the lake is popular.

Boating: The three-lane launching ramp at Lake Cumberland is the most impressive in the state parks system. It is at a cove and literally carved out of the mountainside to create a parking lot, one-way access road, and sloping ramp to the water's edge. Three sides of the area have vertical rock walls. More than 100 vehicles with trailers could park there. The ramp is south of the lodge and state dock.

Lake Cumberland State Dock, which is privately owned, is one of the largest and most complete facilities on the lake. The full-service marina is open 24 hours daily and has a variety of services that include fuel sales, boat lift, mechanical repairs, waste pumpout, restrooms and showers, a snack bar with sandwiches and soft drinks, and rental slips (daily, weekly, monthly, seasonally). The Ship's Store sells groceries, fishing supplies, water skis, life jackets, sunglasses, video rental, apparel and souvenirs.

Houseboating: The marina rents many types of watercraft including ski boats, personal watercraft, pontoons and fishing boats. But houseboat rental is by far the biggest activity at the dock. Dozens of houseboats, some nearly 80 feet long, are rented by the day, long weekend, or week.

The houseboats are luxurious. Some have spas and wet bars, while most have wall-to-wall carpeting, a swimming platform, diving boards, hot water, full kitchens, deck seating, dinettes, full baths, and much more. You have to see to believe some of these huge floating homes. Call (800) 234-DOCK for reservations.

Hiking: The hiking trails at Lake Cumberland are well-marked, easy to moderately difficult, scenic, and heavily used. The primary trail is a four-mile loop around the Lure Lodge complex, passing by the Pumpkin Creek Lodge, cottages, outdoor pool, golf course, and the lake shore. This terrain consists of sharp ridges and beech, oak and hickory forests.

Horseback riding: Perched on a ridge top one mile south of the lodge near a small day-use area, the open-air riding stable operates seasonally and weekends in September and October. All rides are guided and last about 45 minutes, starting hourly. Rates are posted.

Day-use areas: Outlined by a split-rail fence, the older miniature golf course is near the outside public pool and open seasonally. Great picnic sites with tables, grills and play areas are ideal for family outings. Shelters and tables scattered around the park can be rented by groups for reunions or company outings. Two tennis courts and a shuffleboard court are at the Lure Lodge.

Planned recreation: Recreation and interpretive programs are offered year-round at Lake Cumberland. The park's naturalist offers public programs, as does the summer recreation staff. Program examples include crafts, scavenger hunts, a golf tournament, pottery, fish hatchery tours, hikes, natural history programs and more.

Outdoor swimming pool: (Olympic-sized) Unlike many outdoor pools in the Kentucky state parks system, the outdoor pool at Lake Cumberland is not adjacent to the lodge. The L-shaped pool is south of the lodge, in the central part of the park, featuring plenty of deck seating, vending machines, a bathhouse and lots of parking. The deepest part of the public pool is 10 feet. Open seasonally, lifeguards are on duty when the pool is open. There is an admission fee.

Indoor swimming pool: The indoor pool is connected to the lodge and easily accessed. The indoor pool is a terrific area with atrium, retractable skylights, live plants and a heated pool. A game room, exercise room (exercise bike and Nautilus), and six-person spa are also in the large recreational facility. The nine-foot-deep pool is open year-round, 7 a.m. - 11 p.m. Rooms 113-117 are along a balcony that overlooks the pleasant indoor pool complex. The indoor pool, nearby play equipment and game room make the Lure Lodge an excellent getaway for families.

Golf: For one price, you can play all day on the small nine-hole, par 3 course. Gently rolling and not heavily wooded, the course is popular with families and short iron experts. Open year-round, weather permitting, club rental is available.

Nature center: The center is in the lower level of the Activity Center at the head of Lake Bluff Trail. Inside the green-carpeted nature center are a variety of interpretive displays including an aerial photo of the park region, weather maps, a snake display, fish mounts, mammal mounts, steamboat information board, birding information, an electric touch board and a balcony that is often used for programming. From Memorial Day to Labor Day the center is open 7:30 a.m. - 4 p.m. The remainder of the year the hours vary.

Special notes: Three miles south of the park entrance on U.S. 127 is the 240-foot-tall Wolf Creek Dam. The visitor station and power house are open to the public during the summer.

Near the dam is the National Fish Hatchery, where trout are reared for Kentucky waters. The fascinating hatchery is open year-round, with visitation hours 7 a.m. - 3 p.m.

Thrill seekers can try an inflatable raft tour down the Cumberland River. The exciting trips last three to 10 hours depending on the launching site. Call (502) 343-2662 for details.

28 Lake Malone State Park

Land: 338 acres   Water: 788 acres

Lake Malone is in an area of western Kentucky that is rich in history, thick with hardwood trees, and tall with scenic pines and magnificent cliffs. Hiking or boating the area, visitors can expect to see some of the best in Kentucky nature and scenery. From mountain laurel, holly and other wildflowers to steep sandstone bluffs, white-tail deer and cheery song-birds winging above the lake, this unspoiled area is a top choice for an off-the-beaten-path weekend getaway.

The charming small state park is in the 482-square-mile Muhlenberg County on its south-central boundary. This is Kentucky's 34th county, established in 1798. The county was named for Gen. Peter Muhlenberg, who served with distinction during several campaigns of the American Revolution. A Lutheran clergyman, Muhlenberg received a commission in the Colonial Army to recruit, train and lead soldiers of German descent against the Redcoats. Today, the jurisdiction continues to be one of the top coal producing areas in the country. The county was also the center of iron production during the mid-1800s.

More than 40 percent of the county is covered with hardwood forests of oak and hickory, with 39 percent of the land used for farms. Light and dark tobaccos, corn, soybeans, and livestock and poultry are the main commodities. Streams like the Green, Mud and Pond are carving and nurturing the fertile lands. About 32,000 people live in remote Muhlenberg County.

A pleasure ride on the lake that has sharp outcroppings rising from the lake's surface offers viewers a chance to see a natural rock bridge, steep sandstone bluffs along the almost all of the shoreline and thick woods that teem with wildlife and flora. The spring dogwood blossoms are truly breathtaking.

Many of the oldest towering pines in the campground could tell stories of Civil War skirmishes and other legends that abound. One of the best local stories is that Jesse James and his notorious gang holed up in a large nearby cave to escape a pursuing posse after they pulled an armed robbery of a small bank in Russellville. The cave is now under water, and we all know what happened to Jesse.

The lake was developed in 1960. In 1962 the state dedicated 325 acres as Lake Malone State Park. The lake has 26 miles of scenic shoreline.

Information and Activities

Lake Malone State Park
General Delivery
Dunmore, KY 42339-0093
(502) 657-2111

Directions: South of Greenville, 22 miles south of Central City. From Western Kentucky Parkway, exit at Central City. Take U.S. 431 to KY 973 to the park entrance. The campground and marina are open seasonally. The park and campground office is in a red brick, ranch-style house that doubles as the site superintendent's residence. This is a very rural park.

Campground: The rustic campground has 19 modern sites with utility hook-ups, grills and tables. More than 100 primitive sites are available for tent camping. The dark-colored service building has three showers on each side, restrooms and a laundry. The campground is small. The campground roadway is narrow, but some of the sites could accommodate medium to larger RV rigs, especially those sites on the top of the ridge near the bathhouse. Site four is a pull-through camping site.

Sites 16-19 are near the bathhouse; site 11 is somewhat private and elevated. Behind sites 8-10 is a wooded ravine that plunges toward the lake.

Adjacent to the campground is a day-use area with a tennis court, play equipment, basketball court and mowed open spaces.

Fishing: Live bait is sold at the blue and tan marina store. Spring and fall are clearly the best times to try your luck for channel catfish, largemouth bass, black bass, crappie, bluegill and rock fish. Area bait and tackle shops are your best bet for up-to-date fishing information.

Black bass must be at least 12 inches, and you can take six daily.

Boating: Boat traffic on the lake is generally heavy and the park's dock is busy. Fourteen open slips are rented at the dock, where you can also stock up on marine and fishing basics. Fishing boats and motors, pedal boats and pontoon boats are rented by the hour and day. The marina can be reached at (502) 657-2110, seven days during the season. Gasoline is also sold at the floating dock.

A one-lane boat launching ramp is next to the rental docks along the small cove. The maximums allowed on the lake are 18.5 feet boats and 150 hp engines. Pontoon boats are limited to 30 feet in length.

Hiking: The Wildflower Nature Trail is about one mile and can be accessed from behind the campground. Part of the trail is gravel-surfaced,

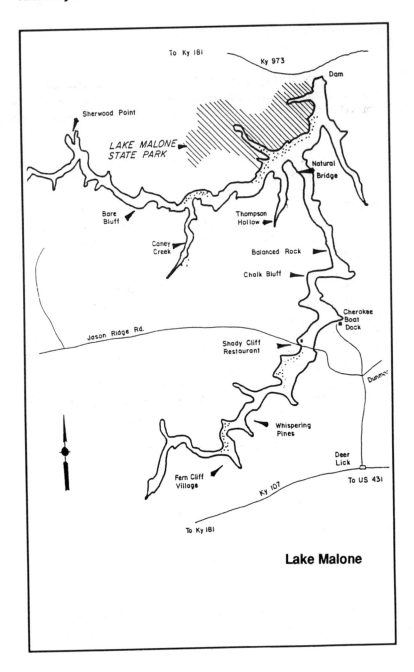

Lake Malone

and meanders down a thickly wooded ravine. The trail is easy to moderate in difficulty.

Day-use areas: A large picnic shelter near woods, open spaces and the lake is available for rent by groups up to one year in advance. This hilltop area is closely mowed and a traditional play area is nearby. Single picnic tables are scattered around the park.

Other day-use amenities include horseshoe pits, three picnic locations, swimming beach and more.

Swimming beach: A scenic lake with rocky shores and tall trees is in sight from the sandy little 50-yard-wide beach that is open during the summer. A newer brick bathhouse has showers and restroom and is near the tiny marina store.

Special notes: The Dunmore Lakeside Golf Course is nearby. Lake Malone Inn is a large and interesting inn and restaurant where William Holden has visited, invested in and donated artifacts. Items inside the lobby include a pair of elephant tusks that weigh 158 pounds each that were taken in 1954 by the actor. This elephant was 11 feet tall at the shoulder and weighed eight tons, and was 60 years old. The tusks are hung over the huge fireplace in the lobby. Two stools made from elephant's feet are also part of the decor. Glen Robertson, noted African nature and wildlife painter, maintains a gallery inside the large inn.

The Jefferson Davis Monument is 46 miles away.

29 Levi Jackson Wilderness Road State Park

Land: 896 acres Water: Little Laurel River

Levi Jackson Wilderness Road State Park pays tribute to the first judge in Laurel County, and to a road that has been recognized as the most significant trail in the westward spread of English colonization. The park also includes the Defeated Camp Burial Ground, McHargue's Mill, the Mountain Like Museum, Wilderness Road and Boone's Trace.

The park has an important and interesting history—and it also chronicles the region's unique role in the development of the rest of the country. After the dedication of the Dr. Thomas Walker Memorial State Park in nearby Barbourville in 1931, Charles Chandler and Lee McHargue, both of Laurel County, returned home with an idea to establish a memorial at the "Defeated Camp," the site of the worst massacre by Indians in the state's history.

After enlisting the help of others, they contacted Colonel Dave Jackson and his sister Ella, owners of the site, about donating a small "six or seven" acres for the effort. According to the records, they were surprised—almost stunned—to receive an enthusiastic and benevolent reply from the Jacksons offering a gift of 307 acres. The only stipulation was that the park be named after their father, Levi Jackson, a judge who died in 1879.

It was their wish that the park "...perpetuate the memory of the pioneers, whose early struggles made possible the settlement and development of the Commonwealth of Kentucky and other (states) to the west, by the hard men and women who traveled that way over the Wilderness Road and the Boone's Trace, which pass through the entire length of the land." These trails carried more than 200,000 settlers into Kentucky.

The story of Defeated Camp is grim. On the night of Oct. 3, 1786, under a hunter's moon, the McNitt party became the victims of a bloodthirsty Indian massacre in which 24 people were killed and scalped. The group of 60 settler's, representing 21 families, had been traveling for months and always put out a night time guard, but for unknown reasons, not on this fateful night.

Indians, both Chickamauga and Shawnee, viewed that area where the McNitts were camping as sacred ground and became angered when they saw the party camping, playing cards, and dancing on the holy hill top. Considering it a desecration of hallowed ground, the Indians viciously attacked the unsuspecting settlers in their sleep. The settlers were no match for the Indians.

Between five and 10 settlers were taken prisoner, including 8-year-old Polly Ford, who spent nearly 15 years with the Indians before being rescued. There are many more interesting details to this story and many other legends and fascinating history of the area—but you'll have to visit the history-based park to learn more!

Levi Jackson Wilderness Road State Park, the 10th park to be added to the system in 1939, is open year-round.

Information and Activities

Levi Jackson Wilderness Road State Park
998 Levi Jackson Mill Road
London, KY 40741-8944
(606) 878-8000

Directions: South of London, off I-75 at exit 38 to U.S. 25. Also, in London is a ranger station for the Daniel Boone National Forest, offering lots of information about the amenities in the area. Call (606) 864-4163.

Mountain Life Museum: Near the museum is a double-winged picnic shelter with a neighboring playground and red wagon climbing structure. Just ahead, a self-guiding tour of the museum begins at the small gift shop where a limited supply of handcrafts and small items are offered for sale. The museum is open April 1- Oct. 31, 9:00 a.m. - 4:30 p.m.

After paying a small admission fee, you exit the back door of the gift shop to start your tour of the seven unique buildings that are filled with historical artifacts, displays and information. Although not the original site of the buildings—many are original buildings.

The first building is to your left and was first used as a two-room school building. It now displays household items and a marvelous display of long guns in the back room. The second, with its hand-hewned wooden plank floors, and third buildings feature a trundle bed used by Levi Jackson and a handmade cradle, old loom and tools, and spinning wheels. Building four is the old Methodist Church of Bald Rock Chapel. The logs in this church are more than 200 years old and has a 200-year-old piano and original pulpit.

Building five is a smokehouse, where meat was cured. Inside you'll see a salt kettle that was used in mining salt petre that was used in making gunpowder and a collection of carpenter tools. Inside building six is the once-busy blacksmith shop with anvils and large bellows. Building seven is a barn with many large farming implements, wagon wheels, covered wagon, and handmade tools of the day.

McHargue's Mill: In the days before cars and supermarkets, settlers who carved a living out of the Kentucky wilderness worked hard to provide the basic necessities of life. One of the most important mechanical devices used by early Kentucky families to make life easier was the mill.

At a time when steam engines and electricity were still in the future, mills harnessed the natural power of moving water. Mills were built for many purposes. Perhaps most common were grist mills, which ground grain for bread and feed for animals. Grain milling is one of the oldest industries of mankind. Once there were hundreds of mills scattered across this geographical region, with McHargue's Mill one of the few still working on the Little Laurel River. It was built in 1938 by the WPA and restored in the 1960s as a special project of the parks system.

The mill is very much like the one operated by its namesake family, the McHargue's, about 10 miles south of the reconstruction. The mill was operated until the 1880s.

The pathway up to the tiny timber-framed mill offers visitors a chance to touch millstones and learn about their shapes, sizes and purposes. It takes the miller about one hour to grind 50 pounds of flour. You can purchase two-pound bags of the freshly ground flour complete with a recipe and information about mills, "bolting," and helpful cooking hints. Children will love the almost Rube Goldberg-like huge wheels and belts that convert water power to grinding power inside the mill building.

One of the greatest problems facing Kentucky millers was where and how to obtain suitable millstones. Rock with exceptional hardness was required. Since suitable rock was not locally available, long journeys with oxen-driven wagons were a likely part of the milling history. Many of the finest millstones were imported from Europe.

Campground: Newly improved, there are about 140 camping sites in the park. Nearby are a mini-golf course under some shade trees and a small grocery store (ice, firewood and small grocery items). The campground is open year-round. Mini-golf and grocery are open April - October.

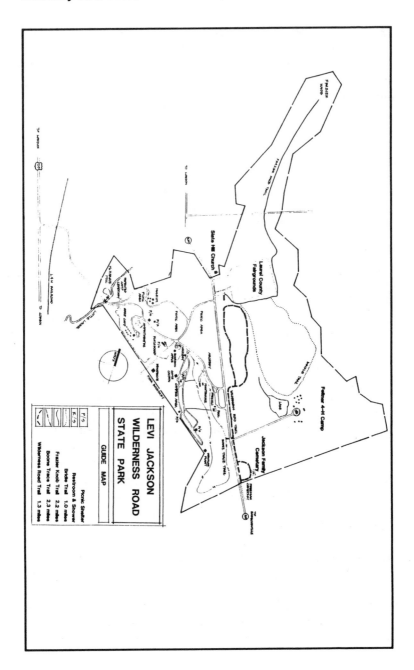

Most of the sites at Levi Jackson are shady and fitted with hard-surfaced pads, fire rings, picnic tables and utility hook-ups. The B loop has grassy pads and is next to a game court area, playground, a bathhouse and the recreation office. This loop is great for families. The play area is away from the road and heavily used by big-wheel riding youngsters.

In the D area, which is said to be the most popular, there are pull through sites on hardsurfaces. Where the H, G and D loops converge are a bath house and laundry building, which is one of three in the campground. In the I loop you will find primitive camping sites under shade trees that are level and heavily used. In fact, the entire campground is popular and always full on holiday weekends.

The M loop, near the back bathhouse, and at the end of the H Loop are the most private sites in the campground. The only caution is for campers to check the levelness of the pull-through sites; some are slightly inclined. If your RV unit can accommodate the incline, they are great sites. Many of the small loops including M, L, K, J and I are narrow, short sections best used by small travel trailers, pickup campers, or pop-up campers. Park staff mentioned that small family reunions or groups often request the entire smaller loops mentioned above, giving them lots of privacy. You can also hop on the Daniel Boone Trace Trail behind the I Loop.

Hiking: Hikers can retrace some of the trails that more than 200,000 settlers once trod on their daring quest to settle Kentucky and the West. The park maintains about eight miles of trails that include original portions of these historic tracks.

Boone's Trace, Wilderness Road and Warrior's Path have often been considered as different names for the same trail; however, they were each distinct trails. The trails do come pretty close together for a short time after emerging from the Cumberland Gap. In the park, Boone's Trace crosses the western portion of the unit, while Wilderness Road, which Kentucky Highway 229 follows, is at the eastern edge.

Boone's Trace, where the ill-fated McNitt party tracked, is of course named for Daniel Boone, the super frontiersman who cut the road through the Cumberland Gap to the Kentucky River in 1775. The track was little more than a bridlepath for much of its 100-mile length. From the

Revolutionary War until 1795 the trail served as a lifeline between the wilderness and the populated colonies in the East.

Plenty of forts and settlements sprang up along the trace, and the danger of Indian attacks was a constant threat to these settlements. Laurel County, the halfway point on the trace named after the shrubs, seems to have been the focus of many assaults and conflicts.

Wilderness Road was created by an act of the Kentucky Legislature in 1795 and enhanced commerce between the new Commonwealth and all of the country east and south.

Day-use areas: A 1,500-seat outdoor amphitheater near a large day-use area hosts many community events, including the weeklong Laurel County Homecoming. Near the park office are game courts, play apparatus, swings and open spaces. You may register for the miniature golf course (open seasonally) at the small campground office. The park also has an archery range that is open seasonally and by permission. There are four reservable shelter houses, a clubhouse for rent, and group camp cabins offered to youth and other organized groups by the night.

Volleyball, basketball courts, shuffleboard, and other game areas are operated by the park. Equipment can be checked out by campers. Planned recreation programs are offered to guests during the summer months. You can get a list of events, activities, times and dates from the park or campground office.

Swimming pool: Open Memorial Day to Labor Day, the three- to eight-foot-deep swimming pool is the perfect place to cool off on a hot day. Deck furniture, a small diving board, concession and bathhouse are at the pool area (a small fee is required).

Special notes: A go-cart track and waterslide are about one mile from the entrance to the park. The Laurel River Lake/Daniel Boone National Forest is nearby. For more information about the U.S. Army Corps of Engineers areas, call (606) 864-6412. Grove Marina, (606) 523-2323.

30 Lincoln Homestead State Park

Land: 120 acres

The heritage of Abraham Lincoln's parents—Thomas (born in 1776) and Nancy (Hanks)—are interpreted at the Lincoln Homestead State Park. The Lincoln's, Hanks, and Berry families migrated to this part of Kentucky over the Wilderness Road in the 1780s and 1790s.

Historians have traced President Lincoln's ancestry through 10 generations on his father's side to the cities of Swanton, Morley, Hingham and Norfolk, England, to Robert Lincoln, who died in 1543.

The President's mother, born Feb. 5, 1784 in Virginia, came to Kentucky as a youngster. Most experts concur that Nancy was the only child of James and Lucy Shipley Hanks, and that after her father's death her mother moved to Kentucky. They lived with Lucy's eldest sister, Rachel

Shipley Berry, and her husband Richard Berry Sr.

As Nancy grew into a young woman, she was noted for her beauty, grace, vivacity and intelligence. Her son said of her that she was intellectual by nature, cool, had acute judgment, and was heroic. Although some historians once claimed she was illiterate, most Lincoln historians now believe she could read and write. In fact, President Lincoln's autobiography tells of his mother teaching him "in letters and morals and especially the Bible stories."

The President's father was raised in Washington County, Kentucky, by his mother, Bersheba. At the tender age of 17 years he served in the Kentucky Militia, a group created to protect the region's settlers against Indian raids. Unlike the tall President, his father was of medium height—but they did share dark eyes and black hair. Young Abraham also inherited his father's well-known ability to spin a yarn, tell jokes, and told stories. Other traits that the President is reputed to share with his father included humility, sobriety, industriousness and integrity.

At 27 years old, Thomas bought 238 acres of land at Mill Creek in Hardin County, about eight miles from Elizabethtown. He lived there for more than five years and worked in the area as a carpenter. In 1803 his mother and sister, Nancy and husband William Brumfield, came to live with him. Three years later, in 1806, before his marriage, he was hired by area merchants to build a flatboat. When it was finished, he was hired to take a load of goods to New Orleans.

Like his son, Thomas was always looking for a new adventure and an exciting challenge. The President once said his father was a "wandering laboring" young man "who grew up without education."

Fresh from his adventure to New Orleans and pockets seemingly bulging with money, Thomas went on a buying spree before his marriage to Nancy Hanks purchasing calfskin for new boots and fancy fabric that would become a suit for his wedding day.

Carl Sandburg, Lincoln's most famous biographer—unless you count Gore Vidal—as detailed in a park reference piece gives the following account of the wedding:

"June 12, 1806 came and the home of Richard Berry at Beechland in Washington County saw men and women on horseback arriving for the wedding of 28-year-old Thomas Lincoln and 22-year-old Nancy Hanks.

"The groom was wearing his fancy new beaver hat, a new black suit, his new silk suspenders. The bride's outfit had in it linen and silk, perhaps a dash somewhere of the one-fourth yard of scarlet cloth Thomas had bought at Bleakley and Montgomery's.

"They have many relatives and friends in Washington County and the time was right to go to a wedding, with spring planting and corn plowing over and the hay harvest yet to come. Nancy Hanks was at home in the big double long cabin of the Berrys. She had done sewing there for Mrs. Berry and it was Richard Berry who had joined Thomas Lincoln in signing the marriage bond, below his name writing "gradin" meaning guardian.

"The six Negro slaves owned by Richard Berry were busy getting ready the food and fixin's to follow the wedding ceremony. The Rev. Jesse Head arrived on his gray mare. He was a man they rhymed about "'His nose is long and his hair is red, and he goes by the name of Jesse Head.' A hater of sin, he liked decency and good order...

"The bride and groom stood up before him. He pronounced them man and wife and wrote for the county clerk that on June 12, 1806, Thomas Lincoln and Nancy Hanks had been joined together in the holy estate of matrimony agreeable to the rites and ceremonies of the Methodist Episcopal Church. Then came the infare." An infare is like today's wedding reception, less the polka band!

The couple lived in Elizabethtown, where Thomas continued his work as a carpenter and cabinetmaker and was said to have owned "the best set of carpenter's tools in Hardin County." Thomas was kept busy making doors, door frames, mantels, general furniture, and his favorite work, corner cupboards.

About 1 1/2 years later the Lincolns' first child, a daughter, Sarah, was born in Elizabethtown. Within the next year Thomas purchased 300 acres of land on the South Fork of the Nolin Creek, about three miles from present day Hodgenville. The family moved to the new farm, called

Sinking Springs Farms—and on Feb. 12, 1809, young Abraham, the future President of the United States, was born.

Young Abe was born into a small, 16-by-18-feet, one-room cabin with a huge outside chimney. The Lincolns were the average pioneer farming family. Only two years after Abe's birth the family moved to the 230-acre Knob Creek Farm, near Hodgenville. Here the family lived until 1816. Knob Creek Farm is the first home the President remembered, maybe in part because his brother, Thomas, was born there, and died in infancy.

Although many believe that the Lincoln family was poor, according to Hardin County records, the family did well at Knob Creek Farm. In fact, Thomas Lincoln's property was valued 16th among 98 others listed on the tax rolls, and sixth of 104 for the number of horses owned. But a swirling controversy about land title got the Lincolns moving yet again when Abe was 8 years old.

They moved to Spencer County, Ind., in late 1816. The President said, "This removal was partly on account of slavery, but chiefly on account of the difficulty of land titles in Kentucky." Two years after the move, a "milk sick" epidemic struck, taking his mother's life on Oct. 5, 1818. About one year later, Thomas Lincoln went back to Elizabethtown and courted an old acquaintance, Sarah Bush Johnson. They married in December 1819.

A visit to Lincoln Homestead State Park will immerse guests in the President's family history and offers great insight into the man. Visitors will also learn about the President's grandmother, and the killing of his grandfather.

Information and Activities

Lincoln Homestead State Park
5079 Lincoln Park Road
Springfield, KY 40069
(606) 336-7461 - golf pro shop/info.

Directions: Five miles north of Springfield, off U.S. 150, via KY 528

to KY 428. From the Bluegrass Parkway take U.S. 150 east of KY 555 south to KY 528. Group rates are available.

The Lincoln Cabin and Blacksmith Shop: The Lincoln Cabin is a replica on the exact site of the original log house in which the President's grandmother, Bersheba, raised her three sons, Mordecai, Josiah and Thomas, and her two daughters Mary and Nancy. The widow Lincoln brought her children to Beech Fork several months after the death of her husband, Captain Abraham Lincoln, who was killed by Indians at their Long Run Farm in Jefferson County.

Thomas Lincoln, father of the President, lived in the humble timber-framed cabin until he was 25 years old. Several pieces of furniture that Thomas Lincoln made are preserved here, including a corner cupboard and a bed that was thought to have been made by Thomas.

Blacksmith shop: Behind the Lincoln Cabin is the replica of the Berry blacksmith shop. It was constructed from logs from an actual log cabin. According to tradition, Thomas learned his trade by apprenticeship from Richard and Francis Berry, who were owners of the blacksmith shop and master craftsmen. Inside the shop are an anvil, tongs, forge with leather bellows, carpentry tools, saws, broad axes, plow hanging on the wall, and millstones.

The Francis Berry House: The President's mother, Nancy Hanks, lived in this house during the time she was courted by Thomas Lincoln. The large, two-story home of Francis Berry is indeed original and was moved to the park from the Beechland section about one mile away. Richard Berry Sr., a Virginian, moved to central Kentucky about 1785. His wife Rachel Shipley was a sister of Lucy Shipley.

Lucy was the mother of Nancy Hanks. Nancy lived with Richard and Rachel Berry until Rachel died. She then moved to the Berry house on Beech Fork to live with her cousin, Francis Berry.

The distinctive frontier home, made of large, hand-hewn timbers, has a full second floor and glass windows, and contains several elegant examples of pioneer furniture and a photo copy of the Lincoln marriage bond. Historians believe Thomas proposed to Nancy in the large living

The quaint gift shop has considerable Lincoln memorabilia.

room before the fireplace.

Mordecai Lincoln House: The Mordecai House is a large structure believed to be built by Thomas's brother, Mordecai, and is now available for rent to small groups. A leading citizen in Washington County, Mordecai lived in the house until 1811. He and his wife had three sons and three daughters, who were all born in Washington County.

Gift shop: The quaint shop is open May 1 - Sept. 30 (weekends in October), 8 a.m. - 6 p.m. daily in a narrow log building. The shop features T-shirts, Kentucky crafts, lots of Lincoln material, copies of the Gettysburg address on antique-looking, thick paper, great cookbooks, post cards, mugs, customized clothing and other small items. You may pay the small fee to view the cabins at the sales counter inside the gift shop.

Day-use areas: Near the museum cabins are a picnic shelter, tables, grills, restrooms and playground with plenty of parking in the vicinity. The shelter may be rented by groups up to one year in advance and is open April 1 - Oct. 31.

An outdoor map depicts the migration of the Lincoln family, where they came from and how they traveled to the central United States. Use caution walking along the rough stone walkway back to the larger Berry House. Also outdoors is an interpretive sign detailing the genealogy of the Lincoln family starting with Samuel and Mordecai Lincoln.

Golf: I wonder if Abe Lincoln would have been a golfer? The 18-hole regulation course accents the gentle rolling hills of the historic setting, offering golfers a challenging course with water and sand hazards. Small greens, bunkers and fairly straight fairways are on 14 of the 18 holes. Four holes have slight doglegs. Tee times are suggested for spring and summer.

The course also has a small pro shop with equipment and golfing supplies, rental carts and clubs, and a small snack bar. The water along No. 6 and No. 9 get the attention of many erratically hit balls. So do the mature trees! The front nine from the blue tees is 3,429 yards, and the back nine yardage from the blue tees is 3,069 yards. The course is open year-round.

Three picnic tables, ice machine and soft drink machine are on the back porch of the pro shop. The homestead cabins are near holes 2, 3 and 5. The course has hard-surfaced cart paths.

31 *My Old Kentucky Home State Park*

Land: 285 acres

The familiar strains of *"My Old Kentucky Home"* moisten many eyes when the crowd stands and the song begins the annual Kentucky Derby. My Old Kentucky Home State Park preserves and honors the mansion that so enchanted songwriter Steven Foster in the 1850s he wrote a beautiful song about it.

The wonderfully preserved mansion was completed in 1818 and rests on the rolling 285 acres that was at the time a working plantation. It was deeded to the Commonwealth in 1922. The home, then known as Federal Hill, was named after the Federalist Party and built by Judge John Rowan, a distinguished man who served on both the Kentucky Court of Appeals and the U.S. Senate. The large house perfectly fit the judge's passion for lavish entertaining, with guests who included Henry Clay and Aaron Burr.

With these and other celebrity guests who visited during this glamorous era, Rowan probably never dreamed his slender cousin from Pennsylvania would make his home world famous. In 1852 Stephen Foster—who during his career wrote more than 200 compositions—visited his cousin and was moved to pen the composition which became one of the most popular songs of the Civil War and the state song of Kentucky.

Today, the home still charms visitors. Although the song I wrote when I visited may not become a hit tune, the splendid home is indeed inspirational. The home's decor, which is much the same as when Foster visited, includes rare furnishings, authenticity and great attention to detail.

My Old Kentucky Home keeps Foster's wonderful songs alive through one of America's favorite outdoor theater productions while also interpreting the history of the colorful Kentucky era.

On Jan. 10, 1864, Stephen was seriously injured in a fall in his room. He was taken to Bellevue Hospital, where he died on Jan. 13, at the age of 37 years. Hs is buried in Allegheny Cemetery in Pittsburgh.

My Old Kentucky Home State Park became part of the Kentucky state parks system on February 16, 1936.

Information and Activities

My Old Kentucky Home State Park
P.O. Box 323
Bardstown, KY 40004-0323
(502) 348-3502
(800) 323-7803

Directions: On U.S. 31E/150 in Bardstown, KY.

Stephen Foster: He was born in Pittsburgh on the 4th of July, 1826, 50 years after the signing of the Declaration of Independence. Also on that, two former U.S. presidents, John Adams and Thomas Jefferson, died.

At the age of 7, young Stephen made his first sojourn to Kentucky with his mother and sister. Because of a deadly cholera epidemic, they stayed only a week in Louisville, and did not visit Federal Hill. As it turned out, it was fortunate that they didn't visit the Rowans, because eight members of the family and eight servants died within a 24-hour period, including the judge's eldest son, William Lyle Rowan. They are all buried in the family cemetery that lies east of Federal Hill.

Stephen demonstrated musical talent early in life and was composing songs as a youngster. At age 18 his first song was published. Just two years later, young Stephen moved to Cincinnati and took a job as a bookkeeper for a steamboat company, which allowed him to travel down the Ohio River and occasionally visit Federal Hill.

While living in Cincinnati, Foster wrote a dozen or more songs, including "Oh Susannah." The song's success offered him a chance to concentrate on music and move back to Pittsburgh, where he married Jane McDowell for whom he later wrote "Jeanie With the Light Brown Hair." Two years later, in 1852, Foster and some friends took a steamboat trip down to New Orleans, and on the return trip, they docked at Louisville and he visited Federal Hill. During the visit, Foster waxed and hummed lyrically, writing the chorus of the song he had been working on and titled it, "My Old Kentucky Home."

John Rowan's wife, Rebecca, offers memories of Foster's visits: "In the bright summer weather they were sitting in the hall, Foster at the writing desk—when he took his flute and commenced to play, taking pen and paper to write. When he finished the song—words and music of My Old Kentucky Home was complete."

My Old Kentucky Home: John Rowan acquired the Federal Hill land from his father-in-law. At that time, it was a small log cabin built in 1798. Rowan and his wife took up residence, but immediately began planning for the big house and development of the land. Rowan's law and political

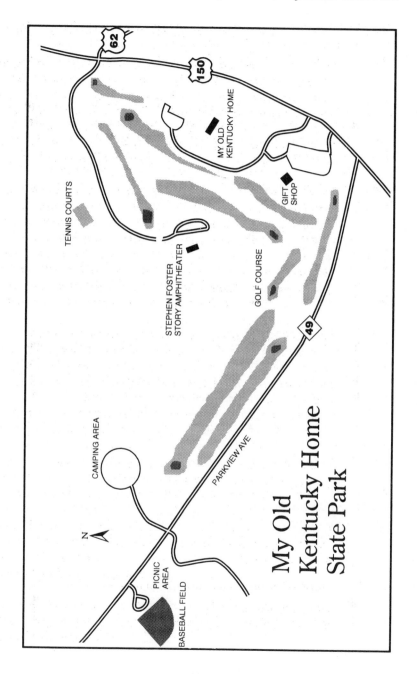

My Old
Kentucky Home
State Park

career took him all over the region, where he observed many evolving American house designs. In about 1815 he decided on the fundamental design for Federal Hill.

Rowan, like many men of his time, was quite familiar with design and building technology. Patriotism also was a major influence on the ultimate design of the new Federal-American style house that was combined with Georgian influences. For example, the 13 original colonies were honored throughout Federal Hill, starting with 13 windows that still greet visitors today. The theme is further carried out by the 13-feet-high ceilings, 13-inch-thick brick walls, 13 windows on each side of the house, and the 13 steps on the stairway. The patriotic spirit didn't end there. In many ways the home is built in the image of Independence Hall in Philadelphia.

The main house includes a basement and 2 1/2 stories. On the first floor are a bright parlor, dining rooms and library. On the second floor are three bedrooms, one of which a large master bedroom. The brick house has seven large rooms, 22 feet square with 13-foot ceilings. Flooring is of yellow poplar. The home was built mostly by slaves and no nails were used in the construction—wooden pegs were used to join the timbers and framing.

Two wells supplied water to the large house. Behind the main house are a carriage house that displays three horse-drawn vehicles and a smokehouse near a lovely formal garden. The sun dial in the garden says, "The sun shines bright in My Old Kentucky Home." From this area you can clearly hear the chimes that play popular refrains from some of Foster's most memorable songs.

Visitors will see period items, including original Duncan Phyfe, Sheraton, Chippendale and Hepplewhite furniture. Much of the house was redecorated in 1977.

Tours: Guides in antebellum costumes lead 20-minute tours through the home daily from 8:30 a.m. - 6:30 p.m., June 1 - Labor Day, and 9 a.m. - 5 p.m. during the remainder of the year. There is an admission fee. Restrooms are handicapped accessible and the first floor is also. Also near the house is the old log cabin-style law office that John Rowan

Tour of the home take about 20 minutes.

used from 1795-1840. Inside is a collection of leather-bound books, grouping of dark wooden chairs, lamps, and rough floors.

Gift shop: There's plenty of bus parking near the gift shop, which is only a short walk from My Old Kentucky Home. It is also near a sculpture of Foster holding a flute and looking back upon the mansion. From the park office or the gift shop, follow the red brick road to the home.

Complete with a bright red roof and reddish-brown brick facade, the gift shop is modern and well-stocked with a wide variety of items. The shop is open 9 a.m. - 6:30 p.m. daily and purveys chinaware, funny mugs, Kentucky handcrafts, painted sweatshirts, toys, Christmas items, refrigerator magnets, wooden post cards, pennants, Foster song books, Rowan family history books and corn-cob pipes.

"The Stephen Foster Story:" The J. Dan Talbott Amphitheatre is home to "The Stephen Foster Story" performances. The musical play is the longest running outdoor drama in the state. The facility is 70 minutes from Lexington and 45 minutes from Louisville.

Colorful flags line the entrance to the outdoor theater, which is carefully placed in rolling wooded terrain with the stage actually nestled into a hillside. There have been more than 3,000 professional performances at the outdoor theater. Today, the nightly shows start at 8: 30 p.m., except for Mondays. About 65,000 people annually see the play; the theater seats 1,404. There are 60 cast members.

The play premiered at the J. Dan Talbot Amphitheatre on June 26, 1959 and was met with immediate critical acclaim. The production was conceived by the people of Bardstown, who, in 1922, had purchased Federal Hill. The Stephen Foster Drama Association, a not-for-profit educational and cultural organization, was formed to produce this musical drama based on the life of Foster.

The Pulitzer Prize winning author Paul Green was commissioned to prepare the script; noted arranger Isaac Van Grove prepare the musical score. The results were hailed as "a tuneful ear."

"The Stephen Foster Story" describes in dramatic detail one year in the life of American's first full-time ballad writer, and presents to us a number of his most beloved songs. For reservations call (800) 626-1563.

Campground: The small 39-site campground is heavily shaded, with sites along the inside and outside edge of a large driveway that forms a loop. A single drinking fountain and the small brown shower building serve campers and are closest to sites 18, 20, 38 and 39. Some small day-use area are offered, as is a small playground for children.

Many of the campers are theater fans. The campground gets lots of use. All sites have hard-surfaced camping pads and other common amenities including fire rings, newspaper vending machines, and nearby ice. Sites 24-26 have a view of the golf course fairway, and site 10 is right next to the 10th tee. Also next to the course are sites 12, 14, 16, 17 and 18. From many sites you can hear the whack as club head meets ball.

Sites 28 and 30 are backed up against a small grass-covered knoll. Site 4 has an extra-wide pad for larger RV rigs and is near the pro shop. Bring your golf clubs to knock the ball around this fine course. This isn't the type of campground where you sit next to your tent or RV; it's a campground to stay in during the evening and explore the wonderful park and area all day.

Golf: Wide and hilly, the fairways are relatively tame, except near the water on holes 12 and 14. The greens are well-tended and of medium size. The golf course, next to the campground entrance, has a modern pro shop with a red roof and wrap-around porch with large practice green out front. Tee times are required on weekends and holidays; call (502) 349-6542. There are four tables near a large bank of windows where lots of 19th hole talk takes place. Carts can be rented at the 18-hole course.

Day-use areas: West of the campground is a popular three-acre day-use area that includes a ballfield and picnic area. A brick picnic shelter that may be rented is near a colorful playground, which includes swings with pumpkin-like tops, red tub slide, rocking teeter-totter, sandbox and plenty of picnic tables.

Special notes: My Old Kentucky Home Dinner Train, (502) 348-7300 is a terrific complement to your park visit.

32   *Natural Bridge*
State Resort Park

Land: 1,900 acres Water: 54-acre pond

High on a hilltop, the grand sandstone Natural Bridge reaches 78 feet from end to end, standing like a watchman guarding the Red River, its tributaries and the heavily wooded mountains that roll off into the hazy distance.

Although the 65-foot-tall arch is Kentucky's most famous, there are actually 150 natural stone arches within five miles of the park's Hemlock Lodge. Natural Bridge isn't even the oldest, largest or most accessible, but it is the most visited and beloved, first promoted as a tourism attraction 1889.

Geologists estimate that the 20-foot-wide rock bridge was created by the forces of erosion over the past 60 million years. Scientists further believe the area was once fairly level and was near the sea. When the Appalachian Mountains were formed, the region was raised hundreds of feet above sea level, with waters running off from the high elevations and carving out the steep walled canyon that we now call Red River Gorge.

Sandstone cliffs on top of the ridges are harder and more resistant to erosion than softer layers below. They stand out in stark relief, giving the gorge its picturesque scenery. Ripped apart by jolting earthquakes and slowly dissolved by rain and running water, the cliffs have been carved into spectacular rock formations, including arches.

You can hike the trails to the arch—or save some of your energy and ride the chairlift (it ascends to within 600 feet of the Natural Bridge) for a dramatic panorama of the steep canyon walls, lush woodlands and other natural formations.

The state park is a great base from which to explore this fascinating part of Kentucky. Natural Bridge is the fourth unit in the state system, donated to the state in 1926 by the Louisville and Nashville Railroad.

Information and Activities

Natural Bridge State Resort Park
2135 Natural Bridge Road
Slade, KY 40376-9701
(606) 663-2214
(800) 325-1710 - toll-free reservations

Directions: Off Mountain Parkway on KY 11, south of Slade. 52 miles southeast of Lexington. In the Daniel Boone National Forest, which was created in 1937 by President Franklin Roosevelt and named after Daniel Boone in 1966.

Lodge: In 1889, the Kentucky Union Railway Co. established a winding rail line through where the town of Slade now lies, connecting logging forests to the markets. The company also saw the potential for tourism in the region and began to develop a park with day-use areas, a rustic campground, and foot trails to the arch and other features in the area. The first Hemlock Lodge was constructed in 1927 of logs and shakes and remained until a fire leveled the structure in 1969. The new Hemlock Lodge was built in 1963 offering a 35-room lodge with a 150-seat dining room and gift shop was built on a ledge looking down a steep wooden valley.

Modern and comfortable, the lobby has a large-screen television in front of comfortable seating. The copper-clad fireplace shines warmly under wood ceilings and warm colors of the medium-size lobby area. Guests can enjoy the view and seating, stroll the gift shop or enjoy a meal at the dining room that opens daily at 7 a.m. The restaurant is one of the more elegant in the park system, offering muted colors, ceiling fans, and a terrific woodland view down to the pool and day-use areas. But, please, come as you are—including a shirt and shoes, that is.

Also exhibited in the lodge are mounts of an American bald eagle and other birds.

Meeting facilities: The unit's Activity Center, a multi-purpose building down a wide hard-surfaced walkway near the lodge, can seat 195 people. The lodge's meeting room can seat 50. A private dining room in the lodge can also be rented for meals or meeting large enough to accommodate 60 people.

Cottages: A narrow, steep road takes visits and guests up to the mini-subdivision of cottages behind the Activity Center in thickly wooded terrain. Cottages 148 and 149 are perched on a high ridge with a wooded view of the valley, with the distant sounds of fun from the large day-use areas in the air. Cottage 147 is at the end of a small gravel road and has a screened-in porch. 142, 143 and 144 are along a ridge below the roadway grade.

Any of the cottages is a delight. All are provided with tableware, cooking utensils, and fresh linens daily.

Campground: There are two campgrounds in the park.

The Whittleton Campground on the northeast side of the park has 45 sites

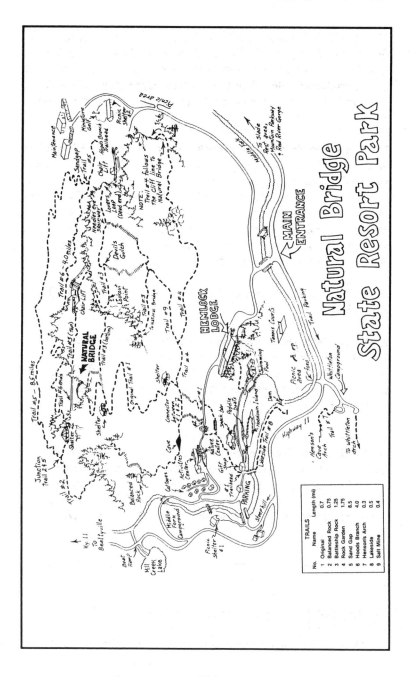

on a hilly loop with a bathhouse and laundry. There are both gravel and hard-surfaced pads. Some of the more private sites are 4, 5 and 7. Most of the sites have shade, and all have access to electrical hookups, but not water. Many smaller units and tents fit well in this camping area.

Sites in the 30s are bound on each side by natural areas. On site 38 you could place your tent on the back portion of the site and have a nice private location for a weekend or a week long stay. Sites 40 and 41 are the two large units for bigger RV rigs.

This is a narrow and often congested campground. Near site 43 is the trail head for the Whittleton Creek Trail, a delightful but moderately difficult hike. This trail is the easiet to hike in the park.

Winding southward, the Middlefork Campground is more open than Whittleton. Most sites are level and there are a number of pull-through sites in the facility. Site 15 is probably the shadiest of the sites in the loop, with 27, 29, 30-36 also nice sites near Red River. Loops are connected by a wooden foot bridge. The Middle Fork Campground is more convenient to the recreation and day-use areas than the Whittleton Campground.

Tent camping is popular in this campground. Each of the tent sites is outlined with wooden timbers, forming a pad-type location to pitch your tent.

Phone, ice and firewood are available from the camp office.

Fishing: There is limited fishing in the Middle Fork, with rough fish and panfish taken with live bait and bobber. Middle Ford is best known for rainbow trout. Anglers can also use a small boat to fish Mill Creek Lake where fishing is considered fair.

Boating: Paddle boats are rented near the snack bar behind the lodge. Small boats may be launched in Mill Creek Lake, off KY 11. Electric motors only.

Hiking: The pathway and stone steps along each of the trails that access the Natural Bridge are worn and polished from use. But the result of the

The park has challenging and scenic hiking trails.

hikes is the same—a dramatic view from the top of the bridge.

The Original Trail (.75 mile) was built in the 1890s by the Lexington & Eastern Railroad and continues to be the most popular route today. It's both the shortest and easiest trail back to the Natural Bridge. The trail climbs more than 500 feet through an impressive forest of hemlock, yellow poplar, white pine and dense thickets of rhododendron.

Balanced Rock Trail (.75 mile) is the steepest trail in the park, a real lung-burner. Beginning behind the lodge, hikers will lose calories on a series of limestone steps to the extraordinary rock formation called Balanced Rock. Along a ridge top, this trail leads to the Natural Bridge.

Rock Garden Trail (1.75 miles) is a winding, lightly used route to the Natural Bridge. The trail follows under the chairlift and climbs gently from the lodge.

At the foot of Natural Bridge.

Six other trails from .4 miles to 8.5 miles long welcome hikers. The 8.5-mile long Sand Gap Trail is a challenging ridge top walk that occasionally drops under cliffs and winds through the park.

A handy trail guide of the parks great hikes is available at the lodge and other offices scattered around the park.

Day-use areas: Under the lodge, nestled in a valley partly filled with a mountain pond, is the central part of the day-use amenities that include the pool, paddle boats, Hoe Down Island, snack bar, free-standing gift shop, miniature golf (18 holes), picnic areas, trailheads, and hillside activity building and nature center.

Skylift: Ride to the sky and come within 600 feet of Natural Bridge for a fee.

Hoe Down Island: Yee haw, mosey on down to the small island for some knee-slappin', toe tappin', and swingin' your partner fun. The open-air dance floor has seating and lights near the snack bar. The island is used each weekend for regular square dances, clogging, line dances, country-bluegrass-gospel singing, and special performances.

Swimming pool: Kidney-shaped and cool in the summer, the swimming pool is free for overnight guests and has a bath house, pool-side lounges, kiddies pool, umbrella tables, and is near the paddle boat dock and lodge. The pool is open seasonally. Behind the pool is an interesting abandoned railroad tunnel, but is not accessible

Nature: The park publishes a list of amphibians, reptiles, wildflowers, ferns, tree's and shrubs, mammals and birds found there. On my first visit to the park, I was lucky enough to see a timber rattler wandering along a trail back to the Natural Bridge. Several people stopped to watch the little snake, but he just kept motoring along not paying much attention to us towering humans. One little boy asked "Is he on his way to the store...Daddy?"

Almost half of this unit is managed as a state nature preserve in cooperation with the Kentucky State Nature Preserve Commission. The 994-acre preserve has a unique landscape and several rare species of

The extensive day-use areas are below the modern lodge.

plants and animals, including the Virginia big-eared bat and small yellow lady slippers. Please stay on trail.

The nature center is in the lower level of a two-story stone and wood building with a balcony. A variety of interpretive programs are conducted for guests, including junior naturalist programs. Other classes and activities are listed in the calendar of events available at the center or lodge. The center features many educational displays.

Special notes: The U.S. Forest Service has maps of the gorge that provide information about amenities, fall colors and much more. Just north of the park entrance are a small amusement park and a nearby privately operated reptile zoo.

The scenic round-trip drive from Hemlock Lodge through Red River Gorge is one of the most impressive in Kentucky. A guide is available.

33 Old Fort Harrod State Park

Land: 15 acres

Old Fort Harrod State Park commemorates the first permanent English settlement west of the Alleghenies, established by Captain James Harrod in 1774. The city of Harrodsburg had many firsts, including the first white child born west of the Alleghenies, the first cultivated corn crop, the first court and school, and the first linen spun. Harrodsburg was also the site of the first Christian religious service and the home to the first physician to practice in the entire region.

The fort was rebuilt in 1927, one-third smaller and just south of the original site. In 1774, James Harrod and a band of pioneers migrated down the Ohio River to this rolling, wooded hills in what would become central Kentucky. By September 1775 the men's families followed and soon the first settlement in Kentucky was created. Eventually the fort became home to waves of pioneers including George Rogers Clark and Daniel Boone. As the fort became established, the town of Harrodsburg grew up around it.

Today, Old Fort Harrod is an experience in living history as it recreates the pioneer settlement with cabins furnished with handmade items, furniture and tools. Artisans in period dress demonstrate pioneer crafts and skills such as basketry, broom making, quilting, woodworking, soap making, blacksmithing and much more.

The fort is quite authentic, offering visitors a window into the pioneer world. Adjacent to the fort, the Lincoln Marriage Temple houses the actual cabin where Abraham Lincoln's parents were married on June 12, 1806. Inside the Mansion Museum are Civil War artifacts, early Kentucky historical items and a Lincoln collection. The James Harrod Amphitheatre, located on the park's ground, features two outstanding dramas during the summer, *The Legion of Daniel Boone* and *Shadows of the Forest.*

Information and Activities

Old Fort Harrod State Park
P.O. Box 156
Harrodsburg, KY 40330-0156
(606) 734-3314
(606) 734-3346 - Reservations for
"The Legend of Daniel Boone"

Directions: The fort is at the intersection of U.S. 127 and U.S. 68 in downtown Harrodsburg. About 32 miles southwest of Lexington and 75 miles east of Louisville. The park is open year-round.

James Harrod: The fort's namesake, a true pioneer and settler, left behind many mysteries—including the time and manner of his death. Historians even argue about his year of birth. Mr. Harrod was quite a guy, and worth learning more about at the museum.

As one of "Captain Cochran's Recruits" in June 1760, Harrod said his age then was 16 years. He also said he was five feet, two inches—which varied so much from his adult height of more than six feet, historians feel comfortable believing that he greatly inflated his age in order to serve. Accounts of his birthdate are vague also, ranging from 1742 to 1746. We do know that he was born in Pennsylvania, had 11 brothers and sisters and was the son of John Harrod and his second wife, Sarah (Moore) Harrod.

Harrod knew the land, several Indian languages and French, learned along his many travels. It's fitting a fort was named after a man who's life was in many ways shaped by Indians. From his father's first wife being murdered by Indians, to his brother's death at the hands of Indians, Harrod actually fled Pennsylvania with his mother seeing burning buildings and hearing the screams caused from attacks. Surprisingly, Harrod never grew to hate Indians. In fact, there are accounts of his kindnesses to wounded Indians.

He was a fine hunter and marksman and, like many pioneers, was drawn westward, where, after several encounters with Daniel Boone, set about establishing the first permanent settlement in Kentucky. Harrod fought for many years to protect the region, including difficult expeditions against the Indians in the Northwest Territory in 1780, 1782 and 1786. After some reasonable prosperity—he owned 1,300 acres—Harrod had a working farm with six slaves who tended scores of cattle, sheep, hogs and horses.

In 1778, when the tall and dark-haired Harrod was in his mid-30s, he married a cultured, attractive 22-year old widow, Ann Coburn, whose husband was killed by Indians. She had a young son when they married. After seven years, of marriage, the couple had a daughter, Margaret.

Once again, Indians savagely impacted Harrods life when they seized his stepson and burned him at the stake.

Finally, Harrod became distraught with grief, taking longer and longer hunting trips until on one trip in the winter of 1792, he disappeared and was never heard from again.

The Fort: Tall wooden walls surround the fort that was rebuilt in the late 1920s. The original fort was 264 feet square, with three corner blockhouses of 25 feet by 44 feet, and with walls that were 12 inches thick.

The original blockhouses had two-foot overhangs from which the defenders could pour lye or shoot at attackers. The fort's gates were of stout timbers opened on the west and north sides. There were seven 20-foot-square cabins, built with one-foot-thick walls. Puncheon roofs, windows and floors were made from logs that had been cut in half, with one side hand-hewn flat and the other side rounded. Many of the cabins had simple dirt floors.

Harrod carefully selected the site for the original fort to include a large spring that ran inside the fort, providing a constant water supply. Many settlers built stations, or small stockades, near the fort complex, and in times of trouble or danger families took refuge behind the sturdy walls of the fort. Although the fort was under siege many times, it always withstood Indian assaults.

Upon paying the small admission and entering the fort, your eyes are drawn to the many tiny cabins, sleepy sheep and other farm animals in the split-rail corral in the center of the fort.

The wide stone walkway that is shaded by tall trees takes visitors past cabins, near wood piles and forges, and next to rendering kettles, a small garden, farm implements, a running spring and much more.

Many crafts produced by fort artisans are for sale in the gift shop. The blacksmith makes wrought iron fire pokers, wind chimes, coat hooks and so on.

Each of the buildings—from the large blockhouse to tiny Mark McGohon's cabin—features exhibits of pioneer life. Baskets, cookware, furniture, rifles, clothing, personal items and many other tools of daily life are featured in the log cabins with wooded pegged flooring and creaking beam rafters made of stripped pine.

The gardens, include a kitchen garden of culinary herbs. For centuries people have used fresh and dried herbs to season meats, vegetables, fruits and sauces. The medicinal garden plot at the fort depicts the variety of herbs used by pioneers to treat medical problems. The herbs grown were

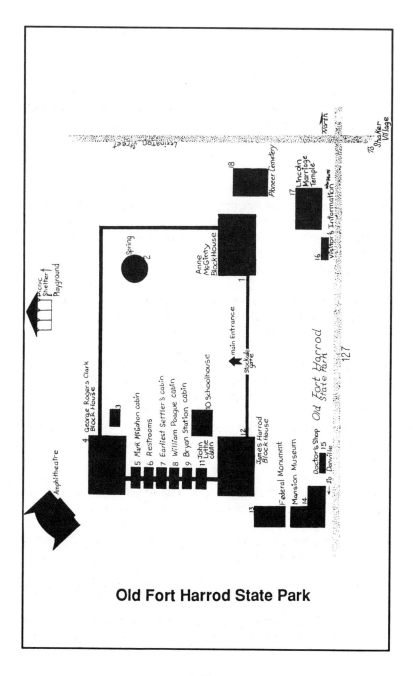

Old Fort Harrod State Park

often used for compresses, pain killers, tonics, poultices and healing wounds.

The exotic herb garden was used for dyes for wool and cotton. The flowers and roots of many wildflowers and herbs produced many bright colors often used by pioneers. The 18th century pioneer woman would gather flower heads when they were in full bloom and simmer them in a kettle of water over an open fire. Skeins of fiber would them be gently lowered in to the colored water, and the result was a pleasantly dyed yarn.

Kentucky's first school is also on display at the fort. The primitive log structure is low and dark, with a large fireplace that is fed long logs from the outside. The clay floor holds rough-made benches where from 1776-1835 school was conducted. Jane Coomes, originally from Maryland, came to the fort with her husband, William, and is credited with opening the school and teaching pioneer children of the fort for nine years.

Mrs. Coomes taught the youngsters from a primitive version of the Old English Horn Book, made of clapboard in the shape of a paddle with its handle whittled to fit the children's fingers. Both the Lord's Prayer and the alphabet were crudely drawn on the flat board. She taught math from a hand-copied book she had brought from over the Alleghenies. After many years of productive life, the couple moved on to Bardstown.

The fort is open year-round, but is closed on Mondays in January.

Gift shop: Air-conditioned, the shop features Kentucky handcrafts, T-shirts, Kentucky-themed souvenoirs, jams, jellies, and a wilde selection of Kentucky books and a good looking recipe book called, "Thelma's Treasures." The shop, inside the fort, is open April 1 - Oct. 31. Restrooms are in the fort and at the Mansion Museum.

Museum: Red brick and white clapboard, its enamel gray porch is a clean and professional entrance to the Mansion Museum that is home to a fine collection of Civil War displays, paintings, guns, documents, Indian artifacts and interpretive material.

The wood floors are tight-grained ash and highly polished, reflecting light and sounds of visitors in one of the oldest Greek Revival house in

Kentucky. The original part of the house was built by potter Felix Matheny in 1813. Major James Taylor, a lawyer, purchased the home from Matheny in 1830 and made many quality additions that were completed in 1836.

The first room to the left upon entering the house is a Union Room with oil portraits, display cases, letters from the President, marriage certificate of the President's parents, and more. Opposite this room on the right is a room dedicated to the Confederacy during the Civil War. With an oil painting of Jefferson Davis and Robert E. Lee, and information about Stonewall Jackson, visitors will find examples of confederate money, swords, rifles, and lots of information about Major General John C. Breckenridge.

Upstairs is a music room, pioneer tools, Indian artifacts, and an impressive display of guns. Under glass are many wonderful samples of handguns, and long guns rest against the walls. From many Kentucky rifles to a small cannon, the gun room has flintlocks, Springfield rifles and interesting small caliber handguns. As you exit the museum, you will see some excellent high-quality examples of dining room and other furniture. The museum is open mid-March to Nov. 30.

George Rogers Clark Memorial: After establishing Leestown (it was later abandoned), fighting Indians and exploring, George Rogers Clark later settled at Harrodsburg in the summer of 1775. Clark was a key figure in the protection of the new territory called Kentucky. He was made a major, given a military command, and helped arrange for Harrodsburg to become the county seat.

Many experts suggest that Clark's military decisions to secure the Northwest Territory, which comprised the states of Ohio, Indiana, Michigan, Illinois and Wisconsin, changed the entire history of the United States.

Fort Harrod was also the site of the first jail established by Clark after his forces subdued the Indians and their French military supporters at Kaskaskia, Ill. and Vincennes, Ind. Clark brought back 26 prisoners and kept them in jail for 13 days. Among the prisoners was Gov. Hamilton.

The monument commemorates the pioneer struggle.

The Federal Monument, which honors Clark and many brave Kentucky pioneers, was dedicated before 75,000 onlookers by President Franklin D. Roosevelt on Nov. 16, 1934. The handsome monument cost $100,000 and commemorates the first permanent settlement to the West, recalls the Epochal Era of the pioneer day. Each historical figure on the monument is a separate study of the map spread before the base. The pioneer figures and map suggest the huge scope of the territory explored and settled. The granite steps and map that depict the rivers, as well as cultural information about the region, makes this one of the finest monuments in the entire state parks system.

Lincoln Marriage Temple: Many visitors first think that the building that encloses the marriage cabin of President Lincoln's parents is a church. But it was actually constructed for the purpose of preserving the very old and tiny cabin that rest quietly on the flagstone floors that are polished from use. The wedding took place on June 12, 1806 and was conducted by the Reverend Jesse Head (for more information about the Lincoln family, turn to the section on the Lincoln Homestead State Park). The cabin was acquired by the Harrodsburg Historical Society in 1911 and moved from its original location at Beechland in Washington County. The building that protects and preserves the cabin is a beautiful structure with a steeple on the northeast corner of the block.

Today, the old logs that comprise the cabin are dry-looking and delicate. Inside the 22-foot-square cabin are simple furnishings that include two small stools, a small bed, a wicker-like chair and a fireplace.

The Doctor's Shop: Next to the Mansion Museum is a tiny physician's office that offers examples of surgical tools, medicine containers, surgical kits and a small fireplace. The entire office is about 15-by-20-feet in size.

Amphitheatre: The James Harrod Amphitheatre, located on west gournds of the state park complex, is large and modern. It features outdoor theater productions from mid-June through August. The box office is open daily for tickets for *The Legend of Daniel Boone* and *Shadows in the Forest* live shows that play Monday-Saturday, beginning at 8:30 p.m. In front the of theater are some great picnicking areas. Check with the box office for dates and times for indoor shows during the spring and fall.

Pioneer cemetery: Just inside the main gate of the fort lies Kentucky's first settlers. About 500 graves are surrounded by a stone wall under the canopy of mature trees. Tiny grave stones mark the plots in the historic cemetery.

Day-use areas: The park has two picnic areas, shelters, play apparatus, a gift shop, craft shop, and the biggest osage orange tree in the country!

Special notes: The community of Harrodsburg is attractive and the many state park facilities—especially the marriage cabin of Thomas and Nancy Lincoln—are excellent.

On summer evenings, Monday - Saturday, the Fort is open until 8 p.m.

34   Old Mulkey Meetinghouse State Historic Site

Land: 60 acres

In April 1804, a seven-member committee was appointed to erect a new meetinghouse in Monroe County. The group decided that the building would be 50 feet long and 30 feet wide, made of logs, and shingled with jointed shingles, featuring symbolic windows and three doors. Construction was completed in 1804, during a period known for religious revival. Old Mulkey is the oldest log meetinghouse in Kentucky.

The dark log structure lies in a flat area now canopied by tall trees. Its 12 corners are said to represent the Twelve Apostles, and its three doors the Trinity. The building is in the shape of the cross.

Old Mulkey is in south-central Kentucky on the Tennessee state line. This wonderful region of the state is gently rolling with extremely fertile bottomlands that produce abundant grain crops. The area attracted prehistoric people who hunted and lived near streams and in deep caves; European settlers in the 1770s clustered along the Cumberland River; and, later, the area became a hotbed of activity during the Civil War.

In 1773 settlers from the Carolinas came to the region led by Philip Mulkey. The park interprets early religion in Kentucky and Mulkey's experience. The area became a state park in 1931.

Information and Activities

Old Mulkey Meetinghouse State Historic Site
1819 Old Mulkey Road
Tompkinsville, KY 42167-8766
(502) 487-8481

Directions: Fifty miles southeast of Bowling Green, 2.5 miles south of Tompkinsville. Off I-65, take U.S. 231 south to KY 100 east or via Hwy 90 East to Ky 163 South.

Old Mulkey Meetinghouse: The last outdoor meetinghouse in the state saw religious revolt, pioneer settlement, great leaders and loving renovation. It is also the oldest wooden structure in the state.

"Now all you who believe as I do, follow me out the west door," said Baptist Minister John Mulkey to his congregation of 200 on Nov. 18, 1809. On this day, Mulkey founded a large group of Christians, later known as Disciples of Christ—in the humble place that became known as "Old Mulkey." This, and other religious movements of the day, defined the era that was to called by historians the "Great Awakening."

The crude log structure, with puncheon floor, pegleg seats, chinked and daubed walls, clapboard shutters and hand-drived shingles, was built without a fireplace. Worshippers warmed themselves with good thoughts and frequent visits to a log fire that was kept burning in the churchyard.

The men who tended the fire also guarded against Indian attacks.

Frigid Sundays encouraged resourceful pioneer women to warm large soapstones and then place them in heavy wool bags. They then placed the hot rocks in the pews to warm cold Christians. Many successful years passed, but slowly the church crowds grew old and the congregation's numbers declined until the group moved to Tompkinsville. In the late 1870s, some of the local residents including John Gee and Frank Pedigo, who had close ties to the church and area, began renovating the old building. It was again renovated in 1890 and in the mid-1920s, and finally became a state park in November 1931.

Hannah Boone: Forty yards from the old meetinghouse is a tiny pioneer graveyard containing the gravesites of Philip Mulkey, 15 Revolutionary War soldiers, and Hannah Boone, sister of Daniel Boone.

Hannah was married to John Stewart, a companion of Daniel on his first trip to Kentucky in 1760. She was the youngest of the Boone family, born in Berks County, Pennsylvania in 1746.

Upon a return trip to Kentucky, Stewart and Boone were captured by a party of Shawnee Indians, who forced the pioneer hunters to lead them back to their camp where they stole furs, supplies and horses. The intrepid pioneer followed the Indians and ultimately rescued two horses during a daring nighttime foray.

Unfortunately, two days later, Stewart and Boone were again captured. According to records, sometime between January and May 1770, Stewart was killed by the Indians. Later, when Boone was blazing the Wilderness Trail, he found Stewart's remains in a hollow sycamore tree. Apparently Stewart was wounded and had hidden in the tree, where he bled to death.

Hannah eventually married Richard Pennington in 1776. Hannah was a member of John Mulkey's "Old Mulkey" congregation.

Gift shop: The gift shop and rest room, built in 1991, is open seasonally, 7:30 a.m. - 4:30 p.m. on weekdays, 9 a.m. - 5 p.m. on weekends. The tastefully decorated shop offers some interesting items for sale. Includes Amish baskets, historial books and Kentucky handcrafts.

35 Paintsville Lake State Park

Land: 1,700 acres Water: 1,139-acre lake

One of the newest units in the system, Paintsville State Park is located on a lake that that is hidden among the steep hills and gorges of eastern Kentucky's Johnson and Morgan counties. Although the developed portion of the state park is actually quite small, it borders on more than 13,000 acres of lands and water that are leased from the U.S. Army Corps of Engineers.

Covering more than 1,100 acres, Paintsville Lake was created by the Corps and opened to the public in May 1984. The park was dedicated two years later. The narrow lake is 26 miles long and up to 100 feet deep in places. It winds through deep and narrow gorges, steep hills and towering sandstone bluffs.

There is no state park office at this day-use park, but you can visit the Corps of Engineers office for lake and area brochures and maps. The small office has a back observation deck that offers a splendid view of the ridge lines that make up the park and the privately-owned marina that is the focal point of the state park. A telescope, bench and drinking fountains make this an excellent first stop if you are touring the park and the surrounding managed lands. The Corps is also developing a small historical village on a hillside near the office.

Information and Activities

Paintsville Lake State Park
P.O. Box 200
Prestonsburg KY 41653
(606) 297-1521 - dock

Directions: Four miles west of Paintsville, off KY 40 from U.S. 460, 50 miles south of I-64. Follow "Paintsville Lake" signs. There is no campground at Paintsville Lake State Park.

Fishing: Walleye and bass fishing is good to very good in the spring and fall, with action slowing as the water clears during the summer. The average depth of the lake is 38 feet.

Largemouth bass have a stable population over the entire lake and receive heavy fishing pressure. Spotted bass fishing is considered good, with the best angling opportunities in the lower two-thirds of the lake. Walleye populations are very good in the spring, while crappie fishing is poor. The best chances for these species are in the upper part of the lake.

Many serious bass anglers fish Paintsville Lake. Topwater buzz baits are popular.

Summer walleye anglers typically jig the deep waters using lead-head jigs tipped with active minnows. Twelve-pound walleye are taken each year at the lake. In the spring, crankbaits can be effective.

Structures, in the form of old Christmas trees, have been placed in the

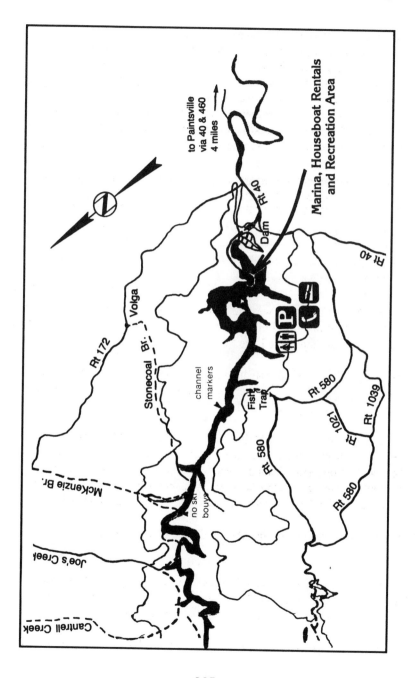

lake, especially around Large and Small Island. A hand-drawn map detailing the locations of the underwater structures is available at the Corps office. A fishing pier that is handicapped accessible near the marina is maintained by the local Kiwanis Club. Some catfish are also taken from the lake, usually fished in the summer shallows using cut baits, dough balls or other stink baits.

Marina: The full-service marina (call, (606) 297-LAKE) is privately owned. It offers 84 open slips, 80 covered slips and a launching ramp that is busy year-round.

Inside the floating marina are a small snack bar, six tables, and some marine and fishing supplies. Other services include complete docking facilites, rental of houseboats, party-sized pontoon and fishing boats, overnight tie-ups, picnic shelter reservations, gasoline and oil, ice, live bait, a pumping station and trailer parking. You can rent 54-foot-long houseboats that sleep 10 for three-day periods or by the week. Jet Skis are offered for rent by the hour, and general pleasure boating is very popular on the clear lake.

Day-use areas: The park features some limited open spaces and scattered picnic tables and trash barrels.

Hiking: The Paintsville Kiwanis Club has built and maintains a 1.25-mile walking trail at the Paintsville Dam that winds through a section of woodland that provides excellent scenic views of the lake.

Nature: Rugged rock cliffs that line the lake and adjoining mountainside are home to various wildlife, including increasing numbers of black bear. The woodlands surrounding the lake also contains hardy stands of persimmon, dogwood, sumac and walnut trees.

Hunting: For squirrel, rabbit, ruffed grouse and other types of hunting, call the Huntington District of the Corps of Engineers for details.

36 *Pennyrile Forest*
State Resort Park

Land: 863 acres Water: 56-acre lake

The most beautiful woods of western Kentucky is home to a lovely hideaway state park and cottage-like stone lodge that is perhaps the finest in the entire park system. In addition to the spectacular scenery of the lush, 15,331-acre Pennyrile State Forest, visitors will treasure the crystal-clear waters of the lake and the unspoiled terrain that teems with wildlife and wildflowers.

Named for the tiny pale violet Pennyroyal plant—often called Pennyrile—that blooms from July through September, the lodge, cottages, campground and golf course are the perfect place to vis. The charm level at Pennyrile is intense. The rustic stone and wood lodge and dining room are set serenely on a high cliff overlooking the green-blue lake, surrounded by perfectly maintained and manicured grounds. This is one of the top getaway resort parks in the entire state.

The park opened for operation in 1937 (then owned by the U.S. Government) and is completely surrounded by the Pennyrile State Forest. In 1954 the lands were transferred to the state of Kentucky. In 1962, the 24-room lodge was built, overlooking the oddly-shaped lake.

The region's first settler, John Thompson, traveled from Virginia with his wife and young son in the fall of 1808. With a yoke of oxen, two-wheeled cart and a strong constitution, the family trekked to Cumberland Gap, where he took the great Wilderness Road that had been blazed by Daniel Boone into the heartland of Kentucky.

He crossed the gentle, rolling hills of bluegrass, the vast plains and prairies, then pushed westward into the glades and jungles of the Tradewater River and its tributaries. On these vast plains he saw huge herds of buffalo and elk. Further west the family saw abundant deer, bear, turkey and other more easily hunted game. Braced by the game and rich lands, he took up residence for the winter under a rock shelter know, now as "Thompson's Cave." Today this site is surrounded by the state park.

Pioneers spirits high, the family cleared a plot of land where the lake now lies, lived mostly off of game and wild edibles, and made it safely to the warmer days of spring. By 1810, eight other families had settled near the Thompsons. The small community thrived in this most rich and productive part of Kentucky. Some of the families settled in what is now the north end of the golf course.

Information and Activities

Pennyrile Forest State Resort Park
20781 Pennyrile Lodge Road
Dawson Spring, KY 42408-9212
(502) 797-3421
(800) 325-1711 - reservations

Directions: 20 miles northwest of Hopkinsville. From Hopkinsville, take KY 109 north. The park is open year-round.

Lodge: From the lovely grounds of the lodge you might hear a passing warbler sing, see the sparkle of the lake waters in the distance, hear the slap of a canoe paddle, or smile at a misty morning that will blossom into a glorious day. The lodge is perched on a tall ridge line above the lake.

The lodge, cottages, swimming pool and beach are clustered for convenience.

The entrance to the 24-room lodge has gleaming coach lamps, wrought-iron hand rails, and stonework that is the perfect entree into the knotty-pine paneled lobby. The colorful, country-style decor accents the fireplace that is flanked by two large brass deer sculptures. Four ceiling fans paddle around and around, casting a cool breeze over the sitting area (with large screen television). Quality framed artworks of horse racing and nature line the walls and add to the pleasant space. The use of brass accessories, multi-pane windows and curtains will delight visitors who like a warm, cottage-like lodge.

Just off the lobby, through the door next to the fireplace, is a small recreation room. You can try a game of pool, play a video game or lottery machine, or rest in rattan furniture that looks out a large window onto a colorful garden and the tree-lined lake in the distance. This small garden has wrought-iron outdoor furniture and an umbrella table. Huge ferns and other hanging plants are tastefully positioned throughout the exterior of the lodge.

From the permanent benches behind the lodge building, you can watch the small boat traffic (no gasoline motors are allowed on the lake) carve a path along the surface of the clear lake waters. This entire area behind the quaint lodge is almost courtyard-like with outdoor accent lighting, wood and stone fences, colorful annual flower beds, bird feeders, closely cropped lawns, and mature trees. Rooms to consider are 201-203, which face the small pleasant courtyard. All of the lodge rooms have patios or balconies with quality wrought-iron chairs and tables. Room 112, an end room, has a great view and would be extra quiet and relaxing.

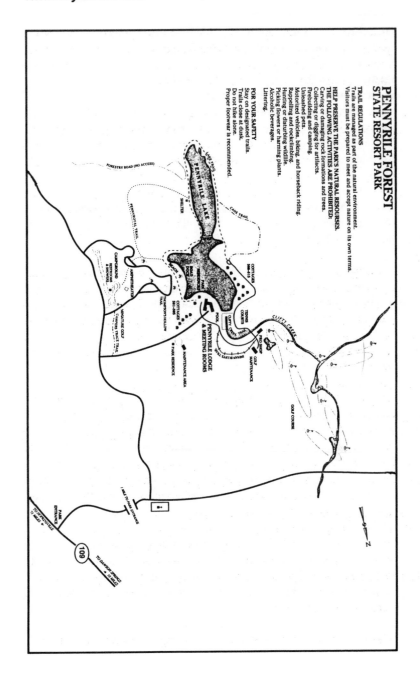

PENNYRILE FOREST STATE RESORT PARK

TRAIL REGULATIONS

Trails are managed as part of the natural environment.
Visitors must be prepared to meet and accept nature on its own terms.

**HELP PRESERVE THE PARK'S NATURAL RESOURCES.
THE FOLLOWING ACTIVITIES ARE PROHIBITED:**

Carving or damaging rock formations and trees.
Collecting or digging for artifacts.
Firebuilding and camping.
Unleashed pets.
Motorized vehicles, biking, and horseback riding.
Rappelling and rockclimbing.
Hunting or disturbing wildlife.
Picking flowers or harming plants.
Alcoholic beverages.
Littering.

FOR YOUR SAFETY

Stay on designated trails.
Trails close at dusk.
Do not hike alone.
Proper footwear is recommended.

Meeting facilities: The E.G. Glover Multiple Purpose Facility is a newer wooden addition to the lodge featuring a rose-colored carpeted room that seats 120 and adapts to many meeting or programming needs. Many special events are held in this building.

Across from the front desk is small gift shop that features Kentucky handcrafts, quilts, rag dolls, T-shirts, books, mugs, jellies and jams, artwork and souvenirs. Pottery and other quality items are contained in the glass cases under the front desk counter.

The 200-seat dining room carries on the county-style decor, using cheerful green and tan colors to enhance the clean and warm feeling of the room with a great view of the lake. The dining room opens at 7 a.m. for breakfast.

Cottages: Pennyrile has six one-bedroom, and seven two-bedroom cottages. Cottages in the 501 -505 loop are in the wooded lodge area. Cottage 503 is a very special little tan-colored cottage with outdoor lighting and beautiful landscaping around the front entrance. It rests in a slight depression, away from the other cottages. Cottage 501 is at the end of the loop with picnic tables and privacy. They are all nice in this loop.

Cottages 508-515 are on the lake; each has a small green fishing and boat dock. Some of the cottages have fireplaces and screened porches. Cottage 508 has a great view and hugs the cliffline, looking down to the water's edge. Cottages 511-514 are directly on the water's edge and popular with guests who want to rent a boat and park it at their door step during their stay. These cottages require guests to park up on the hard-surfaced roadway about 40 yards above the cottages. All of these cottages have picnic tables and grills.

You can take a wandering stone stairway down to the brown wooden cabins that are nestled under tall trees. This loop of cottages is near the tennis courts and lake, but a fair distance from the lodge and other amenities. The Lake and Cane trail heads are accessed from the parking area for these cottages.

Campground: Perhaps the smallest campground store is at Pennyrile.

The landscaping at Pennyrile is one of the finest in the parks system.

Next to the older mini-golf course and playground—west of the lodge complex—the store loans popular board games to campers, sells ice and soft drinks, rents putty golf clubs, and offers information about the state park. The campground has 68 sites with utility hookups, a service building (laundry, showers, restroom and pay phone), two small playgrounds, and primitive camping near the store.

The most level and popular camping sites are 30-45. According to staff, site 30 is the most popular (sites 31-34 are also nice) in the park. Other good sites are 5-10. Most of the campground is lightly shaded. Finding level sites is the main thing to look for in the campground. Each site has picnic tables, grills and hard-surfaced pads.

The campground is always full on holiday weekends. The campground is open March 15 - Oct. 31.

Fishing: The 56-acre Pennyrile Lake—and the 760-acre Lake Beshear, managed by the Kentucky Department of Fish and Wildlife Resources, which has boat access off U.S. 62—are reasonably productive fishing lakes.

Pennyrile Lake has good numbers of largemouth bass, bluegill, and channel catfish. In lily pads and hydrilla beds, bass anglers use rubber worms and flipping, and light-colored buzz and spinnerbaits. Crappies are taken on live bait from shoreline access points. For the best chance of catching fish on this lake, plan on renting a small john boat.

Boating: Pedal boats and john boats with electric motors can be rented. Gasoline motors aren't allowed on the placid lake. There is no boat launching ramp on the lake.

Hiking: Great lodging, good meals, and quiet walks along the park's eight miles of trails (along eight trailways) are great ways to experience Pennyrile.

The difficult *Lake Trail* (1.75 miles) is the most popular trail, with a trailhead that descends from the lower parking lot of the lodge, along the lakeshore to the beach and beyond. Big boulders strewn along the water's edge and tall stairways ultimately lead hikers to a remote shelter for a rest. The trail circles the entire lake.

The Cane Trail (1.25 miles) is moderately difficult and connects to the Lake Trail. The trail is named for the patches of wild cane that can be seen at streamside in the lower reaches. After a moderately steep ascent to an upland forest ridge, the trail flattens out and passes through a mixed hardwood section of the forest.

From the *Pennyroyal Trail* (.75 mile) you may find some of the increasingly rare namesake wildflowers that are part of the mint family. You will meander along a creek, through an oak-hickory and a mixed evergreen-hardwood forest, and crest a ridgetop.

One shorter trails is the *Clifty Creek Trail* (.25 mile) which offers easy walking along the creek under a canopy of tulip poplars. Shagbark hickory trees control the skies. Some of the most beautiful sycamore trees are also along this trail, which crosses the spillway bridge, near a rock shelter and close to the masonry dam. *Camper's Trail* (.25 mile) connects the campground to the lodge. Hikers can visit the original homeplace of the areas first pioneer family on the *Thompson's Hollow Trail* (1/6 mile).

Day-use areas: The park features a series of special events annually that include Easter egg hunts, Christmas open house, photography weekends, New Year's celebration, and arts and crafts. Planned recreation activities include nature hikes, youth programs, mini-golf tournaments, court games, tennis lessons, crazy races, egg toss, sand blast volleyball tournaments, tot time, dinosaur egg hunt, movies and much more.

Next to the lodge is some newer play equipment for children that includes a red, green, and yellow tube slide, and a metal duck small kids can rock on. During the summer foosball and a couple of ping pong tables may be set up in this circular cement area. A small shuffleboard and horseshoe court is used in this mini-outdoor recreation area behind the lodge.

The two tennis courts are across the lake and on a hill. A basketball court is in the campground. Guests may check out tennis rackets, balls and other game equipment at the front desk.

Picnic tables are near the beach, and a rental shelter is available.

Golf: Can you manage your game? Then this is the "thinking man's" nine-hole course for you. Ponds and creeks criss-cross the fairways and well-conditioned greens are protected by sand traps on just about every hole. No. six is a suicide hole with two traps, water hazards, and a 75-yard uphill shot at the green. No. nine is also a touch hole, with water protecting the green. Most golfers need to lay up and take the easy approach shot to the oblong green.

Pennyrile Golf Course might be one of the best in the state park system. It's fairly flat, perfectly conditioned, and 3,270 yards long from the back tees. You can also enjoy seeing deer and wild turkey that often line up along the rough, watching duffers play through. The small pro shop rents clubs and carts, and sells limited supplies.

An older miniature golf course is near the entrance to the campground.

Swimming pool: The smaller pool for overnight guests features a sunning deck with umbrella tables in each corner and scattered deck furniture. The pool's deep end is eight feet deep. The pool is on the west end of the lodge.

Beach: Just south of the lodge is a small sandy beach for swimming that is open seasonally.

Nature: The American pennyroyal (Hedeoma pulegioides) is a pungently aromatic little annual, four to 18 inches high, sometimes called "pennyrile." It has given its name to a major part of the Mississippian Plateau, popularly call the "Pennyroyal."

The pale violet flowers average 1/8-inch to 1/4-inch long and scarcely surpass the calyx. They are arranged in clusters in the leaf axils. The elliptic leaves are up to one inch long. The small plant is commonly found in dry fields, along the roadside, and in open woods throughout the state, July through September. Pioneers used the fresh or dried leaves to make a strong mint-like tea (steep the leaves for 5-10 minutes). Today, all wildflowers in Kentucky state parks are protected by law.

A grove of white pines planted in 1973 is standing pencil-straight along the entrance road to the park. The successful plantation of trees now stands 40 feet tall or more. This and other reforestation efforts are under way.

Special notes: Hopkinsville has many interesting destinations for side trips, including the Pennyroyal Area Museum (502) 887-4270, special events and many other attractions. Call the Hopkinsville Tourism and Convention Commission at (800) 842-9959 for details.

The attention to the park's landscape is great at Pennyrile. If you enjoy colorful flower beds, manicured lawns, flower-lined walkways and lush hanging flower baskets, plan a trip soon.

37 *Perryville Battlefield State Historic Site*

Land: 100 acres

The bloodiest Civil War battle in Kentucky, the Battle of Perryville, sometimes called the Battle of Chaplin Hill, was fought Oct. 8, 1862, around the small town of Perryville in Boyle County. This was the largest military engagement to take place within the Commonwealth during the Civil War, pitting 16,000 Confederate troops against 58,000 Federal troops. The battle broke the back of the Confederacy's Kentucky campaign.

Confederates began the campaign in August 1862. By this time the Civil War was in its second year and the Confederates were weakening, especially west of the Appalachian Mountains. After many defeats including forts Henry and Donelson, and being driven out of Tennessee, their plan was to sweep around the eastern flank of the Federal army under Maj. Gen. Don Carlos Buell—whose troops were in middle Tennessee—-were to invade Kentucky. Fresh Kentucky recruits and considerable public support bolstered the effort. They believed that with Kentucky in their firm grip, they could bring a quick end to the war.

Information and Activities

Perryville Battlefield State Historic Site
1825 Mackville Road., P.O. Box 296
Perryville, KY 40468-9999
(606) 332-8631

Directions: Off U.S. 68 and U.S. 150, two miles north of Perryville. 12 miles west of Danville. The park gate closes at 9 p.m.

The Campaign: From Knoxville, Tenn., Maj. Gen. Edmund Kirby-Smith led a force of 20,000 Confederates into the mountains and foothills of southeastern Kentucky, fighting their way northward to control central Kentucky by the end of August 1862. Gen. Braxton Bragg led his 32,000-man Army of the Mississippi out of Chattanooga on Aug. 28.

By mid-September Bragg's troops got to Munfordville, Ky., and captured a Federal garrison of more than 3,000 men. Anticipating Confederate strategies, Buell took his 50,000 troops from middle Tennessee and rapidly moved back north into Kentucky. Bragg was forced to move northeast, while Buell reached Louisville, picking up 25,000 reinforcements. On Oct. 1 he set out to crush the Confederates. Buell, meanwhile, sent 20,000 troops to the east on Shelbyville Road as a tactical maneuver to occupy Kirby-Smith while he moved the bulk of his troops south toward Bragg's army at Bardstown.

Bragg had temporarily left his men under the command of Maj. Gen. Leonidas Polk and departed to Lexington to meet with Kirby-Smith. They installed Richard Hawes as the Confederate governor in Frankfort, hoping to further public support. When Buell neared Bardstown, Polk and the Army of Mississippi detoured through Springfield and Perryville. As

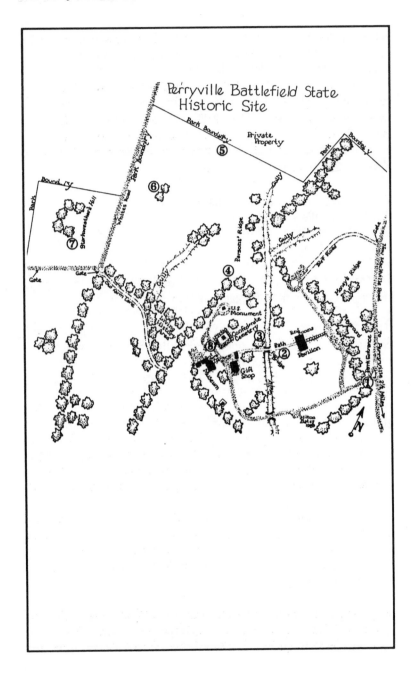

soon as Bragg learned of the move, he commanded both Confederate armies to Harrodsburg, anticipating to engage Buell at Salvisa.

Buell's troops moved through Bardstown after the Army of Mississippi and Polk. By nightfall on Oct. 7 his three corps were near Perryville. Buell was only three miles west of Perryville with other forces only a few miles away. Believing that both Confederate armies were now united in his front, Buell commanded both flank corps of 58,000 men to be ready to attack at dawn on Oct. 8.

Bragg was advised that the Federals had a large column marching toward Perryville on Oct. 7 and ordered Maj. Gen. William Hardee to stop his division at Perryville. Also that day Bragg ordered Polk to take a division back to Perryville, attack and destroy the Federal force, and return to Harrodsburg as soon as possible. The three divisions totaled 16,000 men. Polk and his men reached Perryville in the night and with word of additional Federal forces on their way, he decided not to attack in the morning as ordered by Bragg, but instead spent the dat adjusting his lines. Late that morning, Bragg arrived, hopping mad at the delay. He commanded Polk's men to cross the Chaplin River near Perryville, with an order to attack at 1 p.m.

The plan by Bragg was to open his attack against the Union north of Springfield Road, against their exposed flank. This would force the Federal army back upon themselves along the Mackville Road, where the Confederates could destroy them. For the Union, McCook's Corps arrived and established a line on the left of Gilbert's Corps. A variety of details had Buell hold off the attack that was originally set for dawn on Oct. 8. By midday Bragg had his troops in place and opened artillery fire.

Soon Polk launched an attack from the riverbed on the western bank, of the Chaplin River catching the Federals by surprise. The Confederates, after a desperate and bloody fight, drove back the Union left. Hardee followed up on Polk's move, driving McCook is right back about one mile, with heavy losses on both sides.

McCook's forces were scattered and Gilbert's Corps along Springfield Road was fighting off an attack by Col. Sam Powell's forces, forming the extreme left of Bragg's line. This almost suicidal attack proved that

The museum interprets the battle and Civil War history.

Bragg believed he was facing only a single Federal corps. Bloody hours later, when Buell learned about McCook's problems, he sent two brigades as reinforcements and they were able to halt the Confederate assault.

As darkness fell, the guns grew silent and the full moon lit the ghastly battlefield where the dead and dying of both sides lay everywhere. When Bragg realized he was facing Buell's main army, he fell back to Harrodsburg to unite with Kirby-Smith's army. The battle left Bragg with 510 dead and 2,635 wounded; on the Union side, 845 were killed and 2,851 wounded. Within days Bragg moved his troops back to Tennessee, ending the Kentucky campaign.

Museum: Open April - October, 9 a.m. - 5 p.m., there is a small admission fee. The museum is dedicated to the interpretation of the Civil War and the Battle of Perryville. Displays of interest include information about the operation and firing of cannons, authentic soldier clothing and equipment, camping equipment of the era, examples of weapons, cooking equipment, surgical kit—that included a nasty looking bonesaw—many photographs of men during the Civil War and much more.

Exhibits include examples of swords—officers purchased their own swords and uniforms—frock coats, revolvers, information on how cannons were aimed, cannon loading and its dangers, interesting quotes from officers and soldiers, and detailed information about the battle and the strategies of that fateful day.

Public restrooms are under the museum. The museum is air-conditioned and has two main rooms, located directly across from the Confederate cemetery.

Gift shop: Open 9 a.m. - 5 p.m. daily during the season. The small brown building has a Civil War theme offering mementos (flags, T-shirts, etc.) and information about the period. Videotapes and a good selection of Civil War history books are for sale. Next to the gift shop is a small picnic shelter. The gift shop may be closed during the noon hour.

Day-use areas: The park has plenty of picnic areas and a modern picnic shelter. The large expanses of gently rolling mowed open areas are maintained for reenactment activities that are conducted throughout the year. The sense of space—rolling hills and distant pastures and croplands— helps visitors visualize what a battle in this area might have been like. Historical markers, monuments, cannons and other interpretive signs are scattered around the park that is defined by a low split-rail fence.

Special notes: The main reenactment of the year is held each October closest weekend to the 8th. There are number of antique shops that specialize in Civil War items in the Perryville area.

38 Pine Mountain State Resort Park

Land: 1,520 acres

Pine Mountain is the oldest state park in Kentucky, created in 1924 in the heart of the Kentucky Ridge State Forest in southeastern Kentucky. Today, Pine Mountain is a modern resort surrounded by beautiful mountain scenery. With a unique lodge that displays a large collection of antique knives to modern cottages and rustic camping, the park is popular today, in part due to a rather zany past.

If you thought publicity stunts were only a modern phenomena, the story of Chained Rock, a popular feature at the east end of the park, will change your mind.

It started in the early 1930s when some local folklore turned into a PR stunt that was reported in more than 6,000 newspapers across the country.

According to the legend, children of the town of Pineville, nestled in a small valley below the park, and tourists were told that a huge rock hanging menacingly over the town could not give way and come tumbling down on the city because it had been "chained." This story allowed the town's youngsters to sleep soundly, assured that the boulder would not come crashing down on them in their sleep. In truth, however, the mighty rock had never been chained. Here lies the publicity stunt—for it soon was to be chained.

After reports that some visitors could not see the chain and often left town in a hurry, area resident Pat Caton set about turning the myth into reality. The rock then became a busy tourist attraction and anchor point of the state park.

Caton and his volunteers tried to find a chain "strong" enough to hold the rock and large enough to be seen from the town below. After considerable searching, a suitable jumbo-sized chain was found at a quarry in Hagan, Va. It had been part of a steam shovel owned by the Kentucky-Virginia Stone Company. The links are made of 1 3/8-inch steel and weigh seven pounds each. The chain weighs 1.5 tons and is 101 feet long.

The rusting chain was delivered to the foot of Pine Mountain. Four sturdy mules, harnessed single-file, began pulling one-half the chain up the mountain. When the mules became to tired too take another step, human volunteers form the Kiwanis Club, local Boy Scouts and members of the Civilian Conservation Corps took up the task of dragging the metal snake up the last yards to the summit.

Once at the top of the mountain the halves were welded together. Four-foot-long steel rods were hand-drilled and set into the rock. The chain was suspended between them, "chaining" the rock to the solid mountaintop. Using a triple-set block and tackle, "50 husky men and the spike team of mules tightened and set the chain...It was difficult to accomplish—It took all hands and the cook to do the job," according to an account by H. Handley Gaddie.

The job was accomplished on June 24, 1933. On that day the town became a safer place to live, and now, more than 60 years later, the chain holds fast and tourists still flock to see the secured sentinel over Pineville.

Information and Activities

Pine Mountain State Resort Park
1050 State Park Road
Pineville, KY 40977-0610
(606) 337-3066
(800) 325-1712 - toll-free reservations

Directions: Fifteen miles north of Middlesboro off U.S. 25 East in Pineville at the top of tree-covered Pine Mountain.

Lodge: The two-lane, dipping and diving roadway to the lodge is a tunnel of trees with scattered pulloffs and wonderful vistas of the distant mountains. It's about six miles from the turnoff near 119 up to the lodge.

In 1938 the first lodging facility and several small cottages were constructed. The current bilevel lodge was finished in 1963 and named for Herndon J. Evans, a community leader and parks supporter. The stone and wood craftsmanship throughout the 30-room lodge, dining and lobby areas is cozy and inviting, with two lobbies and fireplaces. You'll enjoy quiet moments and visits with family, friends or business associates. Each of the guest rooms has a private patio or balcony looking out to broad mountain views.

The dining room and gift shop are off the upper lobby that features unique lighted display cases filled with a large collection of antique pocket knives and other small cutting tools. The country-style gift shop features Kentucky handcrafts, books, rag dolls, pillows, candy and souvenirs just steps away from a big fireplace located under a timber-frame ceiling that lends a rustic and warming ambiance to the dining room.

A wall of windows and the aroma of fine Kentucky cuisine greet guests at the 216-seat dining room with a flag-stone porch and wicker furniture. Inside the bucolic lodge are private dining rooms and a larger meeting room featuring the artwork of Ray Harm. About 150 people can use the soothing peach-colored Ray Harm Room and enjoy the many framed artworks by the master nature painter.

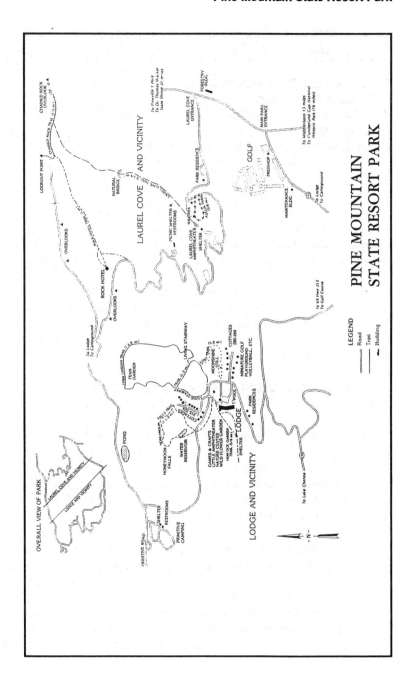

Tours of the historic Cumberland Gap are offered seasonally. The Recreation Room in the lodge is open 9 a.m. - 10 p.m. daily and features a pool table, foosball, video games and ping pong for overnight guests. A small swimming pool south of the lodge is open seasonally. Also nearby are the volleyball court, a basketball goal, small playground and miniature golf course.

Meeting facilities: The C.V. Whitney Convention Center, built in 1991, adjacent to the lodge can accommodate groups of 50 to 300. Food service is available. The wraparound porch from the lodge connects to the Whitney Convention Center and has seating and soft drink machines available.

Cottages: Well-kept, quiet, shady and near the lodge, each of the cottages offers a restful retreat nestled up and down a rolling wood line. Each of the cabins has screened-in porches and air-conditioning.

For families with small children, cottage 286 is across from a tiny playground and sandbox. Each of the cottages has picnic tables and a fire grill.

In the next loop, cottages 215-224 are up an abrupt hillside all the way up to a ridge line. Each of these small log-type cottages is built on a stone foundation. Many of the cottages in this loop have small decks or porches.

This loop is also a good quiet area for families with small children. The most charming little cabin is No. 215, a picture-perfect spot for a restful weekend getaway. All of the cottages are convenient to the lodge and its amenities. The cottages at Pine Mountain are some of the best in the state park system.

Campground: The modestly equipped (no electrical hook-ups) campground is open from April 1 - Oct. 30. Many sites have hard-surfaced pads and lots of shade. Nearby is a timber-framed day-use shelter. There is a small shower house with restrooms that services the rustic campground.

The 30-room lodge features antique displays and a lovely dining room.

Pine Mountains campground is so shady that moss and lichen carpet the forest floor, the bark of trees, and even the campground driveway. In loop 9-22 you will find that each camping site has fire boxes and picnic tables, and is shaded by mature trees. Sites in loop 23-34 are also very shady and each site has gravel pads and is best for tent campers. In fact, this is one of the better tent campgrounds in the system. RV rigs up to 35 feet can be squeezed into the facility.

Hiking: Pine Mountain has a topnotch four-page *Guide to Hiking Trails* that details 10 hiking paths. The publication is available at the lodge or park office.

The brochure starts like this: "It is an unexplainable tenet of wisdom that among the more simple and humble pursuits are nestled some of the most elevating human experiences. Such is the case with walking. Walking inevitably opens up new vistas on the world—granting us the opportunity to view life at a slower, more relaxed pace." The eight miles of trails at the park promise a "spiritual uplift and physical well-being."

Near the lodge you'll find six trails that include: Native Plant Garden (short and easy), Living Stairway (.5 mile, easy), Lost Trail (.5 mile, moderate), Hemlock Garden (5/8 mile., moderate), Fern Garden (1 3/8 miles, difficult), Honeymoon Falls (1.5 miles, difficult).

On the mountainous east side of the park you can hike the Azalea Trail (3/8 mile, easy), Chained Rock (.5 mile, difficult, one way), Rock Hotel (1 mile., difficult, one way), Laurel Cove (1 3/4 miles, strenuous, one way).

Pine Mountain has some of the better foot trails in the region, each offering varied terrain, natural features like huge yellow poplar on Living Stairway, sandstone shelter cliffs, rich forests of leathery rhododendron and airy hemlock, fragrant azalea plants along the Azalea Trail, huge boulders of sandstone, garden-like fern patches and countless species of songbirds and wildflowers.

Day-use areas: Chained Rock is about three miles from the lodge. The Laurel Cove area has some of the best day-use amenities, but there are also many small picnic and playground areas scattered around the park.

Golf: It's about five winding miles to the golf course from the lodge. The regulation course rents carts and clubs and is open year-round, weather permitting. The rolling and wooded nine holes will test your skills! Miniature golf is open April - October.

Nature: Nearly half of all the trees in this part of the 125-mile Pine Mountain range are Eastern hemlock, with some virgin stands that are more than 300 years old.

Special notes: The 3,000-seat Laurel Cove Amphitheater is home of the well-known Mountain Laurel Festival conducted each spring. The event was originally held to honor Dr. Thomas Walker, but has since been expanded to also celebrate the beautiful mountain laurel wildflower.

The annual Dulcimer Convention fills the park and the ears of visitors each September. Wilderness Road tours take guests to areas of great roads and settlements and the Cumberland Gap. Call (606) 248-2626.

39 Rough River Dam State Resort Park

Land: 637 acres   Water: 5,000 acres

Rough River Lake lies within the "Clifty" areas of the Pennyroyal region of Western Kentucky, an extensive, almost flat terrain formed by thick limestone beds and abundant water—both above and below ground—that helped form expansive caverns, sinks and other natural formations. The area is about 11,000 square miles.

Recreation on the lake is extensive and the general topography allows for the development of many man-made facilities. The lake, designed and built by the U.S. Army Corps of Engineers, serves as a unit of the comprehensive plan for the Ohio River Basin flood control program. The lake was authorized by the Flood Control Act of 1938. Construction was initiated in November 1955 and the dam became operational in June 1961.

The dam has earthen core and rock fill reaching 130 feet high, 1,590 feet long, 819 feet wide at its base, and drains an area of 454 square miles. The dam is on the Rough River 89.3 miles above its juncture with the Green River, six miles upstream from Falls of Rough.

The rugged beauty of this part of Western Kentucky has many interesting recreational points. From the blue-green lake to the 500-seat Pine Knob Summer Theater and Abraham Lincoln's Birthplace National Historical Site (502) 358-3137, the entire area is a delightful playground for the entire family.

In 1962 the state leased the ground at the dam, and built the lodge with overnight facilities that include 40 rooms, 15 two-bedroom cottages and 66 camping sites. The park is open all year. The marina is an important focal point of activity where 165 open slips, 30 house boat slips, and 48 covered slips serve the boating community.

Information and Activities

Rough River Dam State Resort Park
450 Lodge Road
Falls of Rough, KY 40119-9701
(502) 257-2311

Directions: 21 miles north of the Western Kentucky Parkway on KY 79. 43 miles southeast of Owensboro, 68 miles southwest of Louisville.

Lodge: A terrific view of the lake enhances the appeal of the stone and wood Rough River Dam Lodge that is perched above the lake on a low, linear ridge line. Each of the 40 rooms in the lodge has a patio or private balcony to enjoy the fresh air and scenery. You can also enjoy some fine Kentucky cuisine in the 167-seat dining room that opens at 7 a.m. daily. The restaurant has a pleasing atmosphere and wonderful lakefront views. Lodge room amenities include cable television, telephones, controlled heating and air-conditioners, shower and tub, and non-smoking rooms.

The gift shop, immediately on your left when you enter the lodge, is open Monday-Thursday, 9 a.m. - 6 p.m. and Friday-Sunday, 9 a.m.- 7 p.m. The compact gift shop features glassware, T-shirts, hats, wooden rocking chairs, post cards, craft items, stained glass and snacks. Hours do vary.

The polished wood floors of the lodge reflect from the huge copper hood over the open fireplace. For some indoor recreation, try the game room where four video games flash near a pool table and ping pong table.

The swimming pool is adjacent to the lodge where overnight guests from the cottages and lodge may enjoy a cooling dip. There are about 20 deck-side lounging chairs enclosed by a black metal fence that circles the small pool.

The day-use areas—fitness trail, blue-surfaced tennis courts, pool, beach, conference center and other amenities—are conveniently and centrally located near the lodge.

Meeting facilities: Rough River Dam specializes in modern and fine quality meeting spaces. The lobby meeting room has an excellent view of the lake. The pleasing colors of the Falls of Rough Conference Center and its ceramic tile lobby reflects the quality and explains the popularity of the conference space. The Grayson and Breckwridge Rooms can each accommodate 150 people for banquets. These rooms can easily be combined for banquets seating 300 guests. Audio-visual equipment is available for use during meetings.

Cottages: Fifteen two-bedroom luxury cottages are in a secluded wooded area near the lake. All of the units have basic supplies including tableware, cooking utensils, and linens provided daily. The cottages have cable television, shower and tub, screened-in porch, air-conditioning and lots more.

Cottages 207-215 are near the entrance off KY 79 and the airstrip. This loop of cottages is terrific for families with children. A small blue, yellow and brown set of play equipment stands ready for action by kids staying in the cottages. The dense grove of mature trees provides lots of shade

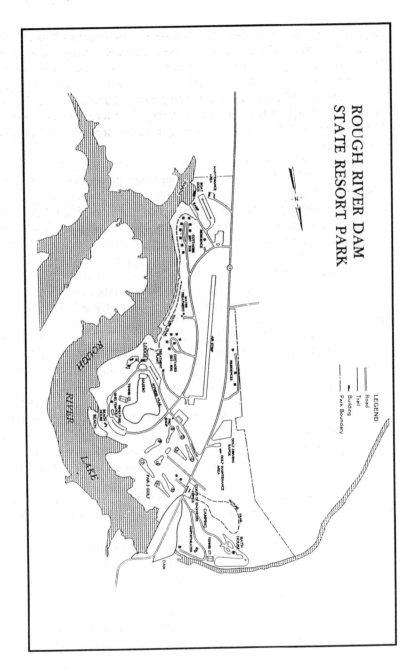

ROUGH RIVER DAM
STATE RESORT PARK

LEGEND

Road
Trail
Building
Park Boundary

and that special feeling that makes a stay in the Rough River Lake cabins memorable. The wood-frame cottages have picnic tables and grills, but little grass.

The most private of the cottages in this loop is 212. In addition it has a "through-the-trees" view of the busy and brightly colored marina and docks. Cottages 213 and 214 have a long-distance view of the water-based action.

Cottages 201-206 are sited in a gently rolling area with occasional steep hills. For dense shade, try cottage 203, with 204, 205 and 206 having wooded forest views and picnic tables and grills in the small side yards. Both of the cabin loops are only a few steps from the nature trail that connects to the lodge and wanders along the shoreline.

Campground: Campers will enjoy the quality of the campground along the lake. All 66 sites can hookup to utilities. Not all of the camping sites have hard-surfaced pads, but they all do have picnic tables and grills and are near the service building.

Campers with larger rigs will want to consider sites, 32, 34, 35 and 36, and the pull-through sites, 42-47. Also in the campground are two tennis courts, a basketball court and a volleyball court.

For privacy-seekers, try site four. Sites 22 and 23 (and other sites) are elevated and look down upon the pull-through sites. Many of the sites in the campground are small, others are not very shady, but all are clean and fairly level. The campground is about 60 percent shady. The campground check-in office has ice and firewood for sale.

Emergency numbers: 1-259-8200; fire and rescue, 257-8200.

Fishing: The lake has many rock outcroppings and is tree-lined along its 67 miles—and 4,860 acres—as it bisects Breckinridge, Hardin and Grayson counties. About 60 species of fish can be found in the long, narrow and meandering manmade lake.

Good numbers of spotted and largemouth bass are taken near the dam, where fishing pressure is high. Because of the increasing number of boaters and anglers on the lake, many locals fish almost exclusively at night. Night or day, try the bridge piers, rip rap, or rock banks where, unfortunately, it is likely many other anglers have already beat the water into a foam. Work a little harder and try finding stumps, scattered rock piles on flats near submerged creek channel drops, and any other structures that other anglers may have missed or passed up. The old river channel is also a good pattern.

Typical lures to try should include plastic worms, small spinnerbaits, jigs and buzzbaits.

In the busy summer season, try for other species than bass, or travel to the upper reaches of the lake and fish near the creek mouths. When in these areas try for walleye in deep water, white bass or panfish. Look for standing timber that holds both bass and bluegill. Drift fishing in the summer with a cricket at 15-25 feet depths off points or casting small spinners is a great way to catch a mess of bluegills.

South of the park, at the mouth of Cave Creek and the mouth of North Fork, are excellent catfishing areas. Cut baits, stink baits, liver and doughballs are used to bring in the cats.

A recreation/fishing map of Rough Lake and adjacent areas is available for a small fee from Room 64, Federal Building, Louisville, Ky., or write the District Engineer, U.S. Army Corps of Engineers, Louisville, Attn.: CEORL-LM-S, P.O. Box 59, Louisville, Ky., 40201-0059. There are also commercially available lake maps from area bait and tackle shops.

Local pan fishermen preferred redworms—they don't nibble off the hook easily—for bluegill (panfish) in Rough River Lake.

Creel limit: Crappies, 9-inch minimum length, 30 per day.

Boating: The south entrance of the park takes you directly to the Rough River Dam State Resort Park marina. The launching ramp is one of the widest in the entire state park system, measuring nearly 50 yards in width. Two temporary mooring docks are conveniently located at the base of the ramp, which is in a quiet cove-like area near the main docks.

From the small yellow marina shop you may rent fishing boats, ski tubes and pontoon boats, and tie up overnight if you like. Ice, lots of live bait and tackle, snacks, and other marine supplies (batteries, oil, tie-downs, plugs, etc.) are sold at the store. Pontoon boats are popular at the smooth lake that meanders through once-wooded valleys. Reservations can be made in advance for boats. You may use your credit card. Call (502) 257-2311.

Excursion boat: The "Lady of the Lake," a rear-wheel, miniature version of a steamboat, chugs over the clear lake daily during the summer, offering visitors a chance to see the rugged shoreline, wildlife and the activity on the lake. There is a fee for the tour.

Canoeing: Rough River isn't. The river is generally high-banked and shaded with willow and mixed hardwoods and can be paddled virtually all year. The most scenic stretches, especially during the fall color times, are from the tailwaters to Falls of the Rough, and from the Falls of the Rough to the KY 54 bridge. These routes have minor ripples. Use local knowledge to find access points and stay clear of the dam.

Airstrip: The newly extended and re-surfaced 3,200-foot lighted airstrip with tie-downs and aviation fuel is popular with sport flyers. A shuttle service is offered from the air strip to the lodge. Pilots may contact the state park at (800) 325-1713. An air-conditioned lounge at the airport is open much of the time for pilots using the facility. The airport elevation is 577 feet. Air camping is restricted to the grassy areas only (for a small fee).

Airplane rides are offered on the weekends, Saturday, 7 a.m. - 8 p.m. and Sunday, 9 a.m. - 7 p.m. There is a fee for the ride.

Day-use areas: Game courts near the beach offer overnight guests and day-use visitors plenty of options for play. From tennis courts to shuffleboard, sports equipment—including bike rentals—are available for checkout. The shuffleboard is on the patio near the dining room at the lodge.

The miniature golf course—which is one of the oldest in the parks system—is near the beach by the edge of the fitness trail and features a

Cool off at the small beach or the swimming pool.

tiny building that oversees and straddles the carpeted fairways. There is plenty of parking in this day-use area, which includes a number of playground apparatus that are popular with the youngsters. You can see the dam, water and lodge from this day-use area.

Planned recreation programs are offered daily during the summer time. A variety of annual special events are hosted at the park, such as a Humor Festival, Old-Time Fiddlers Contest and more. Regularly scheduled activities include lake tours, putting contests, bingo, children's storytelling, Kentucky trivia, chalk art, driving range contest, Frisbee toss, crafts and much more.

Beach: Three lifeguards patrol the small sandy beach on a tiny point reaching into Rough River Lake. The beach is about 50 yards wide. A well-used sand volleyball court is nearby.

Golf: A mere 100 yards from the end of the airstrip is the gently rolling, nine-hole, par 3 golf course. Well-maintained, the executive course has large well-conditioned greens, lake views, hard-surfaced cart paths, and one fairway carved into an area with plenty of rock outcroppings. The golf course operates a driving range for those of you who want to whack the long ball after a round.

Nature trails: Behind the Corps of Engineers' office, north of the golf course off KY 79, is a terrific self-guided nature trail. A handy, yellow-covered, 40-page booklet details all of the stops along the Folklore Nature Trail.

The first pages of the informative little booklet talk about making moonshine by diagramming a typical still and detailing its parts. "She was only a moonshiner's daughter, but I love her still." The book also identifies poison ivy. There are lots of interesting facts to learn.

Some of the following is taken from the Corps' *Folklore Nature Trail* booklet: Flowering dogwood was used to make a tonic and the bark to made red dye. A type of toothbrush was make from peeled twigs and then rubbed on the teeth to produce a whitening effect—yummy. Sassafras was also chewed to whiten teeth and pioneers believed it thinned the blood and cured lung fevers, dropsy, stomach problems, ulcers, skin troubles, sore eyes and gout. The bark of sassafras was also boiled and used as a shampoo to kill head lice and to soothe the nerves of alcoholics.

Sassafras, The Cure All

In the spring of the year when the blood is too thick,
There is nothing so fine as a sassafras stick.
It tones up the liver, and strengthens the heart,
And the whole system, new life doth impart.

Did you know the tulip tree is the tallest tree in the Eastern United States?

Black walnut, a very commercial species today, was an important decay-resistant and easily split wood used by pioneers. The husk surrounding the nut was used to make a rusty-black die and to cure ringworm. People with mental instabilities were also encouraged to eat walnuts—this must be why I love walnut covered brownies!

Spicebush were used to make tea and the twigs of the bush were placed on the bottom of a pan when cooking opossum (yum!). Some pioneers also used the twigs when cooking bear and venison to "soften the wild taste."

For those of you who need a laxative, try a tea made from slippery elm. According to the government-produced booklet, it would also cure stomach disorders, the pain of childbirth, colds and alcoholism. Today, the inner bark of the slippery elm is used to make cherry flavoring in some cough medicines. You'll also learn about the many uses of maple trees, beside maple syrup, including their use in making fiddles and guitars, spoons, butter molds, gunstocks and drawer handles.

Early builders used honey locust—one of the hardest of woods that was decay resistant—to make pegs, dowels, foundation blocks, floor sleepers, fence posts, floating bridges, axles and wagon pillars. The thorns of the honey locust were used as pins, spear points and in animal traps.

White ash trees were considered the best material for rolling pins, yokes, and the handles of hoes and shovels. Hickory was one of the best burning woods, used in fireplaces and for smoking meats. The ashes from hickory logs were used to make homemade lye soap. Thin branches from the hickory were also used as switches in the classrooms of early schools. Ouch!

Special notes: Stop at the U.S. Army Corps of Engineers' office for additional information about camping and other recreational amenities in the area.

40 Taylorsville Lake State Park

Land: 1,625 acres   Water 3,050-acre lake

Taylorsville Lake has some of the best and most productive fishing waters in the state. Nestled in the rolling hills of central Kentucky, the lake takes its name from the nearby town of Taylorsville, which was founded in 1799 and named after Richard Taylor. He was the proprietor of a grist mill and a large landowner. Taylor donated 60 acres of his land at the mouth of the Brashears Creek, which is now occupied by the town and marked the beginning of the recreation area development.

The Salt River, which is now largely controlled by the dam, was named by the early settlers because of a number of salt works which were operated along its banks during the 1800s. For many years salt-making activities took place in the area, due to deposits along this northern range of prehistoric salt licks and terrain. Interestingly, the typical salt operation produced about 50 pounds of salt from 400 gallons of water from the river. But even this production level was good enough, as salt deposits farther west were exploited.

Taylorsville Lake was designed and built by the U.S. Army Corps of Engineers as a flood control project offering general recreation, good fishing and water conservation. Construction on the dam began in the summer of 1974, with impoundment in the winter of 1983. The dam is made from rock and earth fill, reaching a height of 163 feet and a length of 1,280 feet. The drainage area above the dam is 352 square miles. The dam cost $28.8 million to build.

Two of the most important reasons to have the dam are water management and topsoil conservation. The dam ensures adequate water supply, protects against flooding, and helps to reduce topsoil loss and water pollution. The Taylorsville State Park is a great example of a governmental partnership that works—offering quality recreation opportunities while providing a needed service.

Information and Activities

Taylorsville Lake State Park
1320 Park Rd.
Mt Eden, KY 40046
(502) 477-8713
(502) 477-8766 - marina

Directions: 45 minutes southeast of Louisville, 48 miles west of Lexington, and 30 miles southwest of Frankfort. Take I-64 to Gene Snyder Freeway south. Exit at KY 155 to Taylorsville, turn east on KY 44, and drive three miles to the park entrance. There is no camping at this state park.

Information: The newer park office has a brochure rack, interesting aerial photo of the vicinity, restrooms and staff who can answer questions. The ranger's office is also located in this building. The office hours are from 10 a.m. - 2 p.m., but the doors are open longer for access to the restrooms and water fountain.

Corps of Engineers visitor center: East of the state park is the Corps visitor center, which offers a view of the two million cubic yards of earthen dam and tower, brochure racks and a small 18-foot-square interpretive room filled with displays and exhibits. Educational information includes a tree identification display (you lift up the leaf to learn the tree species), boating safety exhibit, aquatic ecology diorama, a "You Be the Operator of the Dam" board display that teaches the importance of expert dam operation, many native animal mounts, nesting box samples, and a very large and interesting hickory tree slab that acts as a timeline. The tree segment was cut down in 1981 and the growth rings are labeled with numbers that match displayed time frames. The oldest tree ring dates to 1861, during the Civil War, this tree was a young sapling.

The center is open weekdays, 7:30 a.m. - 5:30 a.m. and weekends, 10:30 a.m. - 6:30 p.m. There is a day-use area with picnic tables and grill east of the building.

The modern-looking, pyramid-shaped building has a brown metal roof that almost touches the ground and houses plenty of information about the lake and its environs. Interpretive signs detail the dam, its operations, its importance to the area, how the pool is maintained, matters about flooding, and much more.

Fishing: Taylorsville Lake, with about 75 miles of shoreline, is 18 miles long, offering about 3,050 acres of water surface to fish.

The impoundment, unlike many others, was designed to be a good fishing lake long before dam construction began. Kentucky fish biologists learned their lesson well from reservoirs that were not well thought out as they relate to fish management. Considerable planning and many efforts were initiated to maximize the lake and minimize the anticipated heavy fishing pressure from nearby metropolitan areas.

The first thing the biologists did was impose a 15-inch size limit, which helped postpone heavy harvests until the bass were established. The Salt River was also studied to carefully evaluate the species, habitats and populations. These studies helped develop a comprehensive fish stocking program. Biologists also carefully selected areas where the dam contractor would build fish-attracting sites. Nineteen brush and three truck-tire

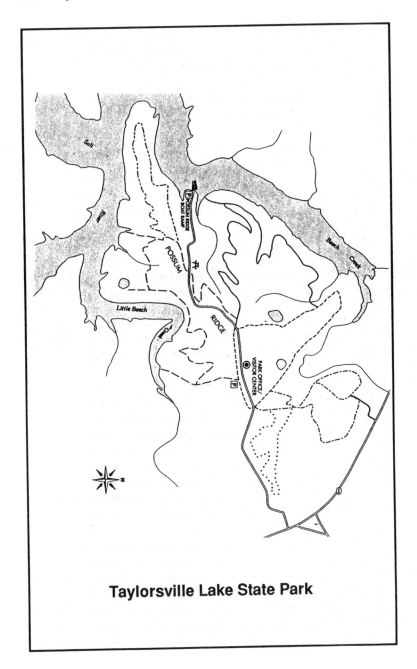

Taylorsville Lake State Park

fish attractors were placed. These artificial supplements, in concert with the flooded timber and other natural cover, have helped make the lake a long-lasting productive fishery.

Attractor sites are around the entire lake, usually near the mouths of creeks in 15-20 feet of water. There are no shallow water attractor sites.

Maybe the most important strategy was to stock multiple-year classes of bass. The first planting was 15,000 fingerling bass in 1983. The lake is well-known for its bass fishing. The lake is truly a classic bass lake with wide broad flats, large stands of flooded timber, thick weedbeds, road-beds, old building foundations, fence rows and the old river channel. Some embayments also have flooded stumps, stick-ups and weed flats.

The bottom is usually mud. There are scattered outcroppings of shoreline rock, where casting at the shale wall can bring up suspended largemouth bass. These bucket-mouth bass are active in the spring and fall, with summer fishing slacking off somewhat. Shad-pattern, orange, white and chartreuse crankbaits fished over points and flooded brush on the flats works well in most parts of the lake. Fish the flooded timber and weedbeds with black, black and purple, or purple plastic worms.

The lake is also an excellent panfishery. Good to excellent catches of bluegill can be taken with waxworms, meal worms, crickets, or tiny jigs along the flooded timber and other structures. Crappie and catfish can also be taken in good numbers. There are many shoreline fishing access points around the lake.

Creel limits: Largemouth bass, 15-inch minimum size, six per day; smallmouth bass, 15-inch minimum size, six per day; white bass, 15-inch minimum size, five per day; crappie, no size limit, 15 per day.

Marina/boating: The Taylorsville Dock is a full-service marina that is open year-round and offers boat rental (pontoon and fishing), slip rentals for houseboats, cruisers, pontoons, and runabouts, and a marina store with gasoline, oil and ice. The small store also has boating accessories, grocery supplies, deli and mechanical services. Call (502) 477-8766 for additional information. There is no motor size restriction on the lake, and next to the marina is an excellent—and busy—two-lane boat launching ramp with plenty of parking.

There are three other ramps on the lake. The Possum Ridge Boat Ramp, west of the state park office, pitches steeply to the water's edge. Two wooden-planked temporary mooring docks are at the foot of the hard-surfaced ramp. There are no rest rooms or day-use areas at this launching ramp.

Hiking: The terrain is gently rolling, with many open fields. The mixed meadows and open spaces near mature timber stands offer hikers an excellent place to birdwatch, look for wildflowers, or just stretch your legs along the park's five trails totaling 17.3 miles. The trails are closed to all bikes and motorized vehicles. Hikers should yield to horseback riders.

The two-mile-long Salt River Vista Loop can be accessed from the Little Beech Loop and offers hikers a waterside hike on a land peninsula near the Possum Ridge Boat Ramp. The 2.7-mile Beech Creek Loop A passes by two small ponds and circles the park's office. The 3.7-mile Possum Ridge Loop has lots of switchbacks and meanders along Beech Creek and up and down some hilly terrain through mixed woodlots and scattered fields.

Bridle trails: Equestrians have a small staging area, with parking and hitching off the main park road at the trailhead entrance. There are no horse rentals at the park. Horses must stay on established trails, which are mowed and lightly used.

Hunting: Hunting is popular in the greater Taylorsville Lake area. Check with the Kentucky Fish and Wildlife hunting guide and the park's staff for details. Species hunted include deer, dove, woodcock and waterfowl. Hunters are required to check in at specified sites on a daily basis. To report poaching, call (800) 252-5378.

Special notes: Near the park is a full service, privately operated campground. You may purchase recreation/fishing maps of Taylorsville Lake and adjacent areas based on USGS topographical sheets from the District Engineer, U.S. Army Engineer District, Louisville, KY, Attn.: CEORL-LM-S, P.O. Box 59, Louisville, Ky., 40201-0059.

41 Waveland State Historic Site

Land: 10 acres

Tall trees seem to touch the clouds around the manicured lawn that flows from the parking lot to day-use areas, and surrounds the L-shaped Greek Revival antebellum mansion. Waveland's gigantic Ionic columns, high ceilings, spacious rooms, wide halls and verandahs are impressive architecturally. So are the builders and heirs of the huge brick home south of Lexington.

Built in 1847, Waveland derives its name from waves of plants blowing in the wind. When the Bryan family accompanied Daniel Boone through the Cumberland Gap to the bluegrass region, they established one of the Commonwealth's first settlements, Bryan's Station.

Daniel Boone allegedly surveyed the terrain for his nephew and namesake, Daniel Boone Bryan, who was an Indian fighter, poet and historian. Young Bryan occupied the 2,000-acre site in the late 1770s and initially built a simple stone house. During the rest of his life he developed the tract into a picture-perfect plantation with blacksmith shop, gunsmith shop, distillery, gristmill, paper mill, female seminary and a Baptist church. Daniel Bryan died in 1845.

Joseph Bryan, Daniel's son, inherited his father's wealth and property and built the historic mansion where the elder's stone house once stood. The Greek Revival masterpiece was home to his wife, Margaret Cartwell, and their five children.

The state of Kentucky purchased the land in 1956 for an agricultural research station. In 1957, the mansion and immediate environs were dedicated as a Kentucky life museum, and in 1971 the lovely homeplace was deeded to the state parks system.

Information and Activities

Waveland State Historic Site
225 Higbee Mill Road
Lexington, KY 40514-4778
(606) 272-3611

Directions: Six miles south of Main Street in Lexington. off U.S. 27 (Nicholasville Road.).

Waveland: The red roof and red-brick exterior walls are the perfect colors and textures for Waveland's elegant design, historical significance and location. The Greek Revival architectural style was popular in the state during the mid-1800s. The bold construction style features grand symmetry, granite steps and a tall, graceful Ionic-column portico.

Waveland exemplifies plantation life in Kentucky in the 1840s. From the mixture of outbuildings that include slave quarters, log cabin, ice house to the formal gardens, porch, smokehouse and deluxe landscaping, Waveland reminds us of the pleasant—and not so pleasant—social climate of the time.

Inside the house are displays of dishware, silver, period clothing, children's toys, needlework, personal effects, handwritten letters, Sheraton and Empire-style furniture, common utensils, tools, and many family heirlooms. From these materials and the tour, guests will get a clear insight into social customs and family life of the privileged Kentucky family of the mid-19th century.

Joseph's son, Joseph Henry Bryan, the next heir to the plantation, had a taste and talent for blooded trotting and pacing horses. He constructed a race course and amphitheater near the estate, and bred and raced many world class horses. One of his most famous was "Wild Rake," a multiple winner that became famous, especially after his sale to William Rockefeller for $7,800.

In 1894, Waveland passed out of the Bryan family.

Tours: Inside the Waveland home is like stepping back into the mid-19th century. The period furniture, hardwood floors, elegant draperies and displays of historical treasures help guests learn about the Bryan family's lifestyles. Tours of the house, outbuildings and gardens are offered March 1 - mid-December, Monday-Saturday 10 a.m. - 4 p.m. and Sundays 2-5 p.m. The interpretive tours last about one hour. There is an admission fee.

Traditional Christmas at Waveland mansion: Maybe the best time to visit the Waveland house is at Christmas time, when the entire house is carefully decorated in 19th century fashion. Delicate ornaments and memories of Christmas are in each of the grand public spaces. The weeklong holiday event features a visit by the Bryan "family." "Mrs. Bryan" and her "grandchildren" visit with guests while refreshments are served and holiday carols play in the background. There is an admission fee.

Day-use areas: The rolling and lush Lexington countryside helps make this a special place for a tour or a picnic on the lawn. A small play area (with youth-sized playhouse) and picnic tables are popular during the warm weather months.

42 White Hall State Historic Site

Land: 13 acres

White Hall, with its gleaming white pillars and ornate trim work, is a crown-like mansion perched atop a rise surrounded by mature hardwoods and small outbuildings from another era. White Hall State Historic Site not only preserves architectural history, also commemorates one of Kentucky's most colorful and historical figures, Cassius Clay, a noted abolitionist, Congressman, statesman and friend to Abraham Lincoln.

The towering brick house called White Hall is actually a house within a house. The "old building," as Cassius Clay referred to the home of his father, Green Clay, was built in 1798-1799 in the Georgian style. The "new" house—White Hall—was built above and around the old building—called Clermont by Cassius in the 1860s. Also of brick, it's a wonderful melding of Georgian and Gothic-Revival-style architecture with Italianate influences.

Clermont had clean design. It was utilitarian and the center of Green Clay's expansive empire which included distilleries, taverns, farms and a ferry service that crossed the Kentucky River. Clermont was a two-story home, with the first floor consisting of a large hallway on one side, a sturdy bearing wall bisecting the structure, dining room and parlor with stairways leading to the second floor. On the second floor were four bedrooms. All seven rooms had fireplaces.

When Cassius Clay visited Russia in the 1860s, he hired architect Thomas Lewinski and builder-architect John McMurty to design and build the ambitious addition. After careful consideration, the new portion of the home was designed so the first floor elevation matched the existing house and old stairways were cleared.

A number of innovations and noteworthy features were incorporated into the design of the house including a wide sweeping stairway of 30 steps, 16-foot-tall ceilings, and a forerunner of central heating, fueled by two fireboxes in the basement with ducts leading to fireplaces in several rooms of the newer section of the house.

The addition also brought the bathroom indoors, divided into three closets, one containing a wash basin, another a commode, and the third a bathtub made of a hollowed-out poplar log lined with copper. Another innovation was that rain water from the roof was funneled into a collection tank on the upper floor of the home and then piped into the bathroom on the floor below.

The house has more than 30 rooms. Upon Clay's death the house went to the Federal Government due to back taxes. Two of his grandchildren purchased the property and rented it to farmers until 1966. In July 1968 the Commonwealth bought the house and began restoration. During the work state officials found two portraits—one of Russian Czar Alexander II and one of a beautiful Russian ballerina. The park opened to the public in 1971.

Information and Activities

White Hall State Historic Site
500 White Hall Shrine Road
Richmond, KY 40475-9159
(606) 623-9178

Directions: From I-75 take Exit 95 at the end of KY 627. Near Richmond in central Kentucky.

Cassius Marcellus Clay: Born in 1810, Clay was an emancipationist, diplomat, the son of a general, and in later years called the "Lion of White Hall."

Clay earned a law degree from Transylvania University and was impressed early in his career by an anti-slavery speech by William Lloyd Garrison. From that time, he launched many outspoken attacks on slavery and aroused bitter hostility, especially among pro-slavery factions of the Whig party. This position occasionally got him into fights. In 1841 he fought a duel with Robert Wickliffe Jr.; neither was hurt. Two years later, Clay was attacked by a reputed hired assassin, who shot at him. According to the story, Clay whipped out his bowie knife and severely wounded the assailant.

After more fights and angry abolitionist speeches, he decided to start his own newspaper, The True American, in Lexington. We choose a sturdy brick building and lined the outside doors with "sheet iron to keep it from being burned." He also said, "I purchased two brass four-pounder cannons...and placed them, loaded with shot and nails, on a table breast high; had folding doors secured with chain, which could open upon a mob, and give play to my cannon...I furnished my office with Mexican lances, and a limited number of guns."

Clay also installed a trap door in the roof and placed a keg of gun powder "with a match, which I could set off, and blow up the office and all my invaders." A committee was organized to suppress the paper, but Clay fell sick with typhoid fever; during his absence a posse, including James B. Clay, packed the newspaper equipment and moved it to Cincinnati.

Undaunted, Clay published from Cincinnati for a time, and later won a judgment of $2,500 against the committee.

After serving as a captain in the Mexican War, Clay returned to Lexington in 1847 and continued his civil rights advocacy, often speaking in the North and eventually corresponding with abolitionists John G. Fee. Clay eventually secured 10 acres of land for Fee in Madison County, where he began a church-school community that ultimately grew to become Berea College.

Clay began a vigorous campaign in the North and in 1860 his photograph appeared in Harper's Weekly along with nine other likely presidential candidates. Clay ultimately supported Lincoln and after the 16th presidents election was appointed minister to Russia. He loved to wine and dine the Russians, impressing the Czar and acting out the statesman's role to perfection. Clay's cultivation of relations with Russia helped bring about the U.S. purchase of Alaska.

Clay returned from Russia for the last time in 1869 to pioneer the Liberal Republican movement and face the fact that his absence from home was destroying his long marriage to Mary Jane, the mother of his 10 children. It wasn't until 1870 that Cassius returned to White Hall, where according to Clay the atmosphere in Kentucky was a great deal more frigid than that of New York: "On my return home, she (Mary Jane) ventured to treat me as a stranger—putting me in a separate room; and, when the weather turned suddenly cold, she moved my clothes, without consulting me, into another room in the new house, where the fireplace was unfinished...and the cold was so intense that icicles froze on my beard."

A short time later Mary Jane left White Hall for good. His 45-year marriage was over. After other family problems, Clay created a sensation in 1894, when at the age of 84 he married a 15-year old tenant farmer's daughter, Dora Richardson.

The community got so upset at Clay that Judge John Cabell Chenault sent a posse to White Hall to demand that old Cassius surrender the girl. Upset, Clay touched off his cannon filled with nails and tacks, jagged horse-shoes, pieces of harrow spikes, grated lead and various nuts and bolts, at the posse.

The leader of the posse, Sheriff Josiah P. Simmons, wrote to Judge Chenault about the incident: "I am reporting about the posse like you said I had to. Judge, we went out to White Hall but we didn't do no good. It was a mistake to go out there with only seven men. Judge, the general (Cassius Clay) was awful mad..."

Alas, Clay's marriage to young Dora lasted only two years, and he was alone again, seemingly becoming more eccentric and suspicious as the years passed. Even his own relatives were warned to approach White Hall at their own risk. Clay barricaded himself in the 30-room house, reportedly firing his cannon at would-be visitors, earning the sobriquet, "the Lion of White Hall."

It's reported that when a sheriff tried to arrest Clay in 1901 for non-payment of taxes, he reportedly shouted from the bastion, "Why should I pay taxes? I get no protection."

Another couple of years passed. Clay became bedridden and close to death. According to the park's interpretive folder, on the night of July 22, 1903, a tornado struck central Kentucky. Buildings were damaged, floods occurred, church steeples in Richmond were toppled, and a statue of Henry Clay in the Lexington cemetery was struck by lightning. On that violent night, Cassius Marcellus Clay, Lion of White Hall, passed away quietly, finally at peace.

If you would like to learn more about the amazing life of Cassius Clay, biographies by H. Edward Richardson and David L. Smiley are wonderfully entertaining volumes.

Tours: The wonderful rolling farmland dotted with tobacco barns and grazing livestock is surpassed only by the professional quality tour of the house. Costumed guides will share with visitors the historical treasures of White Hall and the sometimes zany Clay family. The house was restored in the late 1960s, and open to the public in September 1971.

Guests will have an opportunity to experience the aura of the 1860s, complete with period furnishings and pieces original to the Clay estate.

Gift shop: The cozy shop is open daily April 1- Oct. 31.

43 William Whitley House State Historic Site

Land: 10 acres

On a small rise just south of highway 150, the William Whitley House stands today as a monument to pioneer ingenuity and resourcefulness. The stately home is the oldest brick house west of the Alleghenies and was built by pioneer, Indian fighter and horseman William Whitley in 1787.

From the delicate dentil moldings and frieze board of the cornice along the roof's edge and red bricks that were fired on site and laid in a Flemish bond to the poplar floors, the William Whitley House has endured for 200 years. For a time, the unique home was called "Sportsmen's Hill," referring to the nearby horse racing track. Visitors will make no mistake they are at the Whitley house when they see the "WW" letters made from glazed brick embedded over the front entrance.

These initials and the EW initials on the back of the house are typical of houses in New Jersey and Virginia, which were patterned after buildings in Salem and Gloucester, England. When initials and dates were incorporated in the exterior cladding of the structure, it was usually a way to establish and announce a family dynasty. Whitley got the idea when traveling in Virginia in 1786.

Whitley built the house with exceptionally thick walls. The windows are high above the ground, indicating he was concerned about the safety of his family. In fact, one room is windowless so the women and children would be safe (there is also a secret staircase leading to the upstairs). Glass for the relatively few windows of the two-story house was brought in through the Cumberland Gap by mule pack.

The interior of the house is of walnut and pine fielded paneling. The S-shaped carvings over the fireplace, the crown moldings and chair railings throughout the house and eagle carvings are evidence that Whitley demanded quality and found skilled craftsmen to do much of the work.

The main floor of the house contains three rooms and a large hall, two rooms and a hall on the second floor, and a large attic, with windows, over the entire house. Just left of the entrance is the high-ceilinged family room with its 13 S-shaped wooded carvings over the fireplace. Across the hall is the dining room with Whitley's gun closet in one corner, and behind that is a smaller room which is thought to have been the original kitchen.

The main stairway connecting the lower and upper halls is beautifully carved and decorated with eagles holding olive branches. The second floor may be reached by a hidden stairway or ladder leading from the kitchen to the west bedroom on the floor above. The attic was also a semi-secure place to hide if Indians attacked.

The house, known as the "Guardian of Wilderness Road," was a busy respite for overland travelers including Isaac Shelby, Daniel Boone and George Rogers Clark. The house became part of the Kentucky state parks system on Feb. 25, 1938.

Information and Activities

**William Whitley House State Historic Site
625 William Whitley Rd., P.O. Box 232
Stanford, KY 40484-9770
(606) 355-2881**

Directions: Take Exit 62 off I-75. South of U.S. 150 (and Lexington), two miles west of the town of Crab Orchard. The house museum is open daily, June - August 9 a.m. - 5 p.m., September-May, closed on Mondays. Closed January 1 - March 16.

William Whitley, 1749-1813: In late autumn 1775, Richard Henderson with a party of 40 men were making a second trek to Boonesborough. As the group hurried through the Cumberland Gap and were descending near Yellow Creek, they overtook two small families who where leaving their safe homes in the lush valleys of Virginia for the frontier of the Cumberland foothills. One of the men was leading the way with two small girls, ages one and three. He strided with strength and character. He was pioneer William Whitley.

Whitley was born a son of Irish immigrants, the eldest of four sons (he was said to have five sisters) on Aug. 14, 1749 in Augusta County, Va.

In early spring 1776 Whitley made his first trip into Kentucky, selected a place to settle and return bringing his young family on the 30-day trip to the Cedar Creek. After difficult land clearing, and nearby Indian activity, the Whitleys eventually sought a safe haven at Harrodsburg. There the Whitleys' third child was born.

The family weathered a siege on the fort and Whitley recaptured his horses and learned how to fight the Indians. He eventually joined Captain John Montgomery's volunteer Kentucky company and accompanied George Rogers Clark on his invasion of the Northwest. By early 1779, things had quieted down, and Whitley moved his family back to his station where he completed rebuilding and found that his location on Wilderness Road make a logical place for those who were returning to Virginia to obtain supplies.

In June 1779—Whitley, ever a believer in attacking Indians on their own ground—coordinated with his old friend Logan and raised a company which joined with the forces of Kentucky's County Lieutenant, John Bowman, at the mouth of the Licking River for an attack on the Shawnees. Because Whitley had previously been to Shawnee towns, he was named the "pilot," for this expedition.

One year later, as Whitley began to gather some wealth, he was once again in the forefront of Indian fighting, guiding advances on Shawnee towns, crops, and possessions. The following year small bands of Indians were committing raids, and Whitley and 18 other men were off in pursuit, but to no avail. Well, you certainly get the idea. Mr. Whitley was again and again enlisted to guide, lead and search out Indians who posed a threat in the region for many years. He reached the rank of captain in 1783.

Whitely built his famous clay-surfaced horse racing track in 1788. He required the horses to race counterclockwise—opposite the British style.

His military experienced got him appointed in 1792 by Gov. Isaac Shelby to Major in the Sixth regiment in the Kentucky militia. The next year he became lieutenant colonel. In 1794 Whitley, aggravated by continued Indian raids, led 200 men against a Chickamauga village in Tennessee. After resoundingly defeating the Indians, Whitley gave a barbecue at his newly completed home, "Sportsmen's Hill."

During the next few quiet years, Whitley seems to have devoted most of his attention to his family and land. His 2,800 acres remained intact, later giving each of his sons a good start in life. His large and well-managed land holdings, notable visitors, and fame spread even to his enemies. On occasion Indians came to call upon the family, with many Indians of the region looking upon Whitley as the white chief of the Kentucky frontier.

On one visit, a group of Cherokees challenged Whitley to a shooting contest. Despite of his renown as a fighter, his wife was even better at target shooting—beating them all. After the best Indians were beaten, the deflated Indians asked how it was that she, "a woman," could shoot so well. Ester Whitley is quoted as saying that she learned well in order to kill Indians.

In 1797, Whitley was elected to the state House of Representatives and served one term. He was one of the Lincoln County commissioners of the Kentucky River Company in 1801. Although he was in his 64th year and a longtime veteran of more than 20 Indian engagements, Whitley answered Gov. Shelby's call for volunteers for the War of 1812. He enlisted as a private in John Davidson's company, which formed a part of Richard M. Johnson's Kentucky Mounted Infantry.

In all of his campaigns he was wounded only once, but had often said that "the death he craved to die was in his country's defense." The main engagement took place on Oct. 5, 1813. While other units were dealing with the British, Johnson's regiment assumed the task of engaging a large body of Indians commanded by the noted chief, Tecumseh. When the battle ended, William Whitley was dead, leaving eight daughters, three sons and his strong wife, Ester. Whitley has been suggested as the man who fell Tecumseh.

In 1818 Whitley County was formed named in his honor.

Gift shop: The small shop is behind a freshly painted white wooded door and has kiddy souvenirs and other small items. You may purchase your ticket to tour the home at the sales counter.

Day-use areas: A newer picnic shelter can accommodate about 15 tables and is equipped with grills, four trash barrels and plenty of open spaces. Also next to the house is a small, shady grove of trees with a dozen or so picnic tables scattered about. There is a soft drink machine on site. Behind the house is a small playground.

Special notes: The Big South Fork National River and Recreation Area is about 10 miles from the park. Next door to the historic site is a working farm.

Indiana State Parks:

A Hoosier's Guide to Parks, Recreation Areas and Reservoirs
by John Goll
Indiana's only comprehensive guide to the great state parks! All the details about camping, hiking, scenic areas, lodges, fishing and family recreation opportunities. Maps, photos, directions, 268 pages, $14.95.

Michigan State Parks Guidebook:

A complete recreation guide for campers, boaters, anglers, hikers and skiers by Jim DuFresne
Complete information on Michigan's 92 diverse state parks. Welcome to Michigan's playground! Wilderness retreats, great fishing and the nation's longest freshwater shoreline. Maps, photos, 287 pages, $12.95.

Ohio State Parks Guidebook:

A complete outdoor recreation guide to the Buckeye state.
by Art Weber and Bill Bailey
With 65 maps and 90 photographs. Complete park descriptions, camping, hiking trails, handicapped accessibilities, boating, fishing, rent-a-camps, rentals, lodges, beaches and nature notes. Everything you need to know to enjoy Ohio's terrific state parks! 384 pages, directions, phone numbers, $14.95.

Illinois State Parks Guidebook:

A complete Outdoor Recreation Guide
by Bill Bailey
Detailed guide to the natural features and facilities of the great Illinois state park system. Where to camp, fishing tips and hot spots, trails, watersports, historical and educational attractions, lodging, beaches, cabins, day-use areas, natural history, skiing and more. Photos, maps, 352 pages, $14.95.

Thrill Sports

In the Great Lakes Region, by Bill Bailey
Yahoo! Learn about 13 exciting thrill sports! Facts not myths, about skydiving, parasailing, ultralight aircraft flying, scuba diving, soaring, ballooning, windsurfing, rock climbing, hang gliding, bungee jumping and more. Costs, training, where to go, instructors, books, outfitters and descriptions. Photos, 212 pages, $12.95.

Ask for these books at your bookstore,
or order direct from
Glovebox Guidebooks of America.

To order call (800) 289-4843, or send a check or money order, plus $3 shipping for the first book and .50 cents for each additional book, to:

Glovebox Guidebooks of America
1112 Washburn East
Saginaw, Michigan 48602-2977
24-hour fax order: (517) 792-8363.

About the Author

Bill Bailey is one of America's foremost experts on outdoor recreation, environmental education, parks and public information. He is the author of *Ohio State Parks, Ilinois State Parks, Thrill Sports* (consultant for the *Indiana State Parks* guidebook) and six other books. Bill is a former director of a large environmental eduction center; chief naturalist; communication consultant; publisher and senior public administrator. Bill has been an active member of the Outdoor Writers Assocation of America (OWAA) since 1980. He lives with his wife and two sons in Saginaw, Michigan.